W9-AGY-210

THE FEAR PROJECT

What Our Most Primal Emotion Taught Me About Survival, Success, Surfing . . . And Love

JAIMAL YOGIS

RODALE

Mention of specific companies, organizations, or authorities in this book does not imply endorsement by the author or publisher, nor does mention of specific companies, organizations, or authorities imply that they endorse this book, its author, or the publisher.
Internet addresses and telephone numbers given in this book were accurate at the time it went to press.

Rodale books may be purchased for business or promotional use or for special sales. For information, please write to:
Special Markets Department, Rodale, Inc., 733 Third Avenue, New York, NY 10017

Printed in the United States of America
Rodale Inc. makes every effort to use acid-free ♾, recycled paper ♲.
Book design by Mike Smith

Library of Congress Cataloging-in-Publication Data is on file with the publisher.

ISBN 978–1–60961–175–0 hardcover

Distributed to the trade by Macmillan
2 4 6 8 10 9 7 5 3 1 hardcover

We inspire and enable people to improve their lives and the world around them.
rodalebooks.com

For Amy and Kaifas

CONTENTS

INTRODUCTION

The Roman philosopher Seneca was blunt: "Where fear is, happiness is not." Shakespeare wrote: "Our doubts are traitors, and make us lose the good we oft might win by fearing to attempt."

Judaism, Christianity, and Islam all promote *God fearing,* but true faith, the texts say, dispels fear. John 4:18: "There is no fear in love, but perfect love casteth out fear: because fear hath torment. He that feareth is not made perfect in love."

The Buddhist *Avatamsaka Sutra* emphasizes that to become a bodhisattva, an enlightened being full of compassion, one must transcend the five primary fears: loss of livelihood, bad reputation, death, negative rebirths, and stage fright. The Buddha apparently wouldn't have been surprised that public speaking still often tops fear polls.

William James, who was reportedly afraid of being alone, saw the ebb of fearful situations as part of society's evolution: "The progress from brute to man is characterized by nothing so much as by the decrease in frequency of proper occasions for fear." And Charles Darwin, the agoraphobic who said he might not have finished *The Origin of Species* without his fears (they helped him stay in his study), thought that fear was a trace of our ancestral past that wasn't *always* helpful: "As fear increases to the agony of terror, we behold, as with all violent emotions, diversified results. The heart beats wildly, or may fail to act and faintness ensue. . . . Utter prostration soon follows, and the mental powers fail."

With the exception of when we watch a scary movie or navigate down a treacherous run on the ski slopes, humans generally don't like to feel afraid. And from prophets to philosophers to scientists, there seems to have been a consensus over the years that fear—although helpful for escaping lions, avoiding walking off cliffs, and selling horror movies—can also be an obstacle to evolution, to reaching our potential.

As a pretty shy kid, I've always had an interest in fear and why it holds so many of us back. But over the last few years, what was just a casual interest developed into an obsession, and then into a journalistic and psychological project: a fear project. I've spent years interviewing some of the leading neuroscientists, doctors, psychiatrists, and psychologists, some of them numerous times. I've hung out with some of the world's best extreme athletes, interviewed meditation teachers, gone diving with great white sharks, surfed waves that made me want to vomit, fallen in love, and generally taken chances that I never otherwise would have. This book is the result.

All sentient beings—whether rabbits, guinea pigs, lions, dolphins, or humans—feel fear. Even sea anemones—though it's hard to say what they're sensing—retreat when they sense danger. For humans, fear and stress permeate our busy lives in gross and subtle ways—many, I've learned, that we're not even aware of. Understanding fear changes our lives in extreme ways, but nobody ever teaches us about this basic, primal emotion. I don't recall a single lesson about fear from preschool up to graduate school. More importantly, most of us know very little about how to deal with fear when it stands in our way.

People have come up with all sorts of nutty theories on

overcoming fear. As British scholar Joanna Bourke's book, *Fear: A Cultural History*, recounts, in 1871, one Dr. M. Roth devised a long list of people predisposed to extreme states of fear, including masturbators, sexual deviants, alcoholics, and "people educated on false principles." In 1906, the author of a book called *Bashfulness* attributed women's anxiety to high-heeled shoes. Karl Abraham, a close associate of Sigmund Freud's, thought fear of spiders was an unconscious fear of bisexual genitalia, and it was only decades ago that we were drilling holes in people's skulls and severing sections of their brains from each other—known as a lobotomy—to cure them from excessive fright and anxiety.

One hundred years from now people may look back and think our scientific knowledge of fear was crude. But they probably won't look back at the current neuroscience and say that it was flat-out wrong. At a time when functional magnetic resonance imagery (fMRI) and many other new technological tools allow scientists to look into the human brain as it functions, millennia of theorizing has given way to hard evidence. We're still a long way off from having a flawless, comprehensive neural picture of fear, but the last couple of decades have produced encyclopedias' worth of mesmerizing science that could revolutionize the way we live. *Could,* because, in general, the studies are Greek to us mortals, and academics usually don't spend much time translating them. After reading hundreds of studies, I've realized it would take lifetimes to translate all of this science into everyday English, but with the help of scientists, doctors, and psychologists with a special knack for regular old chitchat—people like Robert Sapolsky, Joseph LeDoux, Daniela Schiller, Rick Hanson, Philippe Goldin, Paige Dunne, Michael Lardon, Howard Fields, David Zald, and

Sian Beilock, not to mention other science writers—I've tried to describe the science that I've found most applicable to everyday life.

Bourke writes, "Fear is fundamentally about the body—its fleshiness and its precariousness. Fear is *felt*, and although the emotion of fear cannot be *reduced* to the sensation of fear, it is not present *without* sensation." In other words, fear is an experience. Over-intellectualizing about it can be useless in terms of living better. Much more often, fear is overcome through action: sports, meditation, music, love, repetitive training, positive exposure to the object of fear, and simply using common sense to investigate what's so scary.

As a fairly obsessive athlete who would probably go crazy if I didn't surf, jog, or swim every day, I've paid special attention to sports in this book, but that's only partly selfish. Fear evolved over millions of years to help us escape physical dangers. It's only recently that taxes have become scarier than lions or not being able to find dinner. I've learned that athletes—the warriors and hunters of the modern era—are often ahead of the curve when it comes to understanding fear. But there are important lessons to be learned from other scary activities, too: preparing for a speech, dating, dying.

I've reported lots of stories in my career, but this wasn't just another assignment. Writing this book changed my life in ways far more profound than I ever imagined. It has been a psychological and physical expedition, and this is why I've chosen to include my own experiences and fears here as well, letting the book roll out in the order that I reported it.

Much as we like to make it into the villain, fear isn't bad. In fact, as we'll learn, it's often our *fear of fear*—our aversion to accepting and understanding this very natural emotion—that can cause fear to spin into unhelpful panic and anxiety disorders. Also, there are still many dangers in the world. There is still much suffering. We have to heed these dangers and strive to alleviate the suffering. Fear, when it triggers compassionate action, can be helpful in doing this. But fear often tricks us into freaking out unnecessarily, making ourselves sick, as well as causing us to underperform.

We now live longer and more pain free than at any other time in history. According to the World Bank's most recent data, even in the developing world, humans are healthier than ever before. We are also richer than ever before and, according to *Foreign Policy* magazine, the world is more peaceful right now than at any time in the last century. But if you look at the statistics on anxiety disorders, watch the news, or check in with your stress thermostat on any given day, it seems that we're more scared than ever. I hope this book will help change that.

CHAPTER 1

HOW I GOT HERE

"Courage is not the absence of fear. It is acting in spite of it."

—MARK TWAIN

I'm 7 years old. It's a blustery, foggy day and I'm on a school field trip. My classmates and I are standing in a single-file line down by the cell of Al Capone, jaws agape, while our guide—a squat, bald man with a world-weary face—is telling us about the history of Alcatraz as if we might someday be inmates. "So kids, you think you could escape from this place?" he asks. "Let me tell you, even if you made it out of your cell, past the armed guards, and over the barbed wire, then you'd have to deal with the sharks. And let me tell you kids—not a chance."

We learn that only one prisoner, John Paul Scott, survived the swim, and he was found unconscious under the Golden Gate Bridge, nearly dead from exhaustion and hypothermia. For years after this day, I have nightmares of toppling into a San Francisco Bay teeming with great whites and giant octopi, about to become fish food.

• • • •

My Alcatraz nightmares are coming true. I'm swimming in the bay with three men—we're flopping upstream like salmon. The currents push at our faces and drag at our toes. We pull, dig, claw at the water, and we are going nowhere. Alcatraz looms behind us, and a police boat is on our heels as if we really are escapees. Men in black uniforms are scowling at us from on deck, holding big guns. Are they here to arrest us or rescue us?

The man leading this swim through the wild currents of the San Francisco Bay is not a convict. He's my cousin's husband, Jamie Patrick, one of the best ultra swimmers in the world. Large, blond, and loud, Jamie is one of the most friendly, enthusiastic people you'll ever meet: a responsible father, a good friend. And he's indisputably insane.

Jamie started swimming competitively at 7 years old, got serious about the sport at 12, and swam at Long Beach State and the University of Hawaii. After college, he fell in love with triathlons, and it wasn't long before he completed an Ironman and became a sponsored Ironman racer. For most triathletes, completing one Ironman is a dream, the hardest thing they will ever do. Jamie decided to do a triple: 7.2-mile swim, 336-mile bike, 78.6-mile run. The swim wasn't hard, Jamie told me, but during the bike ride, it rained for 20 hours. Around the 30th mile of running, at which point he hadn't slept for 24 hours, Jamie developed a blister half the size of his foot. He popped it, wrapped it up with duct tape, and kept going for the other 48.6 miles.

Jamie's idea of fun was to become the first swimmer ever to complete two crossings of Lake Tahoe, a distance of 44 miles at around 6,200-feet altitude. He wanted to use the swim to raise awareness about Tahoe's environmental problems. To prepare, the man woke at 4 a.m., trained for 4 hours, and worked a full day at Patrick and Co.—his family's San Francisco office supplies business—swimming some more on his lunch break. Then he came home to spend time with his wife and daughter. His training for the Tahoe swim included little jaunts like swimming 18 miles across Clear Lake, something else nobody had ever done.

The least I could do was confront my childhood nightmare and swim the 1.5 miles from Alcatraz back to shore. I asked Jamie if we could do the swim together.

"Sure," he said, as if I'd asked him to meet me for coffee. "We'll make a morning of it."

Jamie said he would bring his friend Greg Larson, a former member of the US Olympic swim team. I told my surfing buddy Mark Lukach—a fellow journalist and possibly the only person in the world with more energy than Jamie—about the swim, and he almost jumped on top of me. "I can't even tell you how long I've wanted to do that!" Mark said. "When do we leave?"

My nerves kicked in about 8 p.m. the night before, when Mark called me with a sudden hesitant tone in his voice. "This is a serious freaking swim, you realize that? It's not like swimming 1.5 miles in a pool. Where are we meeting Jamie? Are we going to take a boat out there?"

I didn't know. I figured we would take a ferry to Alcatraz, then—who knows?—jump off the island? I called Jamie to get the details.

"No, no," Jamie said. "You can't do that. We'll just swim out and back."

Our 1.5-mile swim had just doubled to 3 miles.

We arrived the next morning at Aquatic Park, the bay like green glass. The Headlands to the north were vivid in the crisp air. Pelicans splashed down, looking for breakfast, and swimmers in bright rubber caps knocked off their morning laps inside a sheltered inlet. Out beyond this shelter, the water flowed into the bulbous bay, bottlenecking at the Golden Gate, before dumping into the Pacific. I knew that when the tides changed and water flooded in or out of the bay, that bottleneck created extra suction; currents can sweep in or out at up to 8 knots. Jamie's dad, a lifelong sailor, had calculated the best times for us to swim out and back. If we left at around 8 a.m. on a slack tide, we would have a semineutral current on our way toward the island. Then the tide would start to flood, and we would be pushed back to shore at an angle.

Mark and I suited up quickly, hurrying over to meet the real swimmers. We laughed as we jogged in our rubber outfits: We felt like superheroes, how cool.

Jamie and Greg looked serene as we stretched. Mark bounced around like Tigger, human solar panel that he is.

I was oddly chilly, even though the morning air was warm—it crackled with electricity. "Isn't this beautiful!" Jamie proclaimed.

Yeah, I could feel it. Even with my nerves, I was excited. And I felt fairly confident as we entered the icy green soup, beginning a relaxed crawl north. Alcatraz sat low on the horizon. It didn't look *that* far. We could do this. But when we got to the end of the rip-rap jetty, about to enter the open bay, the currents balked. They were clearly pushing southeast, away from Alcatraz, right in our faces.

I looked at Jamie. "What's this about?"

Jamie looked confused too. He asked a man in a wooden skiff, who was overseeing the Dolphin Club's lap swimmers (a group who do the Alcatraz swim regularly but who, curiously, weren't swimming today), if now was a good time for, you know, a little swim to the prison out there. "Sure, if you want to end up in Berkeley," the man said dismissively. "There's a full flood right now." This meant that the tide would push us 6 miles east instead of letting us swim in a line.

We huddled to reassess. Jamie and Greg still thought the swim was doable. Mark and I looked at each other and shrugged. I nervously peed in my wetsuit, but I nodded yes when they asked if I was willing to try. We would swim west of Alcatraz toward the bridge, overshooting, hoping the current would carry us down toward the island. It would mean swimming in an arch, so now we were looking at more like 3.5 or 4 miles. Great.

Jamie led the pack, and once we got going, I felt surprisingly loose and strong. Surfing, my usual form of exercise, had kept me in fair swimming shape. The farther we got from shore, the more supple and free I swam. Sure, I heard the *Jaws* intro music a few times, and it was a tad eerie looking into the endless murky green. But now that I was actually swimming, I felt good. Why had these waters plagued my imagination for so many years? Why didn't I do more open-water swimming with Jamie? All I had to focus on were the elements, and the rhythm of my breath. We were making good headway. The current was strong, but we swam wide and already looked to be about halfway to the island after what seemed like just 15 minutes. I thought of that old Alcatraz guide scaring me as a kid. If he could see me now. What a—

I heard a motor.

"How you guys doin'?" The man in the wooden skiff had returned.

"Good, thanks. Yep, we're pretty good."

"Let me ask you something: What are you gonna do if a freighter comes through?"

Oh, come on. He followed us out here to tell us this? We were doing fine. We were with Jamie Patrick, world-class Ironman!

I looked at Jamie, hoping for a professional response. Jamie said, "Um . . ."

"You guys have a radio?" the man asked.

We didn't have a radio.

"Well, I'm not going to tell you to turn back," the man said, "but we work hard to keep this swim safe so we can keep doing it. We notify the Coast Guard before our swims, and we carry radios so we can communicate with the freighters. A 400-foot steel ship isn't going to be able to stop for something they can't see or hear."

Oh.

And with that, the man motored off. Apparently our radio

had been lost or was unavailable that morning. And although Jamie had done this swim dozens of times before (without a radio), now he was responsible for us. Getting chopped up in the giant propellers of a 400-foot steel boat seemed like a legitimate concern. "The guy's right," said Greg. "Let's head back."

Yes, let's. It felt fine to heed the man's advice. They were a nice group, the Dolphin Club, and we didn't want to mess things up for them. Besides, we'd made it more than half-way to Alcatraz, a respectable swim. This was legit. Had we been trying to escape the prison, we'd have made it, and this is basically what my inner 7-year-old wanted to know.

The San Francisco skyline looked sharp and jagged and clear on the horizon. We swam hard but happily toward the mouth of Aquatic Park, a fairly small entrance, trying to overshoot it to the west again. I looked up occasionally and could tell we were being dragged way off course toward—surprise!—Berkeley, a good half-mile from the only entrance back to land. To get back, we had to swim directly west, up current. As soon as we started, we were going backward.

• • • •

Backward, like salmon flopping upstream. What is that police boat doing on our heels? We're like cartoon characters, windmilling their legs furiously and going nowhere. Well, at least Mark and I are. Jamie and Greg are gaining distance. They stay steady and just keep heaving themselves upstream. Mark and I are falling back. What are we doing? This is just . . . dumb. We are obviously unprepared.

I'm angry with Jamie. This is really uncool. I think of all

the dumb stunts he's pulled, how pained he looked during the last leg of the Ironman when we went to cheer him on in Hawaii. He looked as if he was dying. Why does he put himself through such grueling masochistic acts? Why is he such a—why am I falling so far behind?

Spontaneously—and I swear, I have never done this before—I start chanting "Eye of the Tiger" in my head. *Eye of the tiger*—hands thrust deeper—*it's the thrill of the fight*—feet butterfly. *Rising up*. I am fast. *To the challenge*. I am faster than fast. *Of our rival*. And I must believe this even if it's not true.

It all seems a tad pathetic. But, oddly enough, it works. There are a few moments when I want to stop. But when I push through, it's like someone has plugged in my batteries. Maybe it's Mark next to me, turning up the heat. Maybe it's my ego not wanting to be left in the dust. Maybe I'm channeling Jamie's superhero qualities. The harder I swim, the more I am glad this is hard. I want to *earn* this. I suddenly feel life in my arms. I could go farther now. I could do it all again! Before I am even aware that it is done, it is done. It's over. We round the corner into Aquatic Park, high-fiving and hooting like a bunch of drunken cowboys.

Then we hear a megaphone.

"Don't ever pull a stunt like this again," a Darth Vader voice says. We turn and see the police boat, men scowling with arms crossed. "We don't know what the hell you guys were thinking, but you have to get a permit from the Coast Guard and the police department to swim in the bay. Next time we won't let you off."

We apologize. We wave to the nice policemen, ruefully crawling onto the beach. Should we feel bad? Will the Dolphin Club be punished? These feelings pass quickly when we realize, wait—what better ending for an escape to Alcatraz swim than being chased down by the law? And we won.

• • • •

Even if it's just a piddly thing from childhood, overcoming fear feels good. It makes you feel as if all the other fears and stresses in life might not actually be real. They might just be illusions you can shatter, a scary story on television you can just turn off.

A few months before my Alcatraz swim, I became driven by the need for this feeling. I wish I could say that it stemmed from an overwhelming sense of compassion for the 40 million people who suffer anxiety disorders in the United States every year, or that I'd fought bravely at war and was now trying to understand my post-traumatic stress disorder. But I was obsessed for a far more selfish (and, I thought, tragic) reason: Sara had broken up with me.

I hadn't been looking for a serious relationship in my early twenties. But when a friend introduced me to Sara—an artist with sprightly green-blue eyes and a fantastically silly sense of humor—I was afraid a woman this beautiful and quirky and creative wouldn't come along again. I fell for her. She fell for me. We ran off to Mexico together in love, but officially broke up a few months later when I went to journalism school in New York. I flip-flopped, not sure what I wanted. We got back together when I moved back to San Francisco, then sort of moved in together, then sort of broke up again. We got back together *again* and definitely moved in together. The final stretch lasted 2 solid years in our very own loft apartment on the western fringe of San Francisco. It was a decent 2 years, and we talked about marriage and children. But something just wasn't right.

All we knew was that the color had dulled in our filmic, if frustrating, love story, and we were afraid of losing each other, so we decided on a 1-year separation. We mutually agreed that we should go out there and *explore*—leaving the definition of that term a little loose—then check in a year later. The result, we hoped, would be that (a) we would miss each other terribly and, having explored the horrible alternate options out there, live happily ever after, or that (b) with the clarity of a real break, we'd discover our happiness apart, and remain loving friends forever.

Both of us remembered the ugly and painful divorces of our parents—we divided up our things amiably and promised not to contact each other for at least, well, we'd play that by ear. (For anyone considering this plan, I don't recommend it.) Sure enough, about 30 minutes after Sara left, I wanted her back, desperately. I suddenly realized how my parents did this same dance: fight, separation, another try; fight, separation, another try. Finally, a bitter divorce. I now realized why I'd been so noncommittal early on. My fear of commitment protected me from ever being abandoned. But it also prevented me from finding real love.

After a few weeks, I brought Sara flowers and spilled my heart onto the floor. I told her that it wasn't too late to skip this whole year apart because *what a silly idea it was anyway!* I was ready for all of it: marriage, kids, ready for our lives to finally *begin*. I apologized again and again for being such a pansy at the start. I was different now!

Sara appreciated my display of affection, but she wasn't sure. She needed more time.

I felt as if someone had shot rusty staples into my chest cavity. But I understood. Stick with the plan, I told myself, holding back tears. There was hope. And fortunately my friends had impeccable timing—we'd been planning a surf trip to Indonesia, and it was almost here, thankfully. Another week or two and I would have been camping out on Sara's porch holding a boom box and blasting "In Your Eyes." (I'd done the equivalent at least twice before, and there was no telling how far my inner John Cusack would go on round three.)

As soon as I buckled in on the plane, I felt a little better. I was on my way to a tropical island! We had a layover in Taiwan, and at the airport we bought some of those funny boba drinks with the big straws. We checked the swell forecast on the Internet and it looked great—we high-fived. For surfers, a good swell can nullify just about any global tragedy. I also checked my e-mail, and—oh, here's one from Sara!

Jaimal, the e-mail began. *There's been something I've been wanting to tell you.*

E-mails that started with just my first name were never a good sign. There was almost no reason to read further. Sara had, in fact, not changed her mind about us. She was seeing someone else, someone I'll call John, someone who was one of our mutual friends, someone who I always sensed liked her, someone who, well . . . suddenly, the world spun around me and my chest felt tight. I was sweating. How could she? How long have they . . . ?

Technically, we were broken up. Technically, this was fair play. But that didn't stop me from stumbling around the airport, past Hello Kitty and duty-free shops, nearly puking. I wanted to kill John, or perhaps just permanently damage his face. I wanted to crawl into a hole, or move to Japan, or disappear. I was oddly certain that I would be alone forever, that I was fundamentally flawed, that I had to get Sara back to keep my heart from turning to coal. But I would never get Sara back.

• • • •

On what should have been a dream surf trip, I spent a lot of time underwater, trying to scream the lump in my chest out. My friends helped me keep it together. But back in San Francisco, I retreated into a despair ripped right from a romantic comedy. I drank alone and smoked cigarettes and moved into a windowless studio. I wanted darkness.

I reminded myself that people everywhere endured horrible things: losing children, starvation, earthquakes, tsunamis, layoffs. I was one of the lucky ones. This didn't help. I stopped working on my books and articles. I couldn't write. Everything I had to say seemed contrived. I was a failure. No wonder she left.

After many long, sleepless nights, I distilled my array of feelings into one very simple, primal emotion: fear.

Jealousy: fear that he's better than me

Stress: fear that I'm not good enough at anything and never will be

Sadness: fear that she's gone forever

Depression: fear that I'm stuck here in this dark hole of insecurity and will never clamber out

I realized that I hated fear, or at least the way it worked in *my* brain. Not only was I now stressed and insecure, but I saw how fear of losing each other or fear that we weren't right had kept Sara and me from really enjoying our time together. One of us was always afraid to lose the other or afraid we were settling. I started reviewing all the choices I'd ever made and realized that although I'd never considered myself a scared person, fear had been pulling the puppet strings of my actions much more than I'd ever thought. I also realized that I didn't know what to do about this.

I guess at some point I'd thought I knew. I remembered as a teenager plastering those "No Fear" stickers to my snowboards, skateboards, and surfboards, hawking my body into precarious aerials, unconcerned about broken bones. The answers back then were simple aphorisms that you could wear on a T-shirt or slap on a bumper sticker: *Just Do It. No Fear. Go Hard or Go Home.*

This perspective has been bred into me by generations of military men telling harrowing tales of things far worse than breakups. My dad's grandfather, Charlie, was a 6-foot-4 Lithuanian Catholic who was forced to fight in the Russian army he hated. He stole a horse, rode across Europe, and hopped a ship to Brooklyn. His son, my grandfather, was one of nine men to survive out of some 300 in his battalion in the battle of Anzio in World War II. My dad served in the navy in Vietnam, the air force in Desert Storm, and retired a proud colonel.

These men believed that when you don't feel so good, you should shut up and do something—mow the lawn, fix the car, move to a different state. This has served them pretty well (not always in their romantic relationships, but everywhere else). Grandpa Simon was diagnosed with emphysema decades before his death. I distinctly recall him up on the roof cleaning the gutters in his early nineties when the doctor had insisted he use a walker. I never once heard Grandpa talk about how he *felt*. If he wanted to show you love, he'd fix your air conditioner.

Breakup sentiments are not something we discussed on my dad's side of the family. But I imagined these men's voices in my head, telling me to get it together, have a shot of whiskey, and go do something—anything.

My maternal grandfather was also a colonel and a West Point graduate, but he was a rare breed who loved—adored, really—to talk about emotions. Gramp, who was raised Jewish but became a science-loving agnostic, loved to talk about anything. I have fond memories of him philosophizing for hours about the existence of God, the latest quantum physics discoveries, nuclear proliferation, monogamy. Gramp was about as progressive a military man as you could find. He couldn't fix a thing, but he was a great communicator. When I was a teenager, Gramp instituted something in our family called the Heart Share in which the whole family passed around a candle. When the candle came to you, you had a turn to vent your emotions—whatever was troubling you, but most importantly what you were grateful for. (By this point, my mom and dad were divorced, but if my dad had been with us for these visits, I think he would have passed on the Heart Share.)

Mom became a French teacher and later a counselor and therapist, promoting a view in my sister and me that emotional processing is as important as eating. We grew up talking about our dreams. We learned meditation and yoga. Both my parents, in fact, abandoned their Judeo-Christian roots and became, more or less, Buddhists. I think my dad connected more with the silent stoicism of Zen—*those who speak do not know; those who know do not speak*—and the fact that some of the old Zen masters occasionally got drunk. My mom tended more toward the psychological processing aspects of vipassana, or insight meditation, and yoga.

I was a philosophy and religion major. I even lived in a Buddhist monastery briefly after high school and wrote a whole book about the links between the Zen tradition and surf culture, *Saltwater Buddha*. I've done plenty of talk therapy. This was the processing side of me. On the other side, there was action: the go-hard-or-go-home view that told me to steal a horse and run far away. With all these resources, I'd felt as a kid that I was pretty well prepared to deal with fear. I mean, things always seemed to work out anyway. So why was this breakup, something I'd been through a couple of times before, making me feel as if I was in an inescapable prison? Why did I feel utterly paralyzed?

What I didn't know then was that none of the ways I'd learned to deal with fear were wrong. Humans have been intuitive about dealing with their nerves for thousands of years. But fear also makes us forget what we know. It freezes us. And this fear had covered everything with such severe doubt that I even questioned the basic standby methods I'd used to fix things my whole life. I wasn't sure what I trusted anymore. I certainly didn't trust myself or my family history. I needed to wipe the slate clean and start at the beginning.

And in the beginning, there was fear.

CHAPTER 2

OF FRIGHT AND COURAGE: A TALE OF TWO BRAINS

"Every special date and anniversary, every advertisement, every therapy session, every day in school is an effort to create or modify memory."

—JOSEPH LEDOUX

Daniela Schiller is a tall, fair blonde who, if she were an actress, could have easily taken Cate Blanchett's place playing Galadriel in *Lord of the Rings*. Her wispy hair, soft voice, and striking blue eyes give her an ethereal quality and make everything she says seem wise. But the more time you spend with Schiller—who is not an actress, but a neuroscientist—the more you see a strength beneath the lightness, especially when she tells you how she developed such an obsessive interest in fear.

When Schiller was still living in Israel, her birthplace, she wanted to complete her mandatory military service with an active duty position in the army. There were plenty of avenues for serving out of harm's way, but this wasn't Schiller's style. She wanted to be out on the front lines. Unfortunately, there were a limited number of active-duty positions for women in the army, and by the time Schiller applied, the female quota was full. Placed on the slightly less adventurous army media team, Schiller decided to test her courage by taking a skydiving class. She was excited—and terrified.

When the day came, Schiller remembers being on a tiny plane with no seats. They reached jumping height and the side of the plane flew open. Looking down, the Earth spun beneath her. "The first thing I thought was, 'Oh my God, I'm going to fall,'" Schiller tells me as we sip espresso at her office at Mount Sinai Hospital in Manhattan. "I got half my body outside the airplane—it was a situation I never pictured myself in. Every part of me did not want to be there. But I just did it."

The terror was almost paralyzing, but as soon as Schiller jumped, it was so strange: She felt no fear at all. "Just the pleasure of falling," she says, "and then when I landed, I felt a huge rush. I wanted to go back up. But it only takes 30 minutes to be afraid again."

Schiller was fascinated by these contradictory sides of fear: the thrill, the empowerment, the relapse, the way anticipation could be scarier than action. Over the course of the army class's next 10 jumps, Schiller observed her fear's ebb and flow like a scientist. Every single time, right before she leapt, she was afraid: Her pulse beat faster, she was short of breath, her shoulders tensed up. The more she did it, though, the less nervous she felt and the more the fear was focused at the moment of the jump. The fear didn't plague her before or after. "I got better at handling it," Schiller tells me. "I used new memories. When I stood at the door of the plane, I knew I did it before. And I used that to go through the fear."

It's a universal experience, even if the fear is just in the mind. I've never been skydiving, but talking to Schiller, I'm reminded how, as young kids, my sister and I were scared of a monster that lived under the bed, one that feasted on children's feet. We made a pact that we had to jump a few feet off the bed each time we woke up so that this beast wouldn't ruin our futures as professional hockey players and gymnasts. Eventually, we gathered the courage to peek under the bed. One . . . two . . . *oh my God, look!* No monster. That decreased our jitters a little, but we still hopped off the bed. We checked again. And . . . still no monster. Less fear. A few weeks later, we would have laughed at some kid if he told us a foot-gobbling monster lived under our bed. Pansy.

Most of us take our ability to overcome fear for granted, but Schiller wanted details. How did it work? And why? And why did it work sometimes but not others? Using the same chutzpah that took her up in that airplane, Schiller began the long road to becoming a neuroscientist, ending up eventually at New York University's prestigious Center for the Neuroscience of Fear and Anxiety. Here, as a post-doctoral fellow, she teamed up with two of the biggest names in the business—the director of the center, Joseph LeDoux, and Elizabeth Phelps, lab director of NYU's psychology department—to perform one of the most fascinating studies on fear and memory ever, a study she now is using to develop new therapies for patients with post-traumatic stress disorder (PTSD) at Mount Sinai.

The study, published in the journal *Nature*, is fairly simple, but neuroscience papers have a way of making even the simplest things seem as if they are written in a foreign language. Experiencing the study firsthand is the best way to really get it, Schiller says, taking me down to the ground floor of Mount Sinai where, in a basement room without windows, an intern named Chris attaches wires to my forefinger and index finger with Velcro. These wires, Chris says, will measure the slightest changes of sweat on my skin and thus measure my stress level. When the wires are snugly attached, a red line appears on a computer monitor, traveling up and down in gentle, repeating waves. This line shows the ebb and flow of sweat release on my skin, a measure of my anxiety level. And even though I don't feel the slightest bit nervous, the rise and fall of the red line shows that I actually am a little. "Just the fact that you're participating in a study where you'll get shocked is probably creating some nervous anticipation," Chris says nonchalantly. (I get the feeling he has done this study on one too many subjects.)

I've never been shocked before. And I do feel just slightly anxious as, on my opposite wrist, Chris attaches a piece of metal hooked to a little box with knobs and dials. It's eerily reminiscent of the machine Peter Venkman used to shock his test subjects at the start of the first *Ghostbusters*. "Tell me when the shock becomes aversive but not painful," Chris says, and I let him turn the dial to just above five. Here, the zap is enough to make me jump in my seat but isn't really painful. It's not unlike when my friends and I used to skitter around on the carpet in socks and shock one another with our static-electricity-filled fingers.

I'm fully wired now. Chris asks me to try to find a relationship between the shapes I see on a second computer monitor and the shocks I'm about to experience. A series of blue and yellow squares begin to appear on the screen for about 4 seconds at a time, and it doesn't take long to realize that the blue squares sometimes come with the annoying shock right at the end. The yellow squares seem safe, but the fact that the blue squares only sometimes have an accompanying shock makes it hard to predict and more nerve-racking. Looking at the pattern of the red line, my brain, after just one blue square–shock pairing, has already developed what Schiller calls a conditioned fear response to blue squares. I hardly notice it consciously, but every time a blue square appears, the sweat levels on my skin spike nearly to the same level as when I actually get the shock. In other words, the anticipation of pain—a mere thought—has become as jarring on my physiology as the actual pain.

This is a bit strange when you think about it. The blue square is doing absolutely nothing to harm me. It's just a picture—just like the monster under my bed was a figment of my imagination. But I've made a quick Pavlovian association that blue squares will probably mean pain. And, according to Schiller's research, this relationship has been singed so deeply in my brain's fear center that even if I come back a whole year from now and see that blue square on the screen—whether the shock comes with it or not—I'll break a sweat. And if that's how enduring a minor fear can be, imagine the power of real pain, real trauma, real fright.

This is just the beginning of Schiller's brilliant study. First, if you are anything like me, you need a little context. In an age when neuroscience constantly makes headlines, and fourth graders use the term *prefrontal cortex* the way they once used *Tyrannosaurus rex,* a lot of people now know a lot about the human brain. Until very recently, I haven't been one of those people. And in preparation to meet with Schiller and her colleagues, I spent a few months trying to get a basic understanding of that lump of matter between my temples. The man who helped me was Schiller's mentor, Dr. LeDoux.

• • • •

I first read about LeDoux, a professor who bears a resemblance to George Carlin, in a *New York Times* piece that referred to him as a rock star of neuroscience. I pictured an ultra-serious guy in a lab coat and round spectacles, but when I went to LeDoux's NYU Web page, it wasn't very serious looking. The primary illustration was of a brain hovering in space without a skull, attached to a set of bulging eyeballs. The eyeballs pulsed with worry because they looked right at a coiled rattlesnake. To enter the Web site, I had to click on a neon-green part of the brain, near the brain stem, called the *amygdala.*

I clicked and started reading some of LeDoux's fascinating studies. I ordered his books, *The Emotional Brain* and *The Synaptic Self.* But what really caught my eye was a link to a music video—turns out LeDoux is *actually* a rock star. His band, the Amygdaloids, a group of hard-rocking neuroscientists, had recently recorded the video in the Hamptons. (Daniela Schiller, I would later find out, is the drummer, and they have toured together as far as Texas.)

I clicked that link and watched LeDoux walking coolly through a green field in a black suit and sunglasses, singing in a Leonard Cohenesque voice. The song, "Fearing," mixed lyrics from several Emily Dickinson poems with LeDoux's own lectures on fear. (Dickinson was notoriously afraid of death, which kept her often confined to the house, writing poems about sadness and anxiety.) "Fear is the most primitive and basic emotion," LeDoux says darkly over spooky instrumentals. "It occurs when we encounter danger. An animal can put off the good stuff—eating, drinking, sex—for days. But responding to danger must be immediate, or there will be no more eating, drinking, or sex."

When LeDoux said sex, two animated cartoon pandas started mating at the top of the screen. I couldn't believe my luck. The foremost expert on fear and the brain had a sense of humor.

Of course, being a rock star neuroscientist *and* a rock star doesn't leave you with much free time. I was told I'd have to wait a month or two to speak with him. And this was actually good. I needed time to study.

I dove into LeDoux's fantastically comprehensible books (as brain texts go) as well as a handful of essential works by other neuroscientists (Robert Sapolsky, Sian Beilock, Philippe Goldin, Norman Doidge). I learned, first of all, that it takes a human brain to understand a human brain. In adults, the brain is packing around 100 billion neurons (or nerve cells), and 100 to 500 *trillion* synapses, the little highways through which information travels in your head. The number of possible combinations of 100 billion neurons firing or not firing is 10 to the millionth power, a completely incomprehensible number that is supposedly more than the number of particles in the known universe. It's also the number of possible states of your brain.

We have used this brainpower to learn an astonishing amount about our brainpower. Since the first mapping of the human genome in 2003, we now know that we share about 85 percent of our genes with mice, and 98 percent of them with chimpanzees. This is because mice, chimpanzees, and humans took similar evolutionary roads. Fish swam the seas around a half billion years ago. Some of those fish, responding to their competitive environment, took to drier parts, becoming reptiles; some of those reptiles, genetic mutation-by-mutation, started getting furry and nursing. This was around 200 million years ago, before the dinosaurs, and these early mammals looked more or less like weasels, rats, or shrews.

Since then, through millions of years of dodging predators and avoiding getting obliterated by meteors, ice ages, plagues, floods, and tempests, some of those little rodent-like beings gradually got back in the ocean and developed into dolphins and whales, others into New York subway rats, others into chimpanzees, and others into creatures who send satellites into orbit and delight in Monday night football.

We usually think of the distinguishing characteristics of

mammals this way: We have warm blood, bare live young, and nurse. But it's really our brains that distinguish us, particularly an area of the brain called the neocortex (Latin for "new rind"), which started as a thin, unicellular sheath in reptiles and became a complex six-layered onion-type thing in humans and other social primates. The neocortex is the latest in mammalian technology, allowing for all sorts of oddities: echolocation in bats and dolphins, tool-use in chimpanzees. For us, the part of the neocortex near the forehead called the prefrontal cortex, or PFC, has become especially important. It's why we can do all that human stuff: plan for the future, build skyscrapers and computers, debate about the best slice of pizza, and write books that analyze ourselves.

It's all this human thinking that has made our brains swell to a size that creates some engineering problems. Our skulls are now so large that our necks are easily breakable, and human mothers have to pop their babies about 3 months early, unable to even hold up their own big heads, just to fit them through the chute. In other words, our brain power has become so important that it has been worth a lot of extra physical risk—a rarity in evolution.

Biologists have been able to find an important clue as to why our brains are so cumbersomely big by isolating some of the 2 percent of our DNA that differs from chimpanzees. One of the differing genes regulates neuron production. This single gene allows our brain's neuron production to continue until around 100 billion neurons, whereas chimps stop a few stages earlier, making their brains a third of the size of ours and therefore less complex.

But it's not just this one gene that changed our brains.

The burgeoning field of epigenetics has begun to reveal that the *expression* of our genes is affected by how we act, and by our environments, too—we were forced to get smart in different ways than our hairier ancestors. "We humans are the scrawny, four-eyed nerds in nature's schoolyard," writes Daniel Gardner in *The Science of Fear*. "Our senses of sight, smell, and hearing were never as good as those of the animals we wanted to catch and eat. Our arms, legs, and teeth were always puny compared to the muscles and fangs of the predators who competed with us for food and occasionally looked at us as lunch. The brain was our only advantage."

This isn't completely true, as we'll see in the next chapter, but our brains have been our greatest advantage. And sticking together and cooperating seems to have changed our brains most. We raise our young and bond with partners, sometimes for life. We form large packs, tribes, communities, and kingdoms. All that social networking (not the online variety), personal relationships, and collective hunting and gathering apparently made our brains grow from around 400 cubic centimeters to their current 1,400 cubic centimeters in just the last 2 million years.

But the neocortex doesn't do everything. There are all sorts of old gadgets and gizmos in our brains that are key to survival, gadgets our ancestors had way back when we were reptiles. And if you've noticed, reptiles do pretty well without a neocortex. They seem to be able to survive as well in our lawnmower sheds as they do in the Amazon rainforest, something most of us would certainly be challenged by. More isn't always better. And as LeDoux says in his song, "Fearing," evolution's rule is: If it's not broken, don't fix it. Our early brain hardware worked so well over the last few hundred million years that, as we evolved, we retained many of those old brain parts in there and added more and more cool tricks, more neocortex. Fear is part of that very, very early hardware. And though the old hardware and its new upgrades sync up pretty well—"the brain is a symphony of cooperation," as Beilock later put it to me—occasionally there are technical difficulties.

• • • •

As a high school sophomore, I walked into algebra class on a Monday morning after a great weekend with friends. I was a little late, but no big deal until—oh no. No. Nonononono! I saw my classmates and froze. Everyone was silently taking the final exam, the one I thought was the *next* week. My heart raced; I began to sweat. There seemed to be three good options: (a) run far, far, far away, (b) set the school on fire, or (c) stay frozen for a while.

I eventually chose (d) take the test, unprepared. And I got a D.

The memory of failing that test, then retaking the class, still gives me nightmares about showing up to anything unprepared (and/or naked). And the feeling of walking into that final exam was strangely similar to the sensation I felt when I received that surprise e-mail from Sara that she was dating someone else. It's also similar to the time I was chased by a wild turkey at the age of 6: tight chest, sweaty, pounding heart rate, a brief sensation of paralysis followed by a very strong desire to flee, hit something, or curl up in the fetal position.

Why such a visceral reaction? The panic didn't help me wing it through the test. Studies show, in fact, that most people perform worse on cognitive tests of various sorts under stress. And the panic I experienced after Sara's e-mail didn't help me win her back or feel better. The panic did, however, help me escape the giant wild turkey pecking at my heels. And this is a very key point.

Fleeing from predators is exactly the reason our fear response evolved. The difference between fleeing the turkey and the math test was that my brain had now wired that ancient system, fight-or-flight, to the modern prefrontal cortex. When I showed up to class, I identified the danger: final exam! That information was quickly routed through my visual thalamus and my visual cortex to my ancient reptile brain, which told my adrenal glands to get ready to survive a saber-toothed tiger. The adrenal glands released adrenaline into my blood stream, raising my heart rate and blood pressure so I'd be ready for fast action. My body also began producing cortisol, the primary stress hormone, which got to work pumping extra sugar into my blood stream and limbs and suppressing all nonessential functions: immune response, digestion, reproduction, and growth.

Meanwhile, my modern brain felt all of this adrenal drama and thought, *Oh no, I'm panicking. I'll be more likely to fail.* This "fear of fear," a hallmark of what happens in many anxiety disorders, generated more imagery of how bad it would be if I failed, beginning a downward spiral of adrenaline surges and cortisol pumping. *This is really serious*, my modern brain told my ancient brain, not just one saber-toothed tiger, but several: telling my parents I failed, being grounded, not getting into college. As University of Chicago psychologist Sian Beilock describes in her book *Choke,* all this worry was actually taking up cognitive horsepower in my prefrontal cortex that I could have been using to solve math problems. No wonder I got a D.

The average reptile, I'm guessing, wouldn't have this problem. The thing that distinguishes humans (and perhaps some complex-brained mammals) is that we have taken our innate fear response to an entirely new level, letting *psychological stressors*—mere abstract thoughts—launch our bodies into a red alert system meant for life-or-death threats. The math test was, in a way, a real threat. But not one that merited a survival response. The worst thing that could happen was that I would have to take the class over. (This ended up being a blessing in disguise. I learned the material so well I can still tutor my teenage cousins.) But I didn't see it that way at the time, and most of us don't. Once the red alert system is ignited, it goes to town on its own.

Our complex modern brain can talk to our ancient brain about the complex fears of taxes and terrorists, but our ancient brain has only a few blunt tools to solve the problem, the same ones it's been using for millions of years. It's a noble effort by the ancient brain, but wooden clubs don't really work all that well when you're trying to fix an iPod. When I finally got to interview him from his NYU office, LeDoux said this: "The ancient fear system is not perfectly adapted to modern life. It's being co-opted by all the nonlife-threatening stresses we have in our lives, and there are a lot of them. Animals' lives were fairly simple: get food, find a mating partner, take care of young, avoid predators, etc. Our kids live with us for 20 years or longer; we have to get them into grade school and high school and college. And when you're constantly stressed in this way, then the brain has to adapt."

As LeDoux has shown in his decades of research, the simultaneous brilliance and problem with our fear response is that it's lightning fast and implicit. It can't risk letting us get in our own way and spend time thinking about a reaction. After all, if you thought too long as a cave person, the saber-toothed tiger may have already swallowed. By the time you can say, *I'm afraid*, your body is already well into the stress process.

This is why, sitting in Schiller's lab, I'd developed a fear response of a blue square from getting one shock and couldn't use reason (telling myself that the shock isn't actually bad) to change my sweat level from rising every time I saw a blue square. It's also why you throw your popcorn into the air at a horror movie when the murderer leaps out of the dark alley before you can think, *It's just a movie*. The fear response is faster than what we typically define as conscious, or explicit, thought, at least when it perceives a threat with our senses. Our imaginations can also ignite the very same fear response, which is why you might think there's a monster under your bed. No wonder you can't sleep.

• • • •

The basics of the fear response are nothing new. Harvard physiologist Walter Cannon discovered the fight-or-flight response in the early 1900s when he realized that animals' digestive systems shut down under stress. He studied it further and found the same pattern in all mammals: Heart rate and blood pressure rise to get more blood to the limbs faster, muscles tense, pupils dilate to let in more light, and veins contract to allow more blood flow to major muscle groups ("the chills," since blood is being drawn away from the skin). Also, nonessential functions like sex drive, immune response, and digestion shut down, which is why some people puke or defecate when they're really frightened. Gives new meaning to the term *scared shitless*.

This red alert system says *Hold off on starting any new projects—no point in planning for the future until we're sure there will be one*. It's a lot of power to give to a part of the brain that takes up relatively little real estate. The amygdala is about the size of an almond, but it's very important. It's involved in consolidating memories and adding emotional emphasis to experiences. Some people have gone so far as to say the amygdala gives life meaning. That may be a bit of a stretch, but the amygdala is definitely the brain's primary fear factory.

In the 1930s, scientists realized that monkeys with damage to their amygdalae lacked something. They'd approach live snakes and start batting them around like toys. They didn't recognize fearful expressions on their fellow monkeys' faces. Repeated studies showed that across species, the results were the same: no amygdala, no fear, at least not with the usual fight-or-flight response.

Humans are no exception. A 2010 study in the journal *Current Biology* by Justin Feinstein and colleagues describes a patient they call SM with a very rare congenital disease that had left holes where her amygdalae (there are actually two, but I'll use the singular, amygdala) usually would be. Researchers couldn't believe their luck when they found her and proceeded, of course, to try to scare her silly while she was wired up. They showed her frightening movies like *Silence of the Lambs* and *Halloween,* and took her to the freakiest haunted houses. She laughed. They introduced her to live snakes and spiders. She wanted to hold them. Even though SM *said* she feared spiders and snakes, she didn't show a single sign of biological fear around them. This could be impressive, as one of her sons told the researchers:

> Me and my brothers were playing in the yard and mom was outside sitting on the porch. All of a sudden we see this snake on the road. It was a one-lane road, and seriously, it touched from one end of the yard all the way to the other side of the road. I was like, "Holy cow, that's a big snake!" Well mom just ran over there and picked it up and brought it out of the street, put it in the grass and let it go on its way. . . .

You can almost see the headline: *Amygdala-less Mom to the RESCUE!* But the lack of fear could also make life dangerous. SM had been attacked at knife and gunpoint, threatened with death, and nearly killed in an act of domestic violence. The night after SM walked through a park alone and was attacked with a knife, she walked through the same park alone *again*. SM was immune to the devastating effects of PTSD, the researchers said, but her condition likely contributed to the number of times she got herself into near-death scenarios.

The amygdala can be clutch for keeping us from harm's way. But it also gets us into other sorts of harm. As LeDoux told me, in evolutionary time, the brain has been under pressure to adapt very quickly to the multiplicity of modern stressors. And it is adapting, but not always fast enough. We used to think that the brain only made big changes in childhood. But neuroscientists have made huge breakthroughs in recent years, showing that the brain changes throughout life, "rewiring" itself constantly and learning up through our golden years (albeit a bit slower than in childhood). This negates centuries of theory, beginning with René Descartes, that the brain works like a machine, its parts only able to perform the functions they were designed for. The brain is actually highly plastic, as neuroscientists say now, so much so that if one part of the brain is damaged, the other parts can sometimes be trained to compensate. One study even showed that London cab drivers have an enlarged hippocampus, a part of the brain involved in memory, from memorizing all those city maps. The amygdala too is constantly changing itself to create different emotional responses, and different fear responses. It's likely trying to update itself for the modern world as you read this.

That said, things move pretty quickly these days, and our brains don't always adapt fast enough. Sometimes they adapt in the wrong direction. If you're on a highway and see a semi barreling toward you, quick reactivity is crucial. That's a *good* fear response. If you have the occasional huge deadline and need a little adrenaline to get you through the all-nighter, that could be a good fear response too (provided that the deadline isn't every night). But if you feel like you're in the emergency room every time you open your in-box or talk to your teenager about grades, that's not a good stress response. And when you're constantly stressed, the amygdala basically assumes that you're living in a war zone and that it should be constantly vigilant. It can get jammed in the red alert zone, so to speak, and the brain begins to think, *Oh, red alert is the new normal.* It adjusts its homeostasis to a point where a barking dog can send you flying into the bushes or a dinner party can seem like a torture chamber. It's no wonder that, according to the National Institutes of Health (NIH), 18 percent of the US adult population suffers from an anxiety disorder in any given year, all of which—from PTSD to social anxiety disorder to phobias—the amygdala is highly involved in.

It doesn't matter whether you call it fear, stress, or anxiety because the same bodily process is involved in all three. Famous Stanford neuroscientist Robert Sapolsky has shown over decades of research that the stress hormone cortisol shuts down digestion, sex, growth, and immunity. He says, "If you constantly mobilize energy at the cost of energy storage, you will never store any surplus energy." Result: You'll fatigue more rapidly and dramatically raise your chances of suffering from cardiovascular disease, infections, erectile dysfunction, asthma, and type II diabetes, not to mention insomnia, eating disorders, depression, and, if you're a woman, a miscarriage during pregnancy. Stress can even make you age more rapidly, a fact every US president seems to demonstrate perfectly. Each one of these problems is unique and complex, but the basic gist, Sapolsky says, is that "if you constantly turn off long-term building projects, nothing is ever repaired."

• • • •

But why? Why does a math test elicit the same adrenaline and cortisol rush as a lion confrontation or a major breakup?

LeDoux has found a clue in the two types of fears: learned

and genetic. Genetic fears are *biologically prepared* to be triggered, which is why some people are born with certain phobias. Studies show, for example, that a rat that was born in a laboratory will still be terrified of a cat the very first time it sees one. Similarly, people all over the world feel uneasy about snakes. Even Eskimos, in general, will get sweaty palms around snakes the first time they see one even though there are no snakes near the Arctic Circle. Poisonous snakes still kill as many as 100,000 people per year in the developing world, so you can imagine they caused our ancestors in East Africa a lot of trouble. Evolution, thus, found it useful to build a fear of snakes into our DNA package.

In the United States, guns, cars, and cheeseburgers pose an exponentially higher risk to us than snakes. If you put a gun in front of a monkey or baby who had never seen one, they probably wouldn't scream or react in terror. Unlike the dangers that have haunted us for millions of years—the dark, spiders, snakes, heights—we *learn* to fear guns through experience or observation.

We know from the great physiologist Ivan Pavlov how this works. I experienced it myself with Schiller, learning to fear blue squares with shocks. But interestingly, the brain doesn't have two different pathways for learned and genetic fears. Rats can learn to fear an innocuous tone—beep—when it's combined with a light shock. Every time the rat hears that same tone, it will arch its back and freeze, expecting a shock. But if that rat has its amygdala damaged, it stops freezing when it hears the tone. No more fear. This same rat with a damaged amygdala will *also* stop freezing when it sees a cat. "The brain can deal with novel dangers," LeDoux says, "by taking advantage of evolutionarily fine-tuned ways of responding." And since that seems to have worked from day one of fear's existence in mammals, all our complex, learned fears are still routed through the ancient system. It's almost as if the US president had to send all our new legislation to the pope before asking Congress for approval—simply because that's just the way it has always been done.

Fear of relationship commitment or math tests hasn't been mapped in the brain by neuroscientists. And these fears are probably more complex than fears of shocks. But they do likely work in a similar way, Schiller says. I watched my parents' relationship grow more and more unhappy, then saw the final fight when my parents decided to divorce—I saw the pain on their faces. My amygdala associated pain with relationships, creating a solid associative fear memory. Maybe that's why whenever something bad happened in my relationship with Sara, or when we broke up, I felt like *all* relationships were doomed. I felt the pain of losing our family unit all over again.

The good news: We can change conditioned fear beliefs, at least to an extent. People who are afraid of heights have learned to enjoy rock climbing. People who fear commitment have gone on to fall in love and marry for life. You can even learn to overcome genetic fears. Shyness, LeDoux points out, has heavy genetic origins, but while some introverted children become more and more scared of social interaction if they are teased or abused, those with supportive teachers and parents learn to come out of their shells.

It has long been known that exposing someone to *positive* experiences can make a fear go away, or at least lessen it.

Psychologists call this extinction, and a number of different techniques have been developed. In the famed psychiatrist Joseph Wolpe's *Systematic Desensitization* technique, for example, an ophidiophobe (someone who is afraid of snakes) might be asked to create a hierarchy of his fears. Looking at a photo of a snake could be ranked 1 out of 100, whereas having multiple snakes crawling around his neck might be 100 out of 100. The person would learn relaxation techniques like meditation or take a mild anxiety medication, and then, while using the relaxation technique, gradually expose himself to his fears, starting with the photo and working his way up to holding live snakes. (It's tough to find exact statistics on how successful various therapy techniques are, but exposure therapy is generally accepted as the most successful in alleviating phobias and anxiety disorders. Oddly, however, Goldin pointed out to me that only about 30 percent of psychology and psychiatry PhDs are trained in exposure therapy, a helpful question to ask next time you're meeting your next therapist.)

After therapy, ophidiophobes generally don't change so much that they want snakes as pets, but many can at least learn to be around snakes without panicking. The reason this kind of therapy works has a lot to do with the modern brain. A 2010 study by neuroscientist Uri Nili (who spends most of his spare time rock climbing to test his lab studies on courage) set up a situation where ophidiophobes had a chance to meet their worst nightmare with courage. While lying in a claustrophobic fMRI tube, the phobics could use a lever to bring a live, writhing snake—situated in a window above them—closer to their faces or farther away. When they were able to bring the snakes closer, a part of the brain between the eyes called the sgACC, part of the prefrontal cortex, strongly activated, as if "talking" to the amygdala (or perhaps trying not to listen).

The scientists also logged the ophidiophobes' fear responses by measuring sweat on their skin and interviewing them afterward. Some of the phobics who acted bravely said they felt afraid, but hadn't actually sweated much. Others said they didn't feel so scared, but they had sweated a lot. Both these groups were able to bring the snake closer. It was the people who said they felt afraid *and* sweated a lot who succumbed to their fear. This suggests the modern brain may have to actually disassociate from its ancient sibling screaming "danger"—or shout a bit louder—in order to act in the face of real fear.

Either way, the point is that overcoming fear is possible and that we can use our willpower to do so. But why are some people traumatized for a lifetime while others conquer their fears? Why are some fears—like my fear of commitment—transcended for a brief period only to come right back? The answer has to do with memory.

• • • •

Goldfish actually have decent memories, at least for fish. They can be taught to do tricks for food, go through mazes, swim to certain areas to avoid shocks. In the 1960s, scientists experimented by injecting chemicals called protein synthesis inhibitors (I'll call them protein busters) in the goldfishes' brains. Proteins, the building blocks of life, are chains of amino acids that the brain needs to shuttle messages around. The protein busters broke up these chains, and without the ability to form new proteins in their brains, the goldfish couldn't retain any long-term memories.

They learned, but forgot immediately. And from this, scientists concluded that memories are material. They exist somewhere. Every single thought has real estate.

In the 1990s, LeDoux, already an accomplished professor, used these protein-busting chemicals in his rat studies. Remember that the rats who heard a tone with a shock even once often became afraid of the tone for life. LeDoux found that if you injected the protein buster directly into the rat's amygdala just after the beep and shock, the rat would not become afraid of the beep. The fear memory couldn't consolidate. If you waited too long to inject, however, the memory was allowed to consolidate. Then it was there for life.

This was nothing new. It had become dogma in neuroscience that memories are pretty much a one-time deal. Every time I recalled that panicked algebra test and the resulting D, it was assumed I was relying on that very first horrid memory in the storage bank. Once that *math tests = pain and humiliation* memory was fixed, it was lodged somewhere in there permanently, even if inaccessible to my conscious mind.

Then in walked Karim Nader, one of LeDoux's then-postdoctoral fellows. Nader had an idea: What if you could train a rat to fear a tone, let the memory consolidate, then insert the protein buster later while the rat was *in the midst of remembering* the bad experience? This would be like me drinking a protein-busting shake while remembering the moment I walked into that math test so unprepared. Nader wondered if that would change the *original* fear memory. LeDoux wasn't too sure. The memory was already there, real estate claimed. He said running such a test might be a waste of time and money.

Nader, being a stubborn scientist, did it anyway. He

trained a group of rats to fear a tone. Then he waited 60 days to play back the tone without a shock, as a reminder. The rats froze up. He then played the reminder tone again and, while the rats were remembering the evil beep/shock experience, followed up by inserting the protein buster in their brains.

Low and behold—poof. The fear of the tone had *completely* vanished by the next day, never to return. Huh? Where had it gone? Nader rushed back to tell LeDoux. This could be huge news. It was almost like memory erasure, like *Eternal Sunshine of the Spotless Mind* (which hadn't been filmed yet, but may have been based on this very study). This suggested that a memory was actually re-created—a new biological structure, new proteins—every single time it was recalled, and that, somehow, this new creation was replacing the original memory each and every time it popped up. As LeDoux later put it: "We learn, we store, we retrieve, and when we retrieve the next time, we are not retrieving the original experience—we are retrieving our last retrieval. In other words, upon retrieval a new memory is formed."

Nader and LeDoux re-created the experiment with control variables, and their paper made a huge splash in the neuroscience community. It was initially criticized, but then hundreds of scientists around the world began replicating and adding nuance to the new memory reconsolidation paradigm, testing it on worms, bugs, mice. The results kept pointing to the fact that every time you remember, the memory is being reassembled brand-new.

Then things got weird. Scientists began testing these protein-busting drugs on humans. They found that if someone popped the drug while remembering a traumatic experience, indeed, that memory's trauma could be dulled, almost as if it had never happened. NPR's *Radio Lab* did a story on a woman who had been raped and was so traumatized she couldn't talk about it with anyone. But after taking this experimental drug—usually called a beta-blocker—while remembering the rape, suddenly she felt well enough to talk about the trauma freely on television. She didn't forget the event, but the painful aspect of the memory was erased.

Many of us would find it a tad creepy to take a drug to dull our memories, no matter how painful they might be, and none of these drugs have been approved by the FDA for use on memory. (Beta-blockers have long been used for cardiovascular diseases.) But the fact that the drugs seem to work means that the same memory principle can be used to heal trauma without drugs.

• • • •

Studies began to show that in rats there seemed to be a period of about 6 hours when the fear memory, once retrieved, was subject to change. It was like an open document on your computer that could still be edited before saving it again. Using positive therapy—in the rats' case, exposure to repeated benign beeps without shocks—the fear memory could be changed for the better within the 6-hour window. But outside the 6-hour window, it was too late. The fear memory would reconsolidate. Why the arbitrary 6-hour window? That couldn't be true of humans.

Schiller wanted to know, which brings us full circle. Her study could turn out to be extremely important to how we use therapy to treat anxiety and fear. Schiller and Elizabeth Phelps asked two groups of people, group A and group B, to come into their NYU lab.

Day one: Both groups were shown a series of blue and yellow squares on a computer screen, the blue squares paired occasionally with a shock. By association, test subjects all developed a conditioned fear response to the evil blue square, which meant pain was likely on the way.

Day two: Group A was reminded of their fear memory with a quick flash of the blue square, which made the test subjects sweat. The fear memory, in theory, was now malleable for 6 hours. Schiller and Phelps came back a few hours later, repeating blue and yellow square images without shocks, teaching Group A's ancient brains that the blue square is just a shape on a screen, not dangerous. Group A showed good results. After positive blue square therapy, they no longer showed signs of fear.

For Group B, the scientists waited longer than 6 hours to give positive exposure to the blue square. Group B also healed their fear.

Day three: Both groups were shown the blue square again without a shock. Group A still had no fear, but Group B had relapsed into a typical fear response. Their amygdalae seemed to fall back on their fear association.

"It was pretty astonishing," says Schiller. "It had so many implications for why some therapies only work temporarily.

The original idea was that you could forget but you'd always have the original memory stored somewhere. The new theory is that memory can be updated, and there is a window in which this can be done. Why would evolution create such a window? Probably because it helps us learn more efficiently."

The study suggests that if we want to truly heal permanently from a fearful memory, we have to trigger that memory and work on transforming the memory right away. If I have a bad dream about math tests, I should work methodically on remembering all the math tests I've done well on. Changing the subject or repressing the fearful memory will only allow it to reconsolidate again and remain there until the next nightmare.

The real proof came a full year later, when Schiller and Phelps interviewed the test subjects again. Group B still got sweaty at the sight of the blue square. Group A was fear free.

• • • •

I can't stop thinking about how I grew up a math lover and did well in my math classes. I remember doing math *for fun* as a kid, telling my friends it was my favorite subject. But after that one failed test, I liked math less and less. I went to college as a marine biology major, but the math classes weren't that enjoyable and I switched to a philosophy and religion major. I don't regret the decision—it made me fall in love with writing—but it's a perfect example of how a single fear memory may have altered the course of my life. It makes me think back to my parents' divorce, and how that may have altered the course of my relationships, too.

I've always wondered if these fear memories were unalterable somehow, if I was stuck this way, my course charted by my past experiences. Schiller, LeDoux, and Phelps have shown proof, hard biological proof, that none of us are exactly stuck. And they've shown that the way to overcome these fears permanently is not by avoiding them, but by diving right into them, triggering those memories purposefully, and using our endlessly creative minds to change them.

Of course, they've been working with blue squares, beeps, and shocks, not the complexities of real life. And Schiller cautions me that there is much to learn about complex fears and how they tangle with trillions of synapses, our endlessly complex imaginations. "Probably where fears of different sorts come from is the same basic process," Schiller says, "but the more complex the fear is, the more times you retrieve that memory in different ways and the representation in the brain is more complex. Those memories would be more difficult to retrieve and update. We know a lot about these simple fears, these pain fears, but we don't know much about how complex memories are represented in the brain yet." Now at Mount Sinai, Schiller is using this new type of therapy on patients with PTSD and obsessive-compulsive disorder, but she says it's far too early to make any claims of the therapy being more or less successful than earlier therapies for these disorders. Severe trauma memories, she says, may work differently from normal pain memories, and we have to be cautious about being overly optimistic.

But even understanding a little bit about the way ordinary

memory works, Schiller says, has already helped her in her daily life. "Let's say you have a memory of a place and something bad happened there," she says. "Whereas before I might have avoided that place, now I deliberately go there. I go with other people. I go do different things. I go listening to a song I like. Over time I feel the memory has changed. It requires deliberate action. Avoidance is a natural response to fear, but it's not the one that helps."

CHAPTER 3

IN PRAISE OF MOVEMENT

"All that ever holds somebody back, I think, is fear. For a minute I had fear. [Then] I went into the [dressing] room and shot my fear in the face . . ."

—LADY GAGA

Mark Twain once wrote that Lake Tahoe "would return an Egyptian mummy to its pristine vigor," and even in this hot month of August, the crystalline expanse is chilly with fresh snowmelt after a huge winter. Last night,

Jamie Patrick and Greg Larson became the 22nd and 23rd people to ever swim the length of it. They started off at 4:32 p.m. and swam 22 miles, nonstop, touching the shore at 3:06 a.m. Greg stopped there, went home, and had a hamburger and bath at his hotel, but Jamie turned right around to attempt the first double crossing of Lake Tahoe in history. He swam through the darkness of early morning, his support boat feeding him bread, energy goo, and swigs of water as the sun slowly rose above the Sierra.

He has been swimming for 20 hours nonstop when family members and I accompany Jamie's dad by boat to cheer him on. But now he needs complete silence and focus, his coaches say, so we all just sit quietly, praying. He's swimming 20 strokes at a time, then resting. Twenty, then rest. It doesn't seem like he's moving at all. He's so close to the finish and yet, still 5 miles away, farther than most of us could go if our lives depended on it.

It's not a pretty sight. Jamie's expression is like someone is ripping his fingernails out one by one. His face is bloated and red. His tongue is swollen up like a plum. He's crying at times.

More people want a turn on the boat, a turn to come and see the dying man, so we return to shore and wait on the sand. We have a cold glass of lemonade. We eat a sandwich. We can see the support boat on the horizon, but it doesn't seem to be moving. Family and friends and strangers seem equally captivated and worried, hands folded together. The sun begins to fall behind the western peaks. It has now been 25 hours since Jamie first set out, and we're beginning to wonder if he'll make it. A few people are beginning to shake their heads when, finally—is it possible?—Jamie flops and flaps into shore. Hadley Grace Patrick, his 4-year-old daughter, wades into the lake, her arms spread wide.

Jamie hits the sand like a dead seal. A group of us help him out and sit him down. Television crews surround him. Medics rush in to check his vitals. Jamie looks like he'll fall over any minute, but he turns the medics away and says he'll stop by the hospital on his way home, thank you.

He answers a few questions for the media, smiles for photos, then vomits black bile. Then he wants to buy a round of drinks for his crew. No, wait—he's vomiting more. His wife, Terry, for whom I think the swim was equally hard to watch, insists that Jamie go get checked out before heading to the bar. We rush him to the emergency room in Truckee, and they put Jamie on an IV for rehydration. After running a full checkup, the doctor says that if Jamie had swum one more hour, he might be dead. Jamie, he says, burned around 20,000 calories and had only been able to keep down about 8,000. He hadn't taken in enough protein, especially, so his body was starting to devour itself, leading to near kidney failure. There was no physical reason he should have been able to push through the pain and keep going.

The next day we visit Jamie in the hospital. He's a doughboy, fattened with fluids, but he's smiling and joking as usual. I ask him how he felt during the swim. "Those last 5 miles were the worst of my life," he says. "But the first 40, wow—and what a sunrise."

True to form, Jamie is already thinking about his next ultra swim, a 111-mile trip down the Sacramento River.

"You're not afraid the same thing will happen?" I ask.

"Honestly," Jamie says, "I feel like I could do anything."

• • • •

Months later, after Jamie recovers, I go for a short training swim with him in the bay near the San Francisco Giant's stadium. It's a sunny fall day, and while we dry off in the sun, I have to ask him why he's attempting another big swim. I mean, it's cool and all to be raising money for literacy and the environment by nearly killing himself, but seriously, why again?

Jamie is thoughtful while he dries off his straight blond hair, letting the question hang there for a bit. "I don't want to hurt myself," he says, "and I don't want to encourage that in other people. I want to be clear about that." He has learned from the Tahoe Double, he says. Lance Armstrong's nutritionist, Stacy Simms, at Stanford, will be working with him on his next swim so he knows exactly what foods to take in at what times, and he'll have a doctor monitoring him the whole way.

"Well, that's good," I say, thinking about this briefly before adding: "No, but seriously—what the hell?"

Jamie first gives the standard answers: wanting to do something nobody else has done, pushing the envelope in the sport, pushing his fears. But he has also discovered a new drive. "When I was in that bad state, the last 5 miles of Tahoe," Jamie says, "I kept thinking, I really want people to see that you can overcome these moments when things seem at their bleakest, when you're truly suffering. I kept thinking that I want my daughter to see her dad do something amazing, and hopefully take something positive from that." Since the Tahoe Double, Jamie's swim has been made into an NBC/Universal documentary, and he has received e-mails from all over the whole world:

"You've inspired me to start exercising for the first time," "I'm doing my first triathlon," "I'm doing the AIDS Marathon." He got one e-mail, he says, tearing up a little, from a lady who said she was severely overweight. She wrote to say that she'd started walking again because of his swim. He kept in touch with her over the course of a few months, and she just wrote a week ago. She's up to jogging 5 miles per week.

"Pain is mental," Jamie says, "fear is mental. And if you can push through it, you're amazed at the good feeling on the other side. The anticipation is almost always worse than being in it."

Jamie has plenty of fears that don't involve extreme sports. Like millions of people, he's terrified of public speaking. But he promised himself that after the swim, he would try to speak about the experience. "I had this fear the night before my first Rotary Club talk," he says, "not able to sleep, the whole bit. But I got up there and I said, 'You know, I'm talking about something I love; I'm talking about something I know.' And 30 seconds into it, I was in a very comfortable place. I finished that and said, 'This is something I really enjoy doing, talking about something I love.' Now I'm excited about speaking. So through my athletics, I've learned that if you put the time and energy into something, and you build confidence, that confidence can trickle over into other parts of your life."

Not everyone wants to put his or her life on the line to overcome a physical obstacle, and that's probably a good thing for our species, Jamie laughs: "I think it's important that people tackle small fears," he says, "whether it's that you don't want to go to the gym because you don't look good in your gym clothes. You don't want to approach a big client because that's out of your scope. But you know if people just take one little step forward, they realize, oh this is not so bad. So it's not just athletics. It's every aspect of life. If you can tackle your fear head-on, you're going to be more fulfilled in life."

• • • •

Like all of us, especially those who grew up in the United States, I've heard these inspirational never-give-up pep talks my whole life. Maybe they were from mountain climbers, motivational speakers, or after-school specials. I don't remember. Sometimes they hit me, but often they just seemed cliché. But having watched Jamie struggle through this, having watched that disgusting pain turn to unencumbered joy and confidence, they don't seem cliché at all. And now that I understand more about the neuroscience and evolution of fear, they also make more sense.

For millions of years, our fear response was used for the basics of survival: run after gazelle when you're hungry; run from lion when you're game; fight battle against a neighboring tribe; hike across a desert to escape a natural disaster. To survive these scenarios, the fear system fired up at the first sign of danger to pump adrenaline and cortisol to our muscles, our bodies expecting to work really hard. In the last chapter I quoted Daniel Gardner saying that our big brains were our only evolutionary advantage. That's not exactly true. Slow and lethargic as most of us now seem, when we're in shape, we can run as far and as long, often farther, than any other animal on the planet, even horses. (There's an actual annual race, the Man versus Horse Marathon, that pits horses against humans every year. The winner seems to alternate between humans and horses often enough to make neither species a clear winner.) Long distance running is literally what we're built for; our ancestors were not just super runners, but super athletes in the most complete sense. The great athletic feats of survival were the central focus of life.

Hundreds of millions of years of genetic programming doesn't get erased in a century of lethargy. So it makes sense that we still revere athletes like gods, even if most of us spend more time sitting on the couch than running marathons. As much as we may think that ethically we should reward public servants and scientists with million-dollar contracts (and I think we should), a primal and unconscious part of us is more amazed by LeBron James, Shawn Johnson, and Michael Phelps. These are the survivors. No wonder the Olympics, the Super Bowl, and the World Cup are the most watched events on Earth. It's also no wonder most athletes carry themselves so confidently.

Studies show that as we watch sports, we get an adrenaline and dopamine rush that is similar—albeit smaller—to what the players themselves experience. Dopamine is a feel-good and motivational neurotransmitter in the brain that's released when we fall in love, exercise, drink coffee, have sex, and do many other "feel good" activities. It's meant to motivate us to action, to help us overcome the scary obstacles. When we watched Jamie finally land on shore that day, all of us felt some of his joy, that dopamine rush, and we had a strange feeling we could do more than we thought possible, even though we'd just been standing on shore.

It has long been known that exercise reduces anxiety and

depression, helps people sleep better, lifts mood, and also improves cardiovascular health, thus reducing chances for a stress-related disease later down the line. Feeling physically fit and confident also builds up positive memories to rely on. But scientists are beginning to get new angles on why athletes like LeBron and Usain Bolt might be so incredibly calm and confident on and off the court and how exercise seems to prepare our brains for handling scary new situations.

It used to be thought that the human brain only goes through neurogenesis, or creating new brain cells, in youth. But scientists like Elizabeth Gould at Princeton have shown that we produce new neurons throughout life, especially in an area of the brain used for learning and memory called the hippocampus. Besides adding new neurons, it appears that exercise might produce neurons that are actually better at dealing with stress.

At the 2009 Society for Neuroscience conference, Princeton researchers presented preliminary findings on an impressive experiment. They took a group of rats that ran on a wheel every day and a group that weren't allowed to exercise at all. Both groups were then put through a stressful experience that all rats hate: swimming in cold water. Afterward, the scientists checked out all the rats' brains. In both groups, the neurons showed signs of stress—except the newest neurons, the ones that appeared to have been produced through exercise. Those neurons were as quiet and calm as little Zen masters. Through exercise, the rats seemed to be literally changing their brains to be calmer in stressful situations. Other studies have shown that well-exercised rats are more exploratory in new places, while sedentary rats will tend to try to hide in dark corners and avoid them.

Exercise also provides a key stress outlet that might just make you a nicer person. Physiologist Jay Weiss did a famous series of experiments (again, I'm sorry to report to we animal lovers, rats were the victims). He measured the number of ulcers rats got from stress, a result of the digestive and immune systems shutting down. If two rats received the same series of shocks and experienced the same stress response from them, the rat that could gnaw on a piece of wood, run on a wheel, or—and this is unfortunate—bite the living crap out of another rat would get fewer ulcers than the rat that had no physical outlet for its stress.

Humans share the same need for stress outlets. If we want to avoid beating the crap out of one another or gorging ourselves with potato chips to get over a hard day at the office, a little physical exertion every day—or at least a few times per week—is a good plan.

The studies on the benefits of exercise are endless, but Jasper Smits, director of the anxiety research and treatment program at Southern Methodist University, did a meta-analysis of dozens of the recent studies related to exercise and anxiety, concluding that exercise is far under-prescribed by therapists for anxiety disorders. Exercise, Smits noted, is a lot cheaper than most fancy medications and therapies (not to mention drugs and alcohol), and "for patients with anxiety disorders," Smits said, "exercise reduces their fears of fear and related bodily sensations such as a racing heart and rapid breathing."

In cases like post-traumatic stress disorder and panic

disorder, patients often come to fear the uncomfortable symptoms of fear. As if there aren't enough real and psychological stressors to project about, stress gets added to the list.

Think of playing basketball or jumping rope at recess. You were probably so immersed in the moment that 45 minutes seemed to pass in 5. Even if you just go for a walk with a friend, you may realize, amazed, that you've walked 20 blocks before you can think about it. Exercise gets us out of our heads and into the present so we don't get stuck worrying about what might happen next. And you certainly don't have to swim 44 miles to get the benefits. "After just 25 minutes," Smits wrote in his study, "your mood improves, you are less stressed, you have more energy—and you'll be motivated to exercise again tomorrow."

• • • •

I'm probably a little biased about how great exercise is for reducing stress because it has, over the years, saved me. Growing up, my dad was one of the early surfers on Long Island—surfing through the winter in jeans and a wool sweater. Later, in Hawaii during the Vietnam War, he rode waves whenever his submarine wasn't out to sea. When I was 3, my dad was stationed on these little islands off the coast of Portugal called the Azores. There, he taught my sister and me to bodysurf, and we were instantly hooked. We later moved to Sacramento, California; my parents divorced; and I rebelled in a classic teenage formula: suspensions from school, drunk driving, drugs. I knew I was screwing up. I thought about what I could do to get my life back together, and I had this obsessive drive to get back to surfing. Unfortunately, we lived 2 hours from the ocean.

My solution? I ran away to Hawaii my junior year, leaving a note on my pillow that said, "I'm somewhere in the world. Please don't worry." It was one of those crazy, impulsive teenage decisions; and looking back, especially because I was on probation for a DUI, it could've been a disaster. But once I was in Hawaii actually surfing, I felt calm. Drugs and alcohol no longer had any appeal.

About a week into running away, I felt guilty and told my parents where I was. I added that I was, under no circumstances, coming home—no way. My dad ended up coming over to Hawaii to negotiate with me. I expected a big standoff, something like Luke Skywalker and Darth Vader—not to say my dad works for the dark side, but you know, a classic father-son fight. But instead of fighting, we ended up . . . surfing. And having fun. It was weird.

It was as if playing in the ocean neutralized our anger and stress and fear. Neither of us had been in a compromising mood, but we worked out a compromise (my parents helped me study abroad my senior year in exchange for coming home before my probation officer found out), and it brought us closer than we ever had been before. Going forward, it was surfing—sometimes just the idea of it when I couldn't get to the beach—that allowed me to get through college and graduate school. I would never be able to be an even moderately sane writer now if I didn't take a brief break every day to exercise, whether I play around in the waves, or at least go for a jog.

"Good medicine is bitter to the taste," goes a Chinese proverb, and the funny thing is that initially after the breakup with Sara, I felt so horrible, even surfing lost its charm. I sat around feeling bad for myself. Friends would call me, saying, "The waves are firing!" and I'd make some excuse why I couldn't go. After maybe a month of this—perhaps because my hangovers were only making me feel worse—I had to literally force myself back out in the cold northern California water (something that had never bothered me before). But as soon as I was out there, it was as if I remembered a part of me—a more confident and whole part—that I'd lost.

Apart from all the physiological benefits of exercise, there seems to be a benefit that science may not be able to measure. Think of the way we use language: I'm running to stand still. Her ship has sailed. I'm going with the flow. I'm stuck. The way we think about our emotions is very linked to the physical world. As I got back into surfing, the more calm and controlled I felt in the chaotic and wild sea, the more calm and controlled I felt in my chaotic and wild life. Exercise was certainly a huge part of this, but the ocean is also where I feel confident. I'm sure people who feel confident in, say, cooking or art or science could immerse themselves in those worlds to heal from insecurity too. My world of confidence is that stretch of saltwater where the wind brings breaking waves. And as if I were training for some Rocky Balboa surf-off against the Russians, I started surfing more than I ever had in my life: 3, 4, 5, 6 hours per day. I worked at night so I could surf during the day. I surfed in my dreams. I felt like I was 16 again, showing up on the shores of Maui alone—paddling to be saved.

Since the Sara breakup, I'd had a recurring dream. Noah Borrero, an education professor and one of my best friends, ventures into terrifyingly big surf. The waves are black and so ferocious that they shake the sand. In the dream, Noah urges me to come along with a relaxed grin, but I'm too scared. And when I go to grab my board, it's crumbling and cracked.

I know what the dream means. Part of me still feels crumbling and cracked. And I look up to Noah. He's one of those people who knows who he is. I once asked Noah if he got nervous giving presentations every day in class, and he looked at me as if to say, "Why?" The question never seemed to occur to him. It's hard to know if this confidence comes from being such an incredible athlete (he got a full ride to the University of Miami on a golf scholarship, one of many sports he plays well) or if Noah just doesn't waste time wondering if he can or can't do something. Not that he's unsafe or stupid. In fact, he's more meticulously cautious than most people I know. But Noah has free climbed El Capitan and Half Dome, surfed all over the world, and managed to do all this fun stuff while getting a PhD at Stanford and winning all sorts of awards as an education professor. If running helps rats build brave neurons, it seems Noah has spent his whole life building a brave brain.

I'd like to be more like that—and I'd like a chance to reverse my recurring dream.

• • • •

It's a crisp, cold morning in December, and Noah and I are standing on the dunes near our houses on the western edge of San Francisco, watching a Coast Guard boat on its usual rescue practice rounds. We're in disbelief. As the waves jack and pitch, they dwarf the gray ship, tossing it around like a twig. We figure the ship has to be at least 15 feet tall, so the sets have to be pushing quite a bit more. They fold one after another, thunderous green-black dominoes. Usually this beach has hundreds of surfers spackled about its 3-mile stretch. Today, not one.

We surf here just about every day. It's one of the most exposed areas of northern California, and during winter swells like this, there is often no chance of paddling through. Recently, the Association of Professional Surfers held a contest here, and they discussed letting Kelly Slater and the other dozens of best surfers on Earth use jet skis to get out if the swell got too large. Normally, I'd suggest we try a more manageable break down the coast, but, who knows, maybe my unconscious has been trying to tell me something with that recurring dream. "Want to just try to paddle out anyway?" I ask Noah, trying to beat him to it. He laughs and raises his eyebrows. Of course, he's game.

We suit up and return to the beach with our big-wave boards, the rumble of surf growing louder. Toward the middle of the beach, it looks as if there might be a rip where we have a chance of getting ferried through the squally inside, the most difficult area to paddle through. If we can stay in the current, it might carry us to the outside.

The water is icy, unseasonably so, and we're prepared to get walloped. My stomach is in a knot. But the rip is surprisingly strong, and in under 15 minutes, we're outside, looking around and wondering: where are the sets, the struggle? We laugh at the fact that we're alone out here, nothing around but blue sky and blue sea, an occasional flock of pelicans. My nerves disappear, and wondering if we misread the size of the waves, we chat casually about work, what our schedules are like. Meanwhile, in front of us, the sky turns to water.

Slugging off the horizon, the biggest wave I have ever seen is baring down on us. We scramble for the outside, the thing rising and rising before quaking in front of us: an avalanche of white. We swim down deep, but still get shoved down farther into the darkness. I have no idea how long the wave holds us down, but when I finally surface, I'm gasping.

"All right?" I holler at Noah.

"Yeah," he shouts, but then shakes his head as a teenager might do when he thinks his parents are being unreasonable. "Little bigger than we thought."

It's unexpectedly some of the heaviest conditions we've ever been in. We're not sure if we're in over our heads, but we paddle farther out to sea so we won't be caught again. I'm afraid now, the telltale signs setting in: shoulders rising around the ears, a mix of nausea, jitters, fatigue, clarity. Everything is suddenly uneasy. Do I have enough experience on this board? It suddenly feels unstable, more like a toothpick than an 8-foot piece of fiberglass. What if I am heaved over the top? What if my board hits me? What if my fins gouge me?

The film *Point Break* got a lot wrong about surfing, but the one thing it got right was Patrick Swayze's line: "Fear causes hesitation, and hesitation will cause your worst fears to come true." You certainly have to know your limits in surfing in order not to put yourself into situations that are too far above your ability level. But once you're out there, total commitment is the only way to succeed. Twice I've been injured fairly badly, and both times it was because I froze up at the crest of a wave and fell in a stiff, awkward position. If I try to paddle in, I might find myself right in the impact zone anyway, the most dangerous spot.

This is the pep talk I'm giving myself now, reminding myself that the tension is just ancient brain doing its job. It will send out its signals of threat and keep me on alert. The extra wakefulness and energy may be good, but the system might also try to make me freeze up or run at the wrong time.

Ten or so minutes pass in silence, and when the next wave comes, there isn't much time. I turn my board toward the sand, windmilling my arms. The spray off the lip is blinding, so I just stand in the chaos as the being underneath jack-in-the-boxes. Dropping, dropping, dropping, and still dropping. Belly rising. The wave reaches out its long green arm as it wraps into shore, and I feel like I'm literally on one of those disgusting waves in my dream. But as my board feels its way down, as the speed picks up, and even as the wave grows high above, I'm oddly not afraid. Like neuroscientist Daniela Schiller told me, "once you jump, there is just the pleasure of falling."

The wave morphs at the end. I can see that the whole claw is going to fold on top of me. I point my board toward land, hoping to outrun the monster, but it's too late. The lip falls onto my back as I leap, beating me down against the cold, hard sandbars beneath, down into darkness. This is exactly what I was afraid of, falling with full weight of the wave on top of me, but pressed against the contours of ocean floor, I know there's no use struggling. The ocean is stronger than me. I feel my body relax, conserving air. The sea will let me go eventually; and up in the light, foam crackling—sunshine, sky—I lie on my back and let out a delinquent hoot.

• • • •

"Fear is freezing," Schiller told me. "Just moving lessens fear." The fight-or-flight response is also called the fight-flight-or-freeze response, and Schiller was referring to some animals' tendency to freeze up when they're under stress. While freezing has its benefits for, say, a rabbit camouflaging itself in a bush, it's not the best stress outlet or way to build up strong memories. Unfortunately, I'm starting to realize it's a tendency I might have been born with.

When my dad was stationed in the Azores, I had to start preschool in a foreign country. I shrieked and kicked on my first day, then isolated myself until some gregarious kid asked me to play. At a new kindergarten, I did the same until Marc Mancebo said, out of the blue, "Want to be friends?" Switching schools a third time in first grade, I remember wandering the playground alone, telling myself that's what I wanted to do, until Urijah Faber asked me if I wanted to join the junk club, a crew of boys who hung out in an old tractor tire making toys out of trash. (I'd been trying to hide my jealous stares from across the yard.)

I always ended up with great friends at school, but I was never the one to initiate. I felt paralyzed in these new scenarios. And because I got by like this, aloofness became even more a part of my personality. I leveraged it to be the reflective, artistic guy; I guess it worked. But I'm seeing now how so much of this aloof coolness was based on that original fear pattern, that resistance to approach discomfort, to jump into the game at the risk of getting rejected. If you avoid the thing you're afraid of, you can initially lower your stress response, which will feel good and right, but like Schiller told me, that only teaches you to avoid again.

Not long after talking to Schiller, I spoke with Dr. Michael Lardon, a physician and sports psychiatrist to many top professional athletes. Lardon, author of *Finding Your Zone*, explained how every time we do something in sports—or in life—we're building what he called neural networks, synaptic connections that form our views of ourselves and our capabilities. The research shows that if we combine strong emotions with an experience, it makes the neural network stronger and allows the feeling to permeate that more ancient brain, changing habits. Often we don't have control over our emotions during a particular random event—a breakup, going to a new school, the loss of a loved one—but Lardon, who works a lot with PGA tour golfers, pointed out that you often can control your reaction in sports, which then act as a training ground for other parts of life: "If I make a double bogey," Lardon said, referring to getting a bad score on a particular golf hole, "I don't want to make a big emotional scene and pout because that's going to ingrain the neural network in a negative way. But if I make a double eagle"—that's good in golf—"I want to pump my fist a little because it's going to ingrain a neural network in a positive way."

• • • •

The big swells continue all month, and I start pushing myself harder, waking up early, going back out at sunset, sometimes with Noah and other friends, sometimes alone. Often I'll toy with what Schiller taught me about memory, remembering a bad experience from the past while I'm out surfing, and updating that old memory with the goodness I feel on the water. And as winter turns to spring, that lump of stone in my chest from the breakup is finally beginning to melt, at least a little.

I think I'm also seeing on an experiential level how all fears are connected. Fear of not being a good enough boyfriend is connected to the fear of not being a good enough athlete is connected to the fear of abandonment, commitment, pain, death. It makes sense evolutionarily. Fear developed to keep us alive and procreating—this is literally written into our DNA—so our deepest fears are still physical: pain, death, the lack of a sexual partner. And it makes sense that finding courage and confidence at this basic level spreads broadly to other parts of life.

Or, at least I hope it does. As spring arrives, I no longer feel as if I shouldn't leave my studio for the rest of my life. I decide to start an activity much more frightening than big-wave surfing: dating. The first woman I ask out, a food writer named Dawn whom I met through work, cancels on me 15 minutes before our dinner, saying she's sick. I briefly want to join a monastery or crawl into a hole. I feel that panicked conversation between my prefrontal cortex and my amygdala beginning its downward spiral. Dawn isn't sick at all. She's canceling because she wasn't interested to begin with because she can probably sense that I'm afraid of commitment, which is why I quit the soccer team when I was 12 and also why Sara abandoned me and that's why I'll always be alone . . .

Fear is freezing, I tell myself. Sometimes freezing is overthinking. I need to keep some sort of forward momentum here. I sign up for Internet dating that very night (even though I said I never would). A week later—after winking passively at 17 strangers—I end up on my first date with Jessica. Turns out there's zero chemistry with Jessica, but the date is harmless. We talk about a new museum show and go our separate ways. That wasn't so bad. This is progress. And some friends, sensing my growing openness to the infamous blind date, soon introduce me to Devon.

Devon wears flannel shirts, tight patchy jeans, and cowgirl boots. She's hot and I am surprised by the fact I'm ready to write her a country love song within seconds of meeting her. But I can tell Devon is unsure about me. At a bar with mutual friends, she does that aloof beautiful girl thing—which, thinking about it now, may be similar in an odd way to my aloof artsy guy thing—and I have to send multiple e-mails after our introduction just for a response. Normally, I would stop at one, but each time I feel myself freeze, I think of the old pattern, resist it, tell myself I'll handle her rejection (how bad can it be?), and, to my own surprise, eventually Devon and I are on a real live date. Turns out, the cowgirl boots aren't just a hipster fashion trend. Devon drinks me into a stupor. I have the worst hangover of my life. My crush is cured.

Alexandra is cute with an artsy wardrobe, and I can tell she likes me. But I know right away she isn't, you know, the one. I like hanging out with her, though. She is silly. We laugh. This feels good, but I don't want to lead her on. She is divorced. She doesn't need that. I will say nice to meet you and move on. It's the decent thing to do. Well, maybe we'll go on one more date, I tell myself, and while we're talking and laughing and Alexandra is giving me come-hither looks, I wonder if I'm afraid of being honest. Shuffling around in my seat, I tell Alexandra that I, um, like her but I just got out of a tough breakup and I don't really want a relationship, and

I know that sounds awful and weird but, what I'm trying to say is that, let me see—what am I trying to say?—if she wants to hang out . . .

"That's fine," Alexandra cuts me off. "Let's go out again."

"Really?"

"I'm not really looking for anything serious either."

Leave it to fear's narrow-minded ways to make us assume stereotypical roles. Alexandra, turns out, is more relaxed about casual dating than I could ever be.

• • • •

I've always felt as if I should get over a heartbreak organically, as if I should be perfectly pristine and healthy before even talking to another woman. And I'm sure there's value to not just trying to dull the pain with distractions, but there seems to also be a biological reason that getting out there again is both very scary and very helpful. In almost all primate species—and we are one—there is a phenomenon scientists call voluntary dispersal or voluntary transfer. A monkey, usually around adolescence, will leave the safety of his or her clan and family to go and mate with a monkey from another area, a huge risk. The monkey must leave the familiarity and safety of the clan, travel alone, and expose itself to what may be an abusive or dangerous group of monkeys. Romeo seeking Juliet is the prime human example of this, and while the importance of this brazen act is likely to keep us from all dating our cousins, it may be one of the origins of what we call courage.

"How did voluntary dispersal evolve?" writes Stanford neuroscientist Robert Sapolsky, who has spent years studying primates in the wild, in his book *The Trouble with Testosterone*. "What is going on with that individual's genes, hormones, and neurotransmitters to make it hit the road? We don't know, but we do know that following this urge is one of the most resonantly primate of acts. A young male baboon stands riveted at the river's edge; an adolescent female chimp cranes to catch a glimpse of the chimps from the next valley. New animals, a whole bunch of 'em! To hell with logic and sensible behavior, to hell with tradition and respecting your elders, to hell with this drab little town, and to hell with that knot of fear in your stomach. Curiosity, excitement, adventure—the hunger for novelty is something fundamentally daft, rash, and enriching that we share with our whole taxonomic order."

Sara and I were both of the same northern California clan: Our East Coast parents had moved west and gotten swept up in bohemian San Francisco. Our parents were so similar, we sometimes joked that it felt as if we were brother and sister. This had its perks for holiday get-togethers, but I'm starting to wonder if that voluntary dispersal drive wasn't giving us a warning by making us feel a little, well, bored. Devon and Alexandra had a similar West Coast lean that made me feel safe in a certain way too.

When I walk into Socha Café on a Wednesday night to meet Amy, she is clearly from a different clan—a clan from that distant and entirely alien land of Washington, DC. As we sip wine and talk about nothing of great significance—bullies and penguins are two of the more passionate subjects—I notice Amy moves differently, talks differently, looks differently. And I like it. There is challenge here. I don't know this girl's clan at all.

I could listen for hours to Amy's stellar grammar without interruptions of "like" every other sentence, her knowledge of the classics, her nuanced views of biotechnology. Then again, I could also simply watch her lips move. And, shockingly, Amy seems to feel the same way (probably not about my grammar, but about something).

We hardly sleep in our first month together. (A new love interest is a huge hit of dopamine for the brain. Drugs like cocaine have a similar effect.) We take camping trips and fly off to tropical islands, telling our employers we'll send in our work somehow or other. We go to movies and eat out all the time and stay up late laughing and talking gibberish. And somehow, in the middle of all this, Amy manages to get a bonus at work, and I manage to break months of writer's block, sell my next nonfiction book (this one), and return to my first novel, a project I'd abandoned completely after my breakup.

If fear is freezing, maybe love is what moves us. I should probably leave this talk of love to Amy, who, among her dizzying talents, writes poetry. But there is some biological proof now that love really does conquer fear, at least the freezing part. Falling in love, making love, making babies, giving birth, breastfeeding, hugging, even just thinking of loved ones—all that sentimental stuff releases a hormone in us called oxytocin. It has long been known that the inability to secrete this oxytocin is associated with a lot of problems—psychopathology, sociopathology, and narcissism—and that oxytocin is what helps mothers love their children unconditionally, as well as deal with the pain of childbirth (the word comes from the Greek, *okytokine*, meaning "quick birth"). But now scientists have shown that oxytocin—sort of like love in chemical form—is what helps mammals be brave.

Neuroscientist Ron Stoop and colleagues recently found that if they injected oxytocin into the fear center of rats, the amygdala, and gave them the same shock that usually makes rats freeze with fear, the rats still went into fight-or-flight (raised heart rate, adrenaline, etc.), but these love-boosted rats were far less likely to freeze from fear. They had the ability to act and move and respond, which would make sense evolutionarily. If a cat was attacking these rat mothers' babies, freezing wouldn't do much good. Love literally helps them overcome their normal response to fear.

I have no oxytocin measuring device, but maybe the oxytocin flooding our brains is why, as summer turns to fall, still just months after meeting, Amy and I both feel willing to move. Literally. Tossing off our fears of re-broken hearts (Amy, too, got out of a 5-year relationship exactly a year prior), we move into a house near the beach, a house with windows and views of the ocean. (My studio that I felt so trapped in was a human shoebox.) We spend our mornings staring out at the waves from our bedroom and reading poems over coffee, tickling and giggling like giddy kids, going to work late.

I suspect a better house with windows isn't the answer to lasting happiness. Nor is even a relationship, great sex, or the oxytocin and dopamine boosts that accompany them. And who knows what the future holds for Amy and me. This love stuff seems to be a big, huge risk, and part of me can't believe I'm taking it. (Isn't this how I ended up heartbroken to begin with?)

Despite our euphoria, Amy and I both admit to feeling a little scared about all these rapid changes. It's happening so quickly. But strangely, this isn't the paralyzing sort of fear. It's a fear that motivates us to be kind to each other, the sort that lets the other know: "It wasn't easy to find you; now I really don't want to lose you."

CHAPTER 4

KNOW YOUR MONSTERS

"Fear is the main source of superstition, and one of the main sources of cruelty."

—*BERTRAND RUSSELL*

It's a clear morning, crisp and cold. The jagged stone islands, appropriately nicknamed the Devil's Teeth, are beautiful, in the way industrial areas of Detroit can be beautiful in the right light: not a single tree or stitch of color. Just serrated rock emerging from the Pacific.

The waters aren't barren though. Just 23 miles from San Francisco, the Farallones Marine Sanctuary is one of the most lively areas of the Pacific. Nutrient-rich upwelling draws tidal plankton, zooplankton, phytoplankton, and krill, attracting, it seems, just about every mammal and fish to feed. From the deck of the *Superfish*, a 56-foot former fishing boat, Amy and I watch gray whales breach and flap and roll. Cormorants, loons, petrels, and pelicans crisscross in unruly patterns. Pods of porpoises pull up alongside the boat. We've only been out a few hours and have seen just about every animal we could hope to—everything except the fish we're looking for.

"Hey, Mick," I ask our captain, "what's up with that 2-foot space between the cage bars? Can't the shark come through that?" I point to the shark-diving cage that hangs over the side, the steel bars clanking against the hull with each pitch and roll. The gap is just about, oh, head-level and would easily let a 250-pound human (or two) swim through it. It's reminiscent of the same one that a great white bends and snaps in *Jaws* while Richard Dreyfuss panics inside.

"Oh that," says Mick, a gruff and sarcastic man who is every bit the shark-boat captain. "Shark couldn't fit its tooth through that."

"Except there was that one time," James Moskito, our shark-dive guide, chimes in.

"Oh yeah, that one time," Mick laughs.

This is only sort of funny. Amy, whom I've convinced to come along on this adventure, only half chuckles. After crash-landing in the ocean in a seaplane when she was a girl, Amy has a fear of deep ocean water. Adding great white sharks to this picture doesn't help, and neither does the idea of me prepping to go in the cage if and when we see one of these legends of the deep. I'm not sure how exuberant I am either. The insurance papers we signed in the darkness of early morning included lines like: "I acknowledge and agree that . . . shark diving, cage diving . . . involve the risk of property damage and/or serious injury and/or death." A shark-diving date may not be the best idea to build trust in a new relationship, but heading into our fears has been going so well. If all fears are connected at the root—I might as well dig even farther back.

A shark is actually the first thing I remember seeing that brought on immediate fear. I was 3 or 4 years old and flipping through a picture book called *Creatures of the Deep*, in awe of all the weird life-forms the sea holds, dreaming of someday being one of those Jacques Cousteau characters. Until I got to the middle of the book. There, staring me in the face, was a two-page spread of a great white shark opening its toothy maw. The shark's mouth was as big as my head, and I immediately slammed the book closed, afraid that I'd be devoured. I spent hours building up the courage to open that page for longer than a few seconds.

Since then, I guess I've warmed to sharks. When I saw a 12-foot tiger, one of the most aggressive sharks, in Hawaii while surfing, I paddled briskly to shore but didn't panic. The great white, however, occupies a different status in my psyche; and San Francisco—with its murky, cold, dark water—is smack inside the Red Triangle, one of the thickest populations of great whites on Earth. For years I've surfed in these waters and told myself that I'm not really afraid of them, that I might even *like* to see one. But this conscious feeling differs starkly from the great white nightmares that come, without fail, a few times per year. Brain scans of the dreaming mind show that when we dream, the amygdala is ultra active compared to other parts of the brain, which is likely why emotions in dreams can feel so raw and why nightmares can feel so much scarier than real life. Sharks apparently still represent grave danger in my emotional brain, and this makes sense in regard to research LeDoux has done.

Fear doesn't only come from the amygdala. Other parts of the brain—the hippocampus, largely associated with turning short-term memories to long-term memories, and the prefrontal cortex, associated with reason—also do some fear learning. But there is a disconnect between the conscious, or explicit, fear learning these more modern layers of brain do, and the unconscious, implicit, fear learning the amygdala does. In LeDoux's words, "The anatomical and functional dissociation between implicit and explicit fear learning, which involves different systems . . . explains how it is possible that in some cases the way we rationalize our fears differs from what really causes us to be afraid and to consciously experience fear." In other words, what we *feel* afraid of is not always what we *think* we're afraid of. My prefrontal cortex might have deprogrammed a little of my conscious fear of sharks. But it hasn't reached deep down in the depths.

It's a common scenario. Numerous studies have shown that when people are hooked up to a brain scanner, or fMRI, and shown random faces of different races, white people will often get more of an amygdala/fear response from unfamiliar black faces than from unfamiliar white ones. Some studies actually show that some black people respond with more fear to black faces as well, so it's tough to know if the fear comes from media programming or an inherent fear of "the other." The point, however, is that participants in these studies generally don't think of themselves as racist, not explicitly, but they can't control their implicit emotional reaction.

But recently there have been interesting variations on these neural race reactions. Princeton researchers Mary Wheeler and Susan Fiske found that when test participants looked at random faces of different races as the test participants were asked a question like "What kind of vegetable would this person like?" the fear response didn't vary between races. But when the same participants were asked to categorize black and white faces according to age—"Is this person under 21 or over 21?"—they went back to showing increased amygdala/fear activity for black faces. Fiske wrote that the fear activation only happened when "thinking about the faces categorically and superficially"—as when making a determination of a person's age. The vegetable question, on the other hand, nullified the fear reaction by making the stranger's face *known*, simply another human being. *We all eat vegetables,* goes the thinking. "By placing the person pictured into an age group, participants were categorizing them," Fiske wrote. "We often categorize unfamiliar people, whether as young or old, black or white, rich or poor. And it is when we categorize that our brain's alarm signals kick in." In brief, it's easier to fear the unknown, *the other.*

• • • •

Sharks are definitely unknown, other, and scary. They've been refining their hunting systems since the Devonian period, 400 million years ago, before trees. Great whites, the largest of all sharks, are so efficient they have existed in their current genetic incarnation for about 11 million years. (The first *Homo sapiens* evolved between 100,000 and 400,000 years ago.) From the moment great whites are born, they're in pursuit of their first meal, detecting the faintest electrical impulse in the pulse of their prey from hundreds of yards away. Full-grown females often reach 20 feet in length, 8-feet wide, 6-feet deep. You'd think something the size of a Eurovan wouldn't be terribly agile, but whites have been observed doing 360 corkscrew aerials while simultaneously decapitating a seal.

Of course, from the safety of the boat, this is what makes sharks so fascinating. There are about 10 of us on board who have been looking for white sharks since dawn. It's now 2 p.m. Half of us are seasick and the others are starting to give up hope. "I waaannaa see a shaaark," a guy from Indiana whines to his wife, who is playing Scrabble on her mobile phone. I don't expect the sharks to cooperate with the tourist schedule, and Amy and I are lying in the sun on *Superfish*'s front deck when, suddenly . . . a cry.

"Bloooooood!" the deckhand shouts, a cigarette hanging from his lip. "Twelve o'clock!"

On the horizon, a pack of harbor seals is skittering from the scene. They barely touch water as they flee. Captain Mick revs the engines. There's a crazed shuffle on deck. We're scrambling and leaning over the rails. Soon, we're at the scene of the crime and—

"Oh my God!" a woman shrieks from the stern. "This is the best honeymoon ever!"

We all run to her side, colliding with one another like the three stooges. It doesn't seem as if the woman's new husband, who has been puking over the edge for the last 6 hours, agrees. But the rest of us are enraptured. The shark is as wide as a giant sequoia, but moves with precision and grace, a sort of biological Ferrari. The water is clear, and we can see every scar along his massive gray back.

"Looks like a 15-foot male," James says.

"Now's the time to get in the cage," Captain Mick says flatly.

I start suiting up, wondering why I want to be in the water at all. My heart is racing. I can see that shark from *Creatures of the Deep* coming right toward me. But curiosity—aided by my nominal faith in the steel cage—trumps fear, and I find myself grabbing the oxygen hose and plunging in.

The seal's body has sunk, and I figure the white is down deep again, which is eerie. If he comes, he will come from below. I wait and wait in the silence, and every shadow, every flicker of light in the endless blue, my mind transforms into a fin, an eye, a tail. I am beginning to doubt my vision until, just there, just beneath—a shadow. Only it can't be the shark. It's far too dark, too massive. A submarine? A whale? I can't make it out.

Another few minutes pass, staring out into the abyss. Now something is close. I can feel it, and when the mass reappears just 10 feet from the cage, there is no way to describe the sheer girth, the volume. From top of dorsal fin to belly, the shark looks like an Airstream trailer. I could run around on his back. I could ride a bicycle. His eyes are black, just like you always hear, but they are not malevolent, not empty. They are simply the eyes of a being that has existed on Earth for 11 million years, just like this. I'm looking back in time. I expect to feel afraid but I'm not. This fish is too majestic. He swims by slowly, seemingly making eye contact but without much apparent interest. He doesn't swim up or chomp at the bars. Doesn't ram into the cage. In fact, as he turns, I have the strange desire to get out of the cage and swim after him. But as quickly as he appeared, he's gone.

• • • •

Sharks are the last true living monsters, the last dinosaurs, the last man-eaters. But the shark I saw didn't square with the image I've held for so long. I ask Mick and James about the dissonance, and they just smile and nod. James, who literally wrote the book on shark-dive safety, has dived dozens of times with whites while filming documentaries, often outside of the cage. "They generally ignore you," he tells me, shrugging. "In fact, they can even be shy."

And they're not always the king of the seas, says Mick. On October 4, 1997, when Mick was leading whale-watching trips out here, he saw a couple of orcas near the boat playing. Next thing he knew, there was an unusual burst of water. An orca had hit a white from the side, and the two killer whales were now passing around a great white shark in their mouths, toying with the body. "They'd dive down," Mick says, "pick up the shark, parade around next to the boat and show it off, then let go of the shark and do it all over again." Mick radioed Peter Pyle, a local biologist, who was able to get some of the event on film.

It was unprecedented, the first time an orca had ever

been witnessed killing a white shark. But more surprising than the attack was the reaction of the Farallones shark population. "They all took off for the season," Mick says. Every last shark fled the scene, happy to give up some extra elephant seal for safer waters. Mick says he has since witnessed two other orca attacks on sharks, and the same thing happened both times. Great whites, much like humans, have apparently learned to fear together.

• • • •

With a dark orange sun falling behind the spires of the Farallones, Amy and I are both high on seeing our first shark. Amy didn't feel at all afraid either once she saw how beautiful he was up close. "I'd really like to go in the cage next time," she says after I ramble on about how life-changing my 2-minute close-up was. It's a 180-degree shift from a few hours ago.

"You don't think the deep water will bother you?"

"No, I don't think it would. It was so clear and, I don't know, I can see why people want to do this now."

"I'll believe it when I see it," I tease Amy, who just hours ago was suggesting I skip the cage altogether. But in addition to the experience, in the weeks following, further research convinces both Amy and me, including our emotional brains, that swimming with sharks might not be worth the time for any more nightmares. A little more research shows that sharks are hardly the man-eating monsters they've been made out to be. Swimming in the ocean, even in the great white–infested waters off northern California, is statistically far less dangerous than petting a random dog or going for a bike ride. Nobody is saying you should invite a great white shark into your swimming pool, and there isn't any question it's a little dangerous to paddle around on surfboards—which are sometimes used to lure white sharks—in a place like the Farallones or white shark–infested Point Reyes, just north of here. Still, the numbers are clear: In the entire United States, with all those tens of millions of water enthusiasts, tens of thousands within the Red Triangle alone, the average shark attack fatality rate is *less than one person per year*, statistically on par with people smashed by vending machines annually. Compare this statistic with people killed by dogs in the United States (around 30 per year), lightning strikes (44 on average), bicycle accidents (more than 700 per year), car accidents (more than 30,000 per year), and heart disease (more than 600,000 per year).

Though the media still like to play up killer great white sharks terrorizing beach towns, most scientists now refer to white sharks as social, intelligent, curious creatures that sometimes hunt cooperatively, and that avoid humans. There are videos of divers like "Shark Man" Mike Rutzen swimming freely with great whites, petting their noses and riding their dorsal fins. White sharks, tiger sharks, white tips, bull sharks, and a few other species do occasionally bite people, but very few of these bites are fatal. Scientists say that white sharks tend to use their mouths as we do our hands, so when they do bite people, they're usually wondering what this odd-shaped thing is, then, realizing it's not a seal, spit out the scrawny human and go on their way. (Unfortunately, this sometimes means losing a limb.)

At least, this is what humans have guessed from our fairly scant observation. The reality is that, even after all the shark specials produced by National Geographic and the BBC, we don't actually know much about the fish we've woven into so many tales. Scientists have never seen a great white mate or give birth. We don't know why they migrate to certain areas like the so-called shark café between California and Hawaii. We're not positive about how long they live or many of their social habits, and we're uncertain about their home. The oceans cover 71 percent of the Earth, and yet, according to the National Oceanic and Atmospheric Association (NOAA), the oceans remain 95 percent unexplored.

"That's the reason for all the fear," Peter Pyle, one of the world's most renowned great white shark experts, tells me when I call his northern California office. "We're out of our element on the water. When we're driving a car, we think we have some control. If an SUV comes toward you, you think you might be able to get out of the way. You have a sense of control—even if it's often false. When we're in the water, most of us feel at the mercy of the unknown."

Control and predictability are highly valued by mammals. Physiologist Jay Weiss has shown, for example, that if a rat receives a warning bell that informs it when the shock is coming, it gets fewer ulcers than if it just gets straight shocks without warning because the shocks with the warning are predictable and the rat can relax between shocks. In another study on rhesus monkeys, researchers gave large amounts of food to some new mothers every day, scarce amounts to a second group, and unpredictable amounts (scarce and large) to a third group. The moms with lots of food every day turned out to be the most nurturing to their children. But the moms with small amounts of *predictable* food were almost as nurturing and low stress. It was the mothers with *unpredictable* amounts of food who showed high stress levels and low oxytocin levels, and these mothers were not only less nurturing—they could be violent and abusive.

But there are lots of unknowns out there that could kill you. Why do sharks seem especially intimidating? Jamie Patrick, the ultra-distance swimmer so brave in most areas of his life, until recently wouldn't do open-ocean swims, period. (As testament to how far he has come, however, he recently did a wetsuit-free swim at the Farallones.)

The fossil record doesn't show that sharks devoured many early primates, but there's always a chance that the fear of sharks is lodged in our genes, maybe even left over from our oceanic roots. All life comes from the sea, and it wasn't all that long ago—perhaps as little as 1.5 million years—that the great white's ancestor, *Carcharodon megalodon*, a 50-foot-long shark with 7-inch teeth, was down there, hunting us before we went terrestrial. "It seems reasonable to think that sharks shaped human evolution," writes Susan Casey in her year observing white sharks at the Farallones, "that a megalodon swimming at you like a bullet train was a very good reason for quickly crawling out of the ocean in the first place."

But given that we came out of the sea so long ago, and that it's unlikely sharks ever posed nearly the threat to primates that snakes and insects have, it seems that our terror of sharks has been greatly enhanced by one of the greatest human tools ever invented: stories.

Perhaps to make us feel more civilized—the tamer of nature, the embodiment of the divine—humans have always loved a good monster tale: krakens, leviathans, dragons, sharks. The Greek word for large shark is *lamia*, which is also the name of the Greek goddess Lamia, daughter of Poseidon, the wrathful god of the sea. In one myth, Lamia has an affair with Zeus and Hera kills their children in a jealous rage. Lamia becomes horrible and bitter—with a distorted face and a serpentine tail—devouring other people's children. Mothers in Europe are said to have used the myth of Lamia as a folktale to threaten their children into behaving. And seafarers have passed on shark sea monster tales for centuries. In his 1862 *History of the Fishes of the British Isles*, Jonathan Couch wrote that the great white "is the dread of sailors who are in constant fear of becoming its prey when they bathe or fall into the sea."

It makes sense for sailors to tell scary stories while drifting around the Doldrums, but it wasn't until Peter Benchley's hit novel was made into the best-selling film of all time, *Jaws*, that sharks became a common fear for people who had never even seen the ocean. Online chat rooms are still full of people saying they won't even venture into a pond since watching that 25-foot great white terrorize the peaceful town of Amity.

"There is no terror in the bang," said horror mastermind Alfred Hitchcock, "only in the anticipation of it." And watching *Jaws* again, even though director Steven Spielberg's white looks deadly real, by far the scariest moments are before Jaws is revealed, which happens halfway through the movie. That first scene under moonlight, the swimmer's legs suspended like bait, her frantic screams, all without seeing the shark, showed Spielberg's understanding of our fear system. "If, like a leviathan," Spielberg later said, "the shark had come out of the water with its jaws agape, and come down on her, it would have been a spectacular opening for the film, but there would have been nothing primal about it. It would just have been a monster moment, which we've all seen. . . . I wanted the violent jerking motions to start triggering our imaginations."

For years, only seeing sharks in movies and in newspaper stories about attacks, our imaginations have been constantly triggered. It's tempting to say this is a genetic trigger, but it's clear that nurture plays as much of a role in our fear of sharks as nature. The ancient Hawaiians, who spent real time around sharks—spear-fishing with them, surfing with them, even occasionally wrestling them in ceremonial competitions—believed that sharks could be *aumakua*, meaning ancestor or protector. Sharks were familiar, a blessing, even. Many native Hawaiians still believe this, and I've watched them happily swim among tiger sharks.

When I went out shark diving, I was afraid seeing a shark might make me more afraid of them, that I'd be suddenly unable to paddle out without imagining that Airstream trailer with teeth beneath me. The result has been just the opposite, and sharks haven't made an appearance in my nightmares since. Amy started talking about how she wanted to write a positive children's book about sharks "because they're so beautiful and kids should know."

• • • •

When Europeans first settled the Americas, the missionaries were terrified of the wild forest and beasts. Nature was the enemy, the scary unknown, and they proceeded to fence themselves off from it, trying to tame it and control it—in stark contrast to the Native Americans, who knew nature intimately. Other animals fear predators, of course, but we are the first animal to fundamentally alter nature to protect ourselves. This is an understandable response for an animal driven to survive, but we're also the first animal with the willpower (and the brainpower) to change our innate habits, and we're now seeing the environmental ramifications that have come from this separation from nature, this fear of the wild.

What's happening to sharks is a perfect metaphor for what's happening to the natural world as a whole. "When you remove an apex predator from the system," John McCosker, chief aquatic biologist at the California Academy of Sciences, told me recently, "the whole thing falls apart like a house of cards." The oceans stay healthy by maintaining a certain ratio of predator and prey. Remove sharks, say marine biologists, and the fisheries we depend on for food go haywire. A 2010 survey led by Stanford University marine biologist Barbara Block estimated that there are only about 3,500 great white sharks left in the entire world. If that's true, great whites are as threatened as South Asian tigers, and, according to the International Union for Conservation of Nature, one-third of all shark species are in danger of going extinct.

It was thought that the white sharks in California were safe after Pyle and others helped pass a California white shark protection bill in 1993, but this was when white sharks were thought to stay close to shore all year to feed. Now we know that the California white sharks travel thousands of miles per year: out to the middle of the ocean, sometimes all the way to Hawaii, leaving them exposed to mistaken catches by longlines, fishing nets, and worst of all, shark finners. Though the few shark attacks on humans bring headlines all over the world, you rarely hear that an average of 38 million sharks are killed every year just for their fins. Shark fins fetch upward of $200 per pound in Asian markets for shark fin soup, a wedding delicacy. Finners pull the shark fully out of the water, cut off the fins, and chuck the live, writhing body back into the ocean to die a slow and painful death.

Thanks to the steady flow of scientific studies debunking myths about sharks, the media now often treat shark attacks with more nuance, and white sharks are now protected off the eastern United States and California, as well as in the national waters of South Africa, Namibia, Australia, Malta, and Mexico. The mainstream campaign to end shark finning globally is beginning too. President Obama signed the Shark Protection Act into law in 2011, forbidding shark finning in US waters, and California Governor Jerry Brown recently outlawed even the sale of shark fin soup in California. According to a July 2012 report from Xinhua, the Chinese government's official news agency, China's State Council will even begin prohibiting shark fin soup from official government banquets and functions, and some revered chefs like Peter Pahk have begun spreading their faux shark fin soup recipes to rave reviews. Yao Ming, the NBA star, also has commercials airing in China that encourage people to stop eating the soup too. “Remember,” he says, “when the buying stops, the killing can too.” The question is, with somewhere around just 3,500 white sharks left, and so many other species threatened—will it stop soon enough?

If it doesn’t, it will be clear what wiped a 400-million-year-old fish off the face of the Earth: fear of the unknown.

CHAPTER 5

THE GOOD, THE BAD, AND THE BRAIN

"If you have fear of some pain or suffering, you should examine whether there is anything you can do about it. If you can, there is no need to worry about it; if you cannot do anything, then there is also no need to worry."

—HIS HOLINESS, THE DALAI LAMA

Flybusters, for anyone who hasn't heard of them, wear very similar outfits to Ghostbusters, but we carry giant flyswatters instead of proton packs. And instead of wearing a patch with a ghost crossed out, we hunt flies and wear a patch with a fly crossed out. It's a very clever Halloween costume. All the other third graders are envious. Nothing can stop us from saving the world from flies and collecting candy as a reward—not a special school assembly to warn us about the dangers of trick-or-treating, not even the 5 o'clock news special informing all parents to check their children's candy for razor blades, shards of glass, heroine, cyanide, and strychnine. Wait a minute—now my mom's wondering if she wants us going trick-or-treating at all.

"Mom—*come on*!" my sister and I plead. "You *said*."

"Okay," she says, insisting we bring all our candy home so she can inspect it. "It's just such a crazy world out there."

On the way to meet up with the other Flybusters, it's getting dark out and now this Halloween candy weirdness is starting to strike a chord. Would people really do that? Or is this just some adult scheme to get us to eat less candy? It must be true. It was on *the news*. Which raises the question—which one of my neighbors is a killer? As we go door-to-door that night, we avoid some houses that look a little questionable: cars parked on the lawn and such. What a dark, sinister world we live in. On the upside, though, we score a full pillowcase of candy. Back at Flybuster Jeff's house, we're counting up our riches when Jeff's mom storms into the room: "Wait!" she cries. "Don't eat anything until I look at it!"

• • • •

Deadly Halloween candy has been an annual panic in US households for decades. Every year, those razor blades and poison warnings come up on the news, and we wonder how many poor children have been killed or maimed by Satan-possessed psychos. Joel Best, a professor of sociology and criminal justice at the University of Delaware, made it one of his academic pursuits to investigate this tragedy. Any death or serious injury to a child from tainted Halloween candy would be reported in detail, Best figured. So he searched the databases of the *Los Angeles Times,* the *New York Times*, and the *Chicago Tribune* (covering the country's three largest metropolitan areas) from the year of 1958 onward to find a record of each Halloween sadism calamity. His shocking results? There hasn't been a single death or serious injury due to Halloween sadism, at least not one that Best could find in his exhaustive research.

Sadly, it turns out to be true that 5-year-old Kevin Totson died in 1970 after eating heroin supposedly hidden in his Halloween candy. Less heavily publicized was a follow-up story that Kevin had found the heroin in a relative's home in Detroit.

Similarly, in 1974, 8-year-old Timothy O'Bryan died after eating Pixy Stix laced with cyanide. But a later investigation revealed that he had received the candy from his father, Ronald, who had taken out a life insurance policy on his son. Ronald was tried, convicted, and executed for murder.

Of the other cases Best has unearthed, nearly all were pranks, many carried out by kids who had heard of Halloween sadism and wanted to scare someone with a copycat prank. "My favorite," Best told the *Los Angeles Times*, "was the kid who brought a half-eaten candy bar to his parents and said, 'I think there's ant poison on this.' They had it checked, and sure enough, there was ant poison on it—

significantly, on the end he had not bitten." The kid, of course, had applied the poison himself.

Best has found other tragic cases of children who died after eating Halloween candy—prompting authorities and parents to throw out bags of candy—but after tests and samples failed to find traces of drugs or chemicals, the deaths were attributed to natural causes, or some other illness, not Halloween sadism.

"Halloween sadism," Best writes, in agreement with several other scholars who have looked at the issue, "is best seen as a contemporary legend (sometimes called an urban legend).... That is, it is a story that is told as true, even though there may be little or no evidence that the events in the story ever occurred. Contemporary legends are ways we express anxiety. Note that concerns about Halloween tend to be particularly acute in years when some sort of terrible recent crime has heightened public fears." Not surprisingly, since September 11, Best has found new urban legends of kids finding cryptic terrorism messages in their Halloween stashes. Nothing has been corroborated. Yet.

• • • •

After seeing how blown out of proportion our fears of sharks are, I've been thinking about how easily manipulated we are by fear. An urban legend about Halloween candy isn't terribly serious, but group panics about complete fabrications have resulted in some of the worst horrors in human history. In medieval Europe, between about 1450 to 1750, a panic about witchcraft and its satanic associations—orgies, child cannibalism—led to the execution of between 40,000 and 100,000 people, mostly women, with most of them burned at the stake. The Nazis, of course, spread false fears to win support for their extermination of more than 6 million Jews. Posters with messages like, "Jews are lice; they cause typhus," were plastered all around Europe, and most genocides and ethnic cleansings in history have used the same technique: They play upon a prejudice that already exists, then further stoke our fears with false propaganda that the targeted group poses some potentially devastating threat, giving a twisted moral justification for their eradication.

Sometimes these fears of *the other* are straightforward. Sharks look scary, bite people, and thus create fear. But other times they're more unconscious. Psychologists at the University of Georgia, Athens, for example, showed a group of homophobic straight men and a group of nonhomophobic straight men various sexual videos while a device measured the arousal of their penises. Both groups were aroused by the heterosexual and lesbian porn, but only the homophobic men were aroused by the gay porn. It's unclear whether these homophobic "straight" men were secretly homosexual—and afraid of their own homosexuality—and had converted that fear to homophobia, or whether they were having some yet to be understood reaction. But if it's the former, then Freud's theory that we often fear and detest that which we secretly desire may be dead on.

Popular right-wing commentator Glenn Beck has stated both on television and in his book, *The Real America*, that 10 percent of all Muslims are terrorists. In a world population of about 1.6 billion Muslims, that would mean there are about 160 million terrorists out there. Frightening! But is it true? After September 11, a lot of pundits suggested that Muslims all around the world supported the bombings, and the news tended to cover the people celebrating the towers' collapse. But Gallup's CEO Jim Clifton realized nobody knew what the majority of the world's Muslims actually thought.

So Gallup set out to poll the vast Muslim world. They spent 6 years on 50,000 interviews, representing Muslims from 35 countries. The 2008 results, published by Gallup in the book *Who Speaks for Islam: What a Billion Muslims Really Think*, didn't fit the stereotypes. The poll found that Muslims and non-Muslim Americans were equally likely to reject attacks on civilians as morally unjustifiable, and Muslims said that the most important thing Westerners could do to improve relations with Muslim societies would be to change their negative views toward Muslims. "Conflict between Muslims and the West is *not* inevitable," the researchers concluded, "and, in fact, is more about policy than principles. Until and unless decision makers listen directly to the people and gain an accurate understanding of this conflict, extremists on all sides will continue to gain ground."

I've done a fair amount of reporting in the Muslim world, and it's true that there are militant Muslims out there. The attacks on September 11, 2001, are a frightening reminder of that. But travel around for a while and you'll meet violent fanatics of all sorts. I recently reported a magazine story on militant animal rights activists, and it turns out that in the United States, according to the FBI, it's the leftist Earth Liberation Front and Animal Liberation Front that have destroyed more property (well over $100 million dollars, mostly by arson) than any other domestic terror organization. Fear of fanatics is valid, but lumping Muslims together as members of a *religion to fear* is ridiculous to anyone who actually knows something about the very hospitable Muslim world. Unfortunately, more than a decade after September 11, 2001, a 2011 Ohio State University poll found that 17 percent of Americans were unwilling to allow a Muslim into their home—as in, say, *for tea*.

This aversion to Islam makes sense when you remember how rudimentary our ancient fear system can be. As Schiller's experiment showed, if you see the blue square while receiving a shock, you forever fear blue squares. . . . until, that is, you've had positive exposure to blue squares. On September 11, and in the days following, we all watched the towers fall hundreds, if not thousands, of times; the horrific images were usually juxtaposed with photos of bearded Muslim men or women in burkas. There wasn't much positive coverage of Islam out there to undo those associations, and most Americans didn't have much exposure to the larger Muslim world. It wasn't all that surprising that the FBI reported a 1,600 percent increase in hate crimes against Muslims from 2000 to 2001, likely making Muslims believe that the United States really was hostile to their religion and creating an ideal recruiting tool for Muslim extremist groups. Like the Halloween candy sadist stories that created child copycats, it seemed our fears were manifesting the exact thing we hoped to avoid.

What is the actual risk that you might be killed by a terrorist, Muslim or otherwise? With increased security, it's probably far lower than it was before September 11, but let's assume that things got really bad and all our security failed, as award-winning Canadian journalist Daniel Gardner did in *The Science of Fear*. "Presuming that there had been one attack each month for one full year—with each attack inflicting a death toll equal to that of 9/11," Gardner wrote, "the total number of dead would have been 36,000. This would be horrific but it would still not be a mortal threat to the average American. The chance of being killed in this carnage would be about 0.0127 percent. That's roughly one in 7,750. By comparison, the annual risk of dying in a motor-vehicle accident is one in 6,498."

But those numbers are little consolation after being bombarded with images of the twin towers crumbling to the ground again and again. Our fear response is a powerful thing.

• • • •

The relationship between fear and avoidance becomes interesting when you consider that most of us wake up every morning and read scary news. I personally feel like a bad citizen if I don't read the newspaper. Staying informed is necessary for democracy, and as a journalist, I'll be the first to argue for its importance. But it's up to journalists to not just focus only on ratings-driven "breaking news" stories: another murder, another sex predator, another theft—and it's up to readers not to feed into this sort of fear-mongering reportage. This sort of reporting doesn't reflect the balance of good and bad news out in the real world. It's also bad for our health.

Our fear systems were not built to be bombarded with tragedies every 5 minutes. My grandmother—bless her heart—was constantly glued to the news. As a result, she feared getting on a plane, riding in a car, even going outside.

To deal with all the stress, she sat at home drinking and chain-smoking. More people rely on medication to calm their nerves these days, and while for some antianxiety medication is necessary, it is often overprescribed, and the heavy need for it is dangerous. Prescription drug–related deaths have recently skyrocketed, surpassing even traffic fatalities. Overdose deaths involving prescription painkillers and antianxiety drugs more than tripled between 2000 and 2008, according to the Centers for Disease Control and Prevention (CDC), and the vast majority of the 26,000 overdoses per year are now from prescription medications.

• • • •

I'm starting to get stressed out and worried, which is why I've come to visit Rick Hanson, a man who believes change is possible. It's an overcast fall day when I meet with Hanson in his Zen garden–like backyard, in the green, rolling hills north of San Francisco. Hanson pours me some tea and we admire the scenery: the tall swaying grasses, the carp in his pond, the deer grazing on the slopes. A best-selling author and cofounder of the Wellspring Institute for Neuroscience and Contemplative Wisdom, Hanson is a neuropsychologist who tracks the latest studies about the brain and develops practices around these proven treatments to help people deal with issues like excessive anxiety.

With his maroon sweater, collared shirt, and gentle demeanor, he reminds me a little of my kindergarten Montessori teacher. But from reading his books, I know that Hanson, who started studying at UCLA when he was just

16 years old, is far from elementary in his understanding of the human brain. When he's lecturing at different universities around the world, he often rattles off lines like, "The diencephalon consists of the thalamus and the hypothalamus, which directs your autonomic nervous system and influences your endocrine system through the pituitary gland." But when he is talking to people like me, he leans more toward sayings like, "Just because there's that funny feeling in your belly doesn't mean that there's any threat. Our internal signals are pretty much bullshitting us all day long."

I like how direct Hanson is, so I launch into a direct question of my own: "Why are we so afraid?"

Hanson gets this question a lot, and he starts off by going back to the Serengeti, that area of Africa where anthropologists say humans first evolved. "So imagine this," says Hanson, "you're living in a small tribe, and to pass on your genes, you've got to find food, have sex, and cooperate with others to help the tribe's children, particularly yours, to have children of their own." Hanson calls these carrots, those positive outcomes luring you forward in life. "But you've also got to hide from predators, steer clear of alpha males and females looking for trouble, and not let other hunter-gatherer bands kill you." And these are the sticks, the negatives. But there is a key difference between carrots and sticks. "If you miss out on a carrot today," Hanson says, "you'll have a chance at more carrots tomorrow. Fail to avoid a stick today and . . . no more carrots forever."

From jellyfish 600 million years ago up to modern technophiles, perpetually prioritizing sticks, we've developed what psychologists often refer to as negativity bias.

"Our brains have become like Velcro for negative experiences," Hanson says, "and Teflon for positive ones."

The evidence is easy to find. Psychology researchers at Vanderbilt University recently wired up volunteers and showed them images of positive, neutral, and fearful human faces. People could process fearful faces the quickest—those faces were fast-tracked by the amygdala. When a fearful face flashed, the amygdala lit up even when the face had appeared so briefly that the conscious parts of the brain didn't have time to know what they had processed. But that didn't matter: The fear response was already in full swing. And this wasn't terribly surprising to the researchers. But it did come as a surprise that happy faces took the longest to register. "What we believe is happening," the coauthor of the study, David Zald, said, "is that the happy faces signal safety. If something is safe, you don't have to pay attention to it." In other words, evolution doesn't really care if you notice that brief smile from your barista, that sunset. It cares if you survive. Recognizing—and *feeling*—happiness is more up to you. The fear comes naturally.

Positive or peak experiences also make a lasting mark, but they seem to in a different way. Harvard psychology professor Daniel Schacter recounts in his book, *The Seven Sins of Memory*, how students in his lab recalled both the positive *and* negative images (a smiling baby, a disfigured face) better than a neutral image (an ordinary building), but the students recalled the negative images with more acute detail.

The definitive paper on negativity bias, *Bad Is Stronger Than Good*, was written in 2001 by psychologist Kathleen Vohs and colleagues. The researchers compiled study after study showing, for instance, that people become more distressed from losing $50 than they are joyful about winning $50; a single trauma in childhood is more enduring and pervasive down the line than lots of positive childhood experiences; a piece of bad information about someone is more memorable than a piece of good information; and a bad day's negative mood will extend easily into the following day, whereas a good mood from a good day is less likely to cross the threshold into tomorrow. Many people have also noted that sex, often a positive, can be an equally powerful memory booster as fear or negativity, which makes sense since sex is a biological priority. However, Vohs points to studies that a single negative sexual experience like a rape or trauma is generally more enduring than many positive sexual experiences. The studies Vohs cites go on and on, but "basically," Hanson says, "negativity bias is about survival. Nature likes skittish creatures because skittish creatures survive."

And sometimes this is a good thing. You have a strange feeling about a man in a parking lot and decide to hurry to the car. You feel fatigued and decide to see a doctor. But in today's world, most of the time, Hanson says, our fears are exaggerated. And—as with Halloween candy, sharks, terrorists, and witches—our social structure makes it difficult for us to think or speak independently about the *actual* risk of things. We suffer from groupthink.

In 1955, a psychologist named Solomon Asch gathered male college students for what he told them was a test in "visual perception." The men were asked to judge pictures of lines of varying length and answer which appeared to be longer.

EXAMPLE:

Line A _______

Line B ___________

Line C _________

When each man was tested alone, he got 99 percent of the questions correct. The answers were obvious. But when Asch put the test subjects, one at a time, in a room full of other men who were secretly in cahoots with Asch and answering most of the questions incorrectly, 75 percent of the test subjects conformed to the group's obviously wrong answers at least once. And more modern variations of this study have shown that when we think an issue is really important, we'll abandon the obvious truth *more often*.

Fear has made us this way. Over millions of years of surviving better as a group, we came to understand that belonging to the pack meant surviving. "Exile in the Serengeti was a death sentence," Hanson says, "and one of the most horrible things you could do was shun someone." Believing that the group is generally right was also adaptive. If the tribe all thinks that the crew over the mountain is hostile, it was probably better to trust that information than go and propose an intertribal BBQ. If a handful of your friends saw a lion in the grass and you didn't, well, why not take their word for it?

This group trust may have worked well back in the Serengeti, but now we can do our research and find out that, actually, the group isn't always right. Jews don't cause typhus. Not all Muslims are terrorists. Great white sharks aren't out to eat humans.

That said, there is so much information out there, we can't possibly keep up with all the latest data, which is often contradictory. We have to trust in experts and groups of experts, but this can be challenging too. Experts these days have often been swayed by enormously powerful groups, and decades of research have shown that when people get together in a group, the group tends to reflect *not* the average opinion of the individuals that make it up, but the *more extreme* view. It's doubtful that the witch hunters all believed that witchcraft was a serious threat to society, or that all the Nazis believed Jews caused typhus. But inside the safety of the group, the collective view can become more extreme than the individuals that make it up.

Negativity bias is not just about political or societal issues. It's also about the way we feel about ourselves, individually and collectively, Hanson says, which has to do with those *implicit* and *explicit* memories. From LeDoux, I knew that explicit memories are the conscious ones, the things you could tell a friend about: This is what I ate for dinner last night, and that's what I felt like when I first rode a bike. But the majority of memory is implicit: This is how to walk, and that's how to chew food. With implicit memory, the brain sends its signals to the rest of the body unconsciously. But Hanson explains that implicit memories include much more than just instructions for movement. Implicit memories form the interior landscape of your mind: relationship models, your general outlook and attitude, your beliefs about what you're capable of—all assembled by the traces of your life experiences. And since we're all born with a negativity bias forming part of our interior landscape, these negative beliefs—*I'm a terrible public speaker, I'll always be overweight*—become fairly set in their ways.

These negative feedback loops take up prime brain real estate, and they end up controlling our actions to a much larger degree than we'd like.

In that first essay on negativity bias, *Bad Is Stronger Than Good*, the researchers made sure to note: "This is not to say that bad will always triumph over good, spelling doom and misery for the human race. Rather, good may prevail over bad by superior force of numbers: Many good events can overcome the psychological effects of a single bad one."

New research suggests, however, that it doesn't take *a lot* of good events to begin to change negativity bias—it takes *convincing* events. In a fascinating study, Ray Friedman, a management professor at Vanderbilt, and colleagues asked black and white students to take a standardized test before and after Barack Obama's inauguration speech. Before taking the test, students read that the exam was "created by the Massachusetts Aptitude Assessment Center, and is used as a diagnostic tool to assess verbal problem-solving ability." The students also had to note their race before taking the exam, all of which was meant to trigger the stereotype that blacks perform poorly on cognitive aptitude tests. This setup was all based on previous research on what's usually called *stereotype threat,* and it seems to work with all sorts of common stereotypes. Ask girls to check a box to indicate "male or female" before taking a math test, and they perform worse than they do when they're not reminded in this way of the stereotype that "boys are better at math." Ask white males to take a math test that they're told Asian Americans perform particularly well on, and they perform worse than if they weren't reminded of the stereotype that "Asians are the best at math." So, not surprisingly, Friedman's setup worked. Before the inauguration, white students scored significantly higher on the aptitude test (12.1 for whites compared to 8.8 for blacks). But here's what was surprising: After the inauguration speech, the black students' scores were so close to *the same* as the whites' that researchers considered the difference statistically insignificant. The scores were even closer among students who had watched the speech.

Examples like this are precisely why Hanson says it's possible for us each to debunk negativity bias by emphasizing the opposite, the good stuff. Obama's inauguration was incredibly emotional for many African Americans, and those emotions were able to undo a small portion of negative stereotypes in a concrete way, at least briefly. But we don't need a huge event to happen, Hanson says. "There is good stuff happening all around us that we tend to just ignore," he says. Appreciate the leaves while you walk during lunch break, the novel you get to read before bed. The studies show, Hanson says, that the longer something is held in the mind and the more emotionally stimulating it is, the more neurons in the brain that "fire and wire" together, making the memory stronger. Hanson calls this turbocharging the good, and while it may seem like sugarcoating, it's actually training your brain to emphasize all the stuff evolution has trained it to ignore.

Good thoughts can be as powerful as good events. Hanson recommends starting with thoughts of loved ones. "We're so deeply social," he tells me, "I often start there." The way to do this is by just imagining, anytime of day or night, some person or a group of people who love you and support you. Imagine yourself with those people and how good it feels to be with them. The key, Hanson says, is really letting the emotions of goodness flood your body. By holding this imagery and feeling in your mind, you're actually strengthening neural networks and stimulating oxytocin, the body's bonding hormone, which decreases the fearful freezing response. Doing this often, you'll build a strong base, so you're not so easily swayed by your own negative feedback loops.

If you suffer from anxiety, Hanson also recommends emphasizing memories of times when you felt strong. "For me," he says, "it's rock climbing, or sometimes I remember a time I really had to stand up for my family when someone was being an asshole." Each time you recall a time you felt strong, and really feel that strength in your limbs, you're again solidifying a positive neural network. "What makes people fearful," Hanson says, "is a combination of the appraisal of the world and an appraisal of their own capacities. So, if on a zero-to-ten scale, you appraise your capacities as a two, and the issue in the world is a three, you're going to be kind of scared. Whereas if you appraise your capacity as a seven or eight and this thing, broadly defined, in life coming at you is a three, all right, you might be a little nervous about it, you're on your guard, but you're not going to freak out."

There is a lot of fluffy talk of positive thinking these days, and it's easy to make fun of, but the research couldn't be clearer that positivity helps performance. Neuroscientist Sara Bengtsson recently tested students in cognitive tasks just after priming them with words like *smart* and *intelligent*. She then had them do the same tests after priming them with words like *stupid* and *failure*. The students consistently performed better after being primed with the positive words, and countless variations of studies have found similar results.

Sports are measurable reflections of how positivity can affect performance, and I can't help telling Hanson about my best friend from childhood, Urijah Faber, now one of the top mixed martial arts (MMA) fighters. Urijah and I were inseparable growing up. He was always a good athlete. There were a handful of guys that were better at certain sports in our elementary school class, but there was something different about Urijah.

In second grade, we were all playing four square when a giant sixth grader stole our red bouncy ball. The sixth grader was about four times our height. Okay, we thought, game over. But Urijah walked casually up to the sixth grader, smiling. "I know you're going to give us our ball back." The sixth grader faked a line drive at Urijah's face, but Urijah didn't flinch—he laughed. A worried look descended over the bully's face, who then tried to act like he was just joking around the whole time. He tossed the ball underhand to Urijah, saying, "Just 'cause you're a cool second grader, Urijah," and walked away. I can still catch Urijah laughing like this when he's talking to his opponents in press conferences.

A good portion of Urijah's youth was spent in a gang-ridden part of West Sacramento, and Urijah had to be tough at times, but he never got in a fight. I never saw one. When people saw his unwavering expression, they just thought better of it. Other times, he used his wit to diffuse the situation before it got too heated; probably one reason he was often chosen by the teacher as a leader for class projects was because of his friendliness. My point, though, is that Urijah just believed in himself, and he was always willing to put it all on the line to back up his beliefs.

It wasn't the least bit surprising to watch Urijah become a nationally ranked wrestler through high school and college, and then become one of the top-ranked MMA fighters. He had stretches when he was undefeated for years. It wasn't surprising to see him start clothing lines and management companies or see his face plastered all over Times Square billboards. There wasn't a bone in his body that doubted his ability to land on his feet in every situation, so he always did.

"I remember as a kid, being almost a little bit unrealistic about stuff, about my abilities," Urijah laughed when I asked him recently about that four square game. (We were at his gym, and he'd just kicked my butt in about 45 seconds.) "That kid could have beaten me up. So much of it is the power of the mind and how you perceive things. An optimist, even when life beats you up, you find something good that you did. I have a real ability to focus on the good thing."

Urijah's parents also supported him unconditionally. Theo Faber was as much his son's biggest fan as he was his dad. And he used this strategy to keep Urijah in line. He would correct Urijah when he needed to clean his room or bring up his grades, but it was always in the context of, you're smart and responsible already, so that's what is expected of you. Urijah's mom, Suzanne, "the iron fist," as Urijah often puts it, was more strict. "But there was always this sense that even though we could get in trouble, we first knew that we were going to be supported no matter what,"

Urijah told me recently. "My mom had this attitude that nobody can mess with my kids. My kids can dance, my kids can act, my kids can play sports, get straight A's, do anything. It verged on unrealistic, but we bought into it and so it made those things possible."

In 2008, Urijah lost the most prestigious featherweight title of the time (the World Extreme Cagefighting title) to Mike Brown, missing a reverse elbow by millimeters and getting caught by a blow to the head that knocked him out. In a rematch, Urijah proceeded to break both his hands with unlucky punches. Rather than giving up, Urijah still managed to go all five rounds, throwing knees and elbows but ultimately losing by decision. A lot of the pundits thought Urijah might be done after that. But just a few years later, he's again one of the top contenders for the title and, more importantly, enjoying his career. "It's a good thing to talk about losses," he told me. "It never feels good to have the loss part happen. But you let it motivate you, or you let it bring you down. If I say, 'Maybe I'm just not good enough,' that's permanent. But if I say, hey, 'If I was a little bit stronger here, or I was just careless, that's what cost me the fight,' I can change that. Then it motivates me to train and doesn't make it personal."

Hanson calls what Urijah has a strong base. Positivity came naturally to him because of his environment and innate skill. For the rest of us, there is evidence that focusing on the positive can improve over time with practice, much like strengthening a muscle. Buddhist monks, for example, focus every single day on prayers of compassion, or *metta*, and neuroscientists have begun to demonstrate how this changes their brains. Antoine Lutz of the University of Wisconsin, for example, recently measured the gamma wave activity in the brain of a French-born Buddhist monk, Matthieu Riccard, who had completed more than 10,000 hours of meditation. Gamma waves are a pattern of neural oscillations that some scientists think are related to how consciousness arises and unifies (a hotly debated issue in neuroscience). Whether they are related to consciousness or not, gamma wave oscillations are usually so faint, they're barely observable. But when Riccard's bald head was rigged with 128 electrodes and he began to focus on compassion and loving-kindness, Lutz could see the waves oscillating more clearly than ever. Lutz and the other researchers had never seen anything like it. They wired up more Buddhist monks and asked some nonmeditating college students to come in as controls. When the monks focused on compassion, they produced gamma waves that were 30 times as strong as the controls, and the researchers saw much of the activity in areas of the brain associated with positive emotions.

Hanson, a longtime meditation practitioner and teacher, points out that it's a bit ironic that science is only now figuring out the benefits of meditation since, more than 2,500 years ago, the Buddha taught his students to meditate in a way that some doctors and psychologists are only now finding is so helpful. "A monk," the Buddha tells his students in one of the ancient Pali sutras, "sits down with his legs crossed, keeps his body erect and his mindfulness alert. Ever mindful he breathes in, mindful he breathes out. Breathing in a long breath, he knows, 'I am breathing in a long breath'; breathing out a long breath, he knows, 'I am breathing out a long breath'; breathing in a short breath, he knows, 'I am breathing in a short breath'; breathing out a short breath, he knows, 'I am breathing out a short breath.'"

The Buddha's instructions went on to say that the monk should be mindful of every sensation and thought "whether standing or walking, seated or lying down," and should constantly reflect on compassion for all living beings. And once certain faculties of concentration were built up, the Buddha recommended his students also look into what their thoughts *are*. "Suppose," he said, "in the last month of the hot season, at high noon, a shimmering mirage appears. A person of good sight would inspect it, and it would appear to them to be empty hollow, insubstantial. For what substance could there be in a mirage? So too whatever kind of perception there is . . . a person inspects it, ponders it, and carefully investigates it, and it would appear to them empty, hollow, insubstantial. For what substance could there be in perception?"

What the Buddha was pointing to, says Hanson, is a very scientific idea: that our thoughts, feelings, perceptions, and sensations exist in the mind, but they don't actually *exist* in some hard or permanent way. Fear is not a thing that exists *out there*. It arises in the mind and ceases in mind. It comes into being and passes away: impermanent. So what substance is there in it really?

Hanson says meditation is one of the best tools to debunk negativity bias. Through regular meditation, people can start to become familiar with their mental patterns, observing them rather than just automatically buying into them. And when the mind is constantly scattered, it's difficult to even notice how automatic negativity bias is. When the mind settles down a little through regular practice, it's easier to emphasize the good because we're taking note of what's actually in front of us instead of worrying about the future or past.

People like Tiger Woods and Los Angeles Lakers coach Phil Jackson have long espoused the benefits of meditation for performance, and, fortunately, it doesn't take 10,000 hours of meditation to start seeing benefits. Before meeting with Hanson, I was fortunate to meet Philippe Goldin, a neuroscientist at Stanford who studies the effects of meditation on the brain. Goldin recently took a group of people who suffered from social anxiety disorder (given the unfortunate acronym, SAD) and taught them a very basic meditation technique called mindfulness, which means essentially focusing on your breath and body sensations as the Buddha taught so long ago. People with social anxiety disorder usually have a lot of negative self-perceptions. But after just nine sessions of mindfulness practice, Goldin's brain scans and interviews showed that their anxiety levels decreased markedly and their views of themselves became more positive. Goldin told me that mindfulness works, in part, because it allows people to focus on something else besides their usual negative feedback loops that they get stuck in.

Scientists are still trying to get a complete picture of how meditation affects the brain and body, but similar benefits have been seen in soldiers returning from Iraq and Afghanistan who suffer from post-traumatic stress disorder, or PTSD. A 2011 study published in *Military Medicine Journal* showed that daily meditation reduced PTSD symptoms in the soldiers by half, and recent studies have even revealed that meditation alters the very structure of the brain. A study led by Harvard psychologist Britta Hölzel found that when a group of former nonmeditators practiced mindfulness meditation just 30 minutes per day for 8 weeks, they increased gray matter in the hippocampus, an area important for learning and memory, while decreasing gray matter in the amygdala.

When I heard results like reduction of gray matter in the amygdala, I wondered if meditation might be dulling the fear response. When you look at animals—who can sense earthquakes before they happen—you start to wonder if humans' innate fear response has been getting worn down over the last 2 million years as our prefrontal cortex has ballooned. This wearing down of the fear response may be happening, but Goldin said meditation seems to give the benefits of reduced anxiety *and* better fear instincts. Practitioners of mindfulness meditation, even after just 8 weeks of 30 minutes per day, actually react to a stimulus with stronger emotional spikes, *more* intensity instead of less. Their stress response is actually more robust in the moment. The key difference, Goldin said, is that the meditation practitioners then have an easier time returning to a baseline of calm when the threatening stimulus has passed, which is exactly what most of us want. We want to react to the real tigers with quick reflexes while letting the paper tigers pass without sending us into panic attacks.

Goldin has tried surfing, and he put his findings into a helpful metaphor for me: Skilled meditators, he said, are like skilled surfers. They have an easier time being calm between waves—enjoying the moment—but when a big wave comes, they react with more intensity, grabbing that boost of energy they need to react appropriately. Then, when the wave passes, they return to calm more quickly.

More research needs to be done to understand how different types of meditation affect different people and why, but Goldin is sold on the research he has seen, as well as his own experience as a practitioner. "Meditation makes people more aware of what actually is," he said. "Life becomes more vivid. Emotions like fear become both sharper and more discerning."

CHAPTER 6

PRACTICE, PRACTICE, PRACTICE

"I must be a mermaid, Rango. I have no fear of great depths and a great fear of shallow living."

—ANAÏS NIN

Pillar Point is a blotch of a peninsula that juts out from the California coast slightly north of the fishing town Half Moon Bay. From above, the point looks like a duck's head sipping from the cold

Pacific, connected to the mainland by a squat neck. But look at Pillar Point from sea level and you'll see that the duck's neck has been flattened. This is where the San Gregorio fault line cuts across the land.

Along with nearly severing the duck's head from California, the fault line's many quakes and quivers have cut grooves along the continental shelf. This probably isn't of much interest to you unless you're a fisherman, oceanographer, or surfer who charts a rare phenomenon that happens about a half-mile out to sea from the duck's beak.

A wave is created by wind over the surface of the ocean. The longer and harder the wind blows, the more ripples are kicked up. Those ripples, like sails, catch more of the wind's energy, becoming larger and larger swells as they spread out and begin their swirling trek across the ocean. During a massive winter storm, these swells reach enormous heights, but they also have a swirling underwater energy, like legs, that reaches hundreds of feet beneath the surface of the sea. Usually these giants break gradually as their legs stumble into shallower and shallower water, the head cresting with more of a crumble than a pitch.

Off Pillar Point, however, it's a little different. Those seismic grooves from the fault line channel the swells' power like a martial arts master focusing energy into one strike. The grooves guide these mountains of water from the depths to a sudden shallow point in the reef about 20 feet beneath the surface, making those long legs trip so abruptly that the swells heave up and over themselves into some of the largest, most powerful waves on the planet.

These mutants happen to take the exact form surfers like to ride. Erase those pretty tropical waves from your mind. Instead, imagine a wall of dark, cold water 60 feet high with a feathering lip as thick as an elephant. If one of these waves hit your house, it would blow it to smithereens. If it collided with a Mack truck, it would roll it like a Tonka. This is a place known as Mavericks.

A Mount Everest of the surfing world, there are only a select few surfers, out of some 20 million worldwide, who have ever ridden Mavericks. Even fewer have braved it during its most treacherous winter swells. Mark "Doc" Renneker has been surfing there for more than 2 decades in every sort of condition. Sharing our regular surf break in San Francisco, I've known Doc for 7 or 8 years, and I've watched him log far more days at Mavericks than any of the young pros, half his age, who are actually paid to go out there to be photographed. Doc's out there for himself.

About a year before finishing this book, I was over at Doc's house on Ocean Beach, the western fringe of San Francisco, listening to tales from his long history of pelagic adventures. Aging Mavericks guns—nearly twice the length of normal short boards and appropriately named after a weapon—were propped about Doc's stairwell and hallway. His shelves were stocked with great literary works, maps, medical texts, and travelogues about expeditions near the North and South Poles, some of Doc's favorite vacation spots. When the waves off the California coast fade—and when he can take a break from his many medical patients—Doc often heads up to the Aleutians, southern Alaska, Iceland, or Greenland to try his hand on the dinosaur-size surf in those parts. Usually the first to have surfed these barren zones (or attempted to), Doc will buy old nautical maps, estimate where the waves should be breaking, and have a bush plane or local fisherman drop him off for a couple of weeks to hunt around.

The danger involved in such acts boggles the mind, but Doc doesn't see himself as a daredevil in the slightest. "I'm not the guy to say, 'Hey, there's a storm brewing, let's go to sea,'" he told me. "I'm not stupid."

The latter statement is true at least. During medical school at the University of California, San Francisco, in the '70s, Doc was a star, becoming director at large of the California division of the American Cancer Society, a ridiculous accomplishment for someone who wasn't even a doctor yet. But Doc studied big waves just as diligently, if not more diligently, than medicine. Most medical students at UCSF find it hard to find time to sleep, but in between studies, Doc surfed every day, sometimes twice a day. While dissecting cadavers, he'd even position the corpse by the window so he could watch the waves at Ocean Beach. At night when he finished his studies, he often pored over oceanic data and maps, allowing him to be the first to ride a number of northern California's unexplored big-wave spots.

So when his friend Jeff Clark, the first man to ride a wave at Mavericks, tipped Doc off to this new maniacal playground off Pillar Point, Doc didn't think much of it. He and his friend John Raymond paddled out there alone one day in 1990 and "had the time of our lives," as Doc said. This is not the experience most surfers have on their first day at Mavericks. In fact, 2 years later, one of Doc's friends, Mark Foo, a Hawaiian big-wave surfing legend, drowned at Mavericks on his first day out. Doc was with him. But even after witnessing Foo's death and countless other injuries—and often acting as the doctor to try to repair those injuries—Doc told me that, to this day, the waves at Mavericks don't haunt him.

The reason, he said, is simple: preparation. Doc grew up

bodysurfing grizzly places in Southern California like The Wedge, a thick slab of a wave that breaks in ultra-shallow water and regularly claims surfers' lives. And when he was first training to surf big waves, "I always had strategies for all the things that could happen out there," Doc told me. "Two-wave hold-downs, rips, snapped leashes, and I would seek out those experiences." Doc knew all about how the amygdala worked, fight-or-flight, and factored it into his training. In the summer when the waves were small, he'd paddle out a few miles into open ocean, then pretend he lost his board and swim back to shore with the board in tow. A two-wave hold-down is one of the scariest experiences for big-wave riders: You're pummeled by one wave, held to the bottom, run out of air from the adrenaline pumping through you, then just as you're fighting to the top, dying for air, the next wave slaps you down. Instead of waiting to find out how horrible this would be, Doc used to rehearse hold-downs. "I'd go out to Ocean Beach on a big day and stay down for two waves on purpose," he said, "just to ablate the fear, because what I know of fear is that it will increase your heart rate, and it will increase your oxygen usage, and you won't last as long."

Doc made little games out of training. On his way to Mavericks, he'd hold his breath between the turnoff from Highway One to Pillar Point. This took about 2 minutes if he forced himself to drive the speed limit, 35 mph. "The interesting thing is," Doc said, smiling a little at how weird he is, "if you don't take a perfect breath, then you find yourself—unknowingly—pressing down on the gas pedal to go a little faster, to get to the end of the road sooner. So what I started doing is, when I really want to breathe, I'd let off on the accelerator, down to 30, 20, and it seems to take forever, and that's what simulates a long hold-down. Much as you want to get to the surface, you just have to wait. But you can definitely uncouple or desensitize a superficial fear response."

It sounds a little obsessive, Doc laughs, but being obsessive has paid off. Not long after Foo died, a 30-foot wave caught Doc inside at Mavericks. He tried to swim deep, but the impact was so hard, it cracked him straight to the reef, 20 feet down. "I bounced three times off the bottom," Doc said, "going backwards." He initially went limp, trying to conserve oxygen. But after his third bounce, something unexpected happened. He was tumbling down farther, farther, farther off an underwater cliff or crevasse. He thought it was some sort of abyss, until, "wham! I slammed so hard on the rock, I hurt my heels." This was new. If all the water was pushing down hard on the reef, when it got to the east end, there was an underwater cliff where the force of the wave waterfalled off the back. He was deeper than he'd ever been, and Doc could still feel the pressure of the wave bearing down. He pushed off the bottom and started breaststroking up: one stroke, two . . . three . . . four (he was deeper than he'd thought) . . . five . . . six . . . seven (How was he not to the surface yet?) . . . eight. . . . He wanted to breathe so, so badly. He felt the involuntary spasms in his throat and lungs. He was starting to panic. If there was another wave, he was screwed.

But then he caught himself. "And this was the override button on the amygdala," he told me. As he was beginning to freak out, he reasoned that if he swam up too quickly, he was more likely to get caught by that next wave in the set and pounded back down. So, against all his natural biology, Doc slowed. Then, finally breaking the surface calmly, he peeked around for the next wave. It had passed. "But if I hadn't caught myself, it would've changed me," Doc said. "If I hadn't realized that I was panicking, it would have changed my feeling about Mavericks and the risk of Mavericks. It was the same thing that I'd been practicing driving along the runway. Okay, now things are bad—slow it down."

• • • •

It may sound weird, but the longer I live with Amy, the more she reminds me a little bit of Doc. She doesn't wear socks with flip-flops or come close to 6 foot 4 with a silver ponytail, but she has an uncanny ability to stay calm in the face of enormous stress (with the exception of deep water and the sight of her own blood, anyway—we all have our issues). I'm constantly in awe of how she can, say, prepare dinner for 30 while navigating a conference call with potential investors and still manage to wink at me when I come into the kitchen.

When I met Amy, she seemed all cute and innocent, but I've gradually realized that she is a terror of success: a nationally ranked lacrosse player through high school, multilingual, lots of extracurricular volunteer work, Ivy League degrees, an invitation from the White House to work in the administration, which, by the way, she has turned down to focus on the start-up she helped whip together after business school. Wall Street firms want her. She was the driving force behind landmark legislation like California's Proposition 71. She has testified before Congress. She loves to ski. I am not lying.

Amy doesn't brag about this stuff. She's incredibly modest. But I've gradually pried it out of her. And I'm convinced that one of the reasons she is in such demand is her ability to handle *very high* stress, which developed, much as it did for Doc, from doing well in sports and going to some of the best schools in the world. Also like Doc—whose father was a well-known psychologist in Los Angeles—Amy had excellent stress-management role models. Both her parents are lawyers, and they were able to juggle high-powered legal careers (mostly in government) while also raising three children and staying deeply in love. Amy's father, Bill, was a football star at Yale, and after law school, he went on to coach high school football and rugby—while still working full days at the office. Amy's mom somehow managed to prosecute rapists and murderers all day for the DC district attorney's office—while DC was the murder capital of the country—and still usually come home in time to cook a healthy dinner for her family. Meanwhile, Amy's parents never pressured her or her two brothers to achieve—they didn't even check Amy's grades in high school—but Amy continually saw, by example, that it was possible to maintain composure and love in the most stressful of careers.

So it's no surprise Amy now feels prepared to handle whatever obstacles life throws her way. Like Doc, she seeks out obstacles, knowing that's what makes her grow, what makes life exciting. And if she doesn't feel like she can handle something, she trains like a ninja. Whenever she has a big board meeting or a speech about something she doesn't understand, it's almost as if she goes into a trance and emerges calm.

I feel slightly, well, unprepared, in comparison. Things are going well in our new house together, but we're still in the probationary relationship phase, and I'm convinced that if I'm going to have a shot with this woman for the long term—which I am nervously and secretly beginning to plot—I'd better learn to be a little more of a ninja myself.

I now have some tools in this department. I know how to debunk negativity bias by emphasizing the positive. I know how to reprogram old fearful memories through gradual positive exposure to the object of fear. I know love can keep you from freezing. I know that anticipation of something scary is usually worse than just acting, and that movement and exercise reduce fear and stress. Meditation can keep the mind from spinning unnecessary webs of dread, and I know not to just automatically buy into groupthink about the world's so-called monsters. And when everything is going well—when I wake up on the right side of the bed and I'm not behind on rent—I'm starting to feel pretty darn good. The whole heartbreak thing seems a distant memory. I feel, generally . . . okay.

But, as Mike Tyson once said, "everyone has a plan until they get punched in the face." Even in this generally good state, I hardly have developed nerves of steel. The smallest thing—a scary ending to a movie, too many deadlines or dinner parties on the calendar, or just a bad cup of coffee—to say nothing of the big things, can still throw me completely out of whack. I need to learn how to remain calm in the midst of high stress, which is actually why I visited Doc to ask him about surfing. I recently read a study that if one rat receives 50 shocks and the other rat 10 shocks, the one who received more shocks will be more stressed out. But if you give both rats 25 shocks the next day, the one that received 50 shocks the day before thinks it's no big deal. And maybe this is Doc and Amy's trick. They've been through it. Which is why for the last few months, I've been secretly training for my own stress inoculation. I've been training to surf Mavericks. I've never been so terrified.

• • • •

Doc thought Mavericks suffered from negativity bias. If you were prepared—meaning that you had a decade or so of obsessive surfing under your belt—then it wasn't as bad as people said. But articles, books, and every other Mavericks surfer I talked to all depicted the place as sinister—"a death wave," it was often called. To top it off, the place was also a great white shark hunting ground, and several Mavericks surfers had already had their boards sampled. I took Doc's points to heart, but just in case, I figured I'd fall back on my ancestral biology and assume the 99.9 percent of the group was right in deeming Mavericks life-threatening.

Studying people's reactions under life-threatening circumstances is very difficult for the obvious reason that when someone has, say, a gun to the head, you don't often have time to shove the person into an fMRI tube. But we do know that people vary widely in how they react under life-threatening stress (or any stress for that matter). Some people freeze, others run; some scream, others fight; some get tunnel vision, others don't; some try to protect their loved ones, others use their loved ones as shields; some remember everything in detail, others remember nothing. But the general consensus from the military and police force, who have been working on this problem for a while, seems to be that most people react *automatically* in the heat of life-threatening danger, even when highly trained. (Three-quarters of trained police officers, for example, reported reacting "automatically" under gunfire, according to a study by psychologist Dr. Alexis Artwohl and police veteran Loren Christensen.)

This makes perfect sense. The fear response is faster than explicit thought, which is why the military and police train, train, and train some more for every possible bad scenario, making those fake POW camps or war games seem as real as possible so the brain won't freak out at the first sight of the real thing. Training is the only way to ensure that once you're under fire—or under the lip of a 50-foot wave—your brain will fall back on the right implicit muscle memory. And the same holds true for making a presentation at work that may feel life-threatening, at least to your ancient brain that desperately wants to avoid being shunned by the tribe. Of course, even then you can't be sure.

We all start off at different levels in sports, academics, arts, and just about any skill there is. Sian Beilock, a University of Chicago psychologist and the author of *Choke: What the Secrets of the Brain Reveal about Getting It Right When You Have To,* told me that no matter where you start on the genetic totem pole, research shows that training is what makes you excel. Contrary to popular belief, even the most gifted athletes and thinkers seem to result more often from better training regimens than from genetics. In a well-known European study, which Beilock highlights in her book, elite soccer players outperformed the average person in soccer-related activities—no big surprise. But when the skill was simply pushing a button in response to a flashing light, the soccer players showed no special reactionary abilities. They performed, on average, just like anyone else. In other words, though genetics definitely plays a role in our skill levels, elite athletes don't necessarily have superhero capabilities. To a large degree, they've simply trained more. Training that involves more academic thinking seems to be similar. Psychologist and chess master Adrianus Dingeman de Groot showed this way back in the '60s. He found that chess masters could reconstruct pieces on a chess board from memory much better than inexperienced chess players. But when the pieces were arranged in a random way, so that the arrangements had no meaning to the game, the chess masters had no special memory capabilities compared to the average person. They had only *trained* to recognize chess patterns.

My dad was in the navy and the air force and often used to tell me his war-game training stories. The military and police can't very well practice under actual life-threatening circumstances, he said, or they would give their trainees PTSD or kill them before they got to battle. Instead, they use what's called stress inoculation, introducing increasing levels of stressful training to raise soldiers' thresholds. In Beilock's lab, she has shown that people who learn to do golf putts while being watched perform better under stress than those who learn to putt alone. And similarly, police officers who do their shooting training by reacting to real people (using pellets, not real bullets), versus those who shoot at cardboard targets, shoot more precisely in a simulated, high-stress battle. The more you train under stress, the more you grow your comfort zone. And there's even preliminary evidence that how you frame stress helps you perform better.

One of Beilock's graduate students recently measured students' cortisol (the stress hormone) levels after taking a difficult math test. For students who reported a fear of math, the higher their stress level was, the worse they did on the test. But for students who liked math, the higher their stress level was, the *better* they performed on the test. The math lovers might have perceived the stress as excitement. The students who had done poorly on math tests in the past probably interpreted the stress as a reason they would fail. Stress, in other words, is not always the culprit. It's how we frame it, and this has enormous implications for work of all sorts. Stress in a job you're passionate about might affect you very differently from stress in a job you just do to pay the bills. (Beilock is already planning similar studies for sports, and more research needs to be done for any conclusions on the framing of stress.)

Because of individual variations, it's impossible to standardize how people will function under high stress. But leave it to the military to give it a shot. Lt. Col. Dave Grossman, a West Point psychology professor and army ranger, has found in studies on soldiers that, at least during physical tasks, performance can be predicted often by stress-induced heart-rate changes. A normal resting heart rate is 60 to 80 beats per minute, which Grossman calls "condition white." This is the ideal for most office work environments as well as for tasks that require *fine motor skills:* sending a text message, threading a needle. Once stress sets in and the heart rate rises to 115, the fine motor skills begin to deteriorate, but there are other benefits from the increased arousal. From 115 to 145 beats per minute, "condition red," *complex motor skills* are in their prime as well as visual and cognitive reaction time.

Say the stressor is a fight. A complex motor skill would be grabbing a guy with one hand while protecting a child with the other, or in Urijah Faber's case, doing a complex double-leg take down. Above 145 beats per minute, complex motor skills begin to deteriorate and you start to lose peripheral vision, which is likely why people often report tunnel vision during high stress. You're getting into survival mode here, and once you pass 175 beats per minute, "condition black," you might end up freezing, voiding your bowels, or attacking your friend by accident. It's the irrational zone, but it's also the best zone for *gross motor skills*—sprinting, charging, lifting a huge rock off your foot, punching. This is why weight lifters sometimes scream or slap themselves before a big lift. The super strength doesn't last long, but very brief bouts of intense stress can be a benefit under the right circumstances. Being trapped in an avalanche comes to mind, and if you ever find yourself in this situation, experts say to fight with everything you have. But if you're in the avalanche of a 50-foot wave, do the exact opposite. Relax and let the wave pass. Every scenario, in other words, has to be specifically trained for.

The ideal combat heart rate seems to be the middle zone, condition red. Here you can benefit from the physiologic arousal but still keep your wits about you, and soldiers are trained to regulate their breathing to keep within this zone during battle. For example, a simple breathing exercise soldiers use is inhaling through the nose for a count of four, holding for a count of four, exhaling through the mouth for a count of four, holding out for a count of four, then repeating. This exercise—and other steady breathing techniques like inhaling and exhaling for even counts—brings most people's heart rates down, and the more these methods are practiced *in the midst of high stress*, the better soldiers get at bringing their stress level down quickly, much as trained meditators have been shown to do.

Not only can people improve at lowering their stress levels, they can also get better at pushing the limits of their stress responses. Professional NASCAR drivers, Grossman points out, have trained themselves to do precision driving with heart rates of 175 beats per minute and above, and, in battle simulations, the most elite military fighters, even when they are shocked by Tasers or attacked by real opponents, have been able to operate precision weapons with heart rates of 175 beats per minute and above. Again, more research is needed in this area, but it appears that nothing is set in stone when it comes to our ability to act well under high stress. The difference comes down to training.

• • • •

To understand a little more about how this applied to sports, I called Dr. Michael Lardon, who works with elite athletes—from PGA tour golfers to NFL football players. Lardon told me that every athlete is different: Some have what he called a high autonomic tone, meaning they're very reactive and tend toward high anxiety, while others—Tiger Woods and Pete Sampras, for example—have nerves of steel. For the high-anxiety athlete, who's probably more likely to choke under pressure and more likely to come see a sports psychologist in the first place, Lardon uses the same tools Grossman does with soldiers—breathing. "Yogis and Buddhists have been doing this for centuries," Lardon told me, "but it's not so easy to get John Daly to meditate."

What's a sports psychologist to do? Give them video games. The HeartMath Institute has developed games in which you hook your ear up to a device called the emWave that measures your heart-rate variability. Heart-rate variability, or HRV, is a measure of the downtime between heartbeats and is a more precise way to measure stress than just plain old heart rate. The science of HRV is complex, but the basic gist of the emWave is that it tells you if you are in the green zone, which HeartMath calls high coherence, or the red zone, called low coherence. Achievement of a good game score depends on how well you can stay in the green zone—which indicates how well you're managing stress. In one game, for example, the more you stay in the green zone, the more little critters appear in a peaceful meadow—this is not exactly what you'd expect pro football players to be doing with their spare time, but Lardon said he has gotten even his NFL guys to do this stuff (he keeps the names confidential), and clients who use the games for just 10 minutes per day get better at bringing their stress levels down when they're on the field. Some pro golfers and NFL kickers even carry their pocket-size emWave devices with them, watching to see if their HRV gets out of the green before making a putt or taking a kick.

Music is another frequent go-to for Lardon. Music keeps positive thoughts flowing, and keeps athletes from overthinking actions they already know how to do implicitly—the main cause of choking in sports. (The more you've learned a movement well, the more you let the motor sensory parts of your brain, the implicit ones, handle the movement, and the less the slow prefrontal cortex can interfere.) But the other benefit of listening to music is that music influences heart rate. Heart rate increases with faster music and slows with slower rhythms, so Lardon has started actually custom designing music for each of his clients to get them into their ideal HRV for their particular constitution and sport. This requires a visit to an HRV specialist, but once Lardon has the athlete's specific HRV recipe, he then merges the custom tunes with a highlight reel—for an NFL kicker, this would be all the best field goals the kicker nailed—so the athlete can watch those positive moments before a game while getting into ideal HRV. Every bit of this is rewiring the athlete's brain, Lardon said, to stay in the zone.

But staying in the zone isn't always about lowering stress. For NFL players like, say, linebackers, who need to rely more on those gross motor skills—slamming a running back into the dirt—it's often more important to get their heart rate up, which is why you see guys like NFL linebacker Keith Brooking screaming liked crazed warriors before a game, Lardon said. But notice how the golfers, gymnasts, fencers, and quarterbacks—who need precision and creativity—aren't screaming like crazed warriors. The key is knowing yourself, your general anxiety level, and the specific situation you're training for.

• • • •

More than 2,000 years ago, Chinese military strategist Sun Tzu wrote in the *Art of War:* "If you know the enemy and know yourself, you need not fear the result of a hundred battles." I know myself pretty well. I didn't need a heart-rate monitor to know that just thinking about Mavericks made me feel as if I was going into condition black (particularly the voiding one's bowels part). I wanted to stay within conditions red and white. In the ever-changing landscape of the ocean, you never want to lose rationality. This would be especially challenging because my head was already full of fear stories about these giant waves. From the age of 12, I'd watched videos and read magazine articles that depicted Mavericks as the grim reaper. If I could have looked at my brain, I was pretty sure I'd see a superhighway running directly between my prefrontal cortex and my amygdala, filled with every possible worst-case scenario at Mavericks, even death.

"So make a list," Paige Dunne told me. Paige, a sprightly, fit mother and triathlete, was Jamie Patrick's sports psychology consultant. He could never say enough about how much of a miracle worker Paige Dunne was. Jamie told me he'd had times when he wanted to quit swimming altogether, and Paige would snap him out of it just by smiling. "She's like a dose of pure positivity," Jamie told me.

Paige was kind enough to meet me for coffee while she was 8 months pregnant, and Jamie was right that she had a smile that could light up a city block. But Paige was also realistic, and when I started rattling off my theories about what my brain might do when I got out to Mavericks—how I might freeze, and what this meant for my HRV—Paige gave me some sage advice: stop. Thinking too much just gave me more things to worry about, leading to analysis paralysis. I wanted the exact opposite of this.

Paige recommended listing all my fears about surfing Mavericks. As psychologists like Beilock have shown, writing down your fears before a high-pressure test can improve test scores significantly. Paige combined this benefit with action. The fears I had no control over? "Just scratch them off the list," she told me. "Why worry about them if you can't control them?" Paige said the very act of voiding them from the list would help me put them out of my mind. For the fears I *did* have some control over, I would script out an action plan for each one. Not only would this improve my training, it would remind me that I'd covered all my bases and would keep me from overthinking what my body already knew how to do.

It feels a bit weird to make a list like this, Paige assured me, but she'd seen too many times how necessary it could be. She had one client, a first-time triathlete, call her the night before the big race and say: "I just can't stop thinking that I'm going to get a flat tire on the bike."

Paige started with the obvious. "Well, do you know how to change a flat tire? Have you ever practiced?"

"No," the client admitted, "but . . ."

"That's why you make a list in advance," Paige said.

I liked this list idea because I was pretty sure I was already ahead of the game. I'd been doing long swims with Jamie, so if I broke my board a half-mile out to sea, I knew I'd be fine. I'd diffused my fear of sharks enough not to panic about their existence (as for an actual shark attack, this was in the *out of my control* category, so I scratched it off the list). I'd diffused some of my fear of falling under the lip of a skyscraper-size wave by surfing obsessively for the last 15 years and surfing many of Mavericks' less frightening cousins around the globe.

But there was a problem, I realized. None of these places I'd surfed—even the most gnarly, terrifying ones—were actually Mavericks. No matter how much I simulated Mavericks, there would always be the unknown.

"So imagine it," Paige said.

Olympic athletes have used visualization for decades. For a long time science disregarded it as fluff, but the biological evidence is rather shocking. In one recent study by biomedical researchers Guang H. Yue and Kelly J. Cole, published in the *Journal of Neurophysiology,* one group of test subjects was asked to do a pinky-finger exercise five times per week for 4 weeks. A second group was asked to do the same exercises in their minds and not flex the pinky at all, and they wore an electromyography to confirm that no muscle movement was taking place. The physical-training group did well, improving their pinky muscle strength by 30 percent, but the mental group improved by nearly as much—*22 percent*. And this isn't just true of pinky-finger workouts. Research has begun to show that when we imagine ourselves doing something, or even when we dream, the brain goes through a similar cognitive process as when we actually do it. The difference seems to be that the volume of the nervous impulses sent down the spinal cord to the muscles is turned down. Thus, the more detail we can include in the picture, the more effective the imagery will be for training.

"You know what Mavericks looks like," Paige said. "You've seen how big it is in those movies and magazines. You've felt how cold that water is. So let's script out your best session at Mavericks with as much detail as possible: When you wake up, what do you eat for breakfast? What does that taste like? Will you do some stretching or yoga, and what does your body feel like? What does the beach feel like, the sand between your toes? How cold is the water? What kind of conversation are you having in your head, and how do you feel when you ride that first wave? Write it all down, memorize it, and just keep going over it."

I admit I resisted visualization at first. It's not that I didn't believe visualization could help top athletes get an edge. It was just that Mavericks just seemed too bone-crushingly real to pretend a few happy thoughts would help little old me out there. And indeed, when I finally started to imagine surfing Mavs weeks later, I was horrible at it. I couldn't help visualizing myself falling right at the crest, air-dropping 40 feet into the wave's gut, spearing myself on a fin, and finally being pushed deep into some pitch-black underwater crevasse, dying. Visualization seemed to make me *more* nervous, especially because I wasn't doing it right. But like anything, repetition helped, and soon, every night before I went to bed, I pictured myself charging 40-foot waves. What the hell, I even threw in some imagery of me winning the annual Mavericks contest, spraying champagne all over my fans. It was my visualization. I could do what I wanted.

I still had a few months before Mavs season started, so—again, after dragging my feet—I made that list Paige suggested and developed an action plan for each fear. Interestingly, like the triathlete who forgot to practice changing a flat tire, I'd forgotten to train for one tiny, insignificant little fear—drowning. It was by far the easiest way to die at Mavericks, and that was probably why I'd been avoiding it.

So, cuing the Rocky Balboa theme song, I did it all: I met up with Mike Madden, a professional diver, who helped me raise my breath retention from 2 minutes to 4 minutes with some special free-diver techniques (watch the film *The Big Blue* to see the method). I trained on my Mavericks gun every chance I got. I jogged. I did yoga. I meditated every day. I followed Daniela Schiller's advice that I should watch videos of Mavericks that scared me and then go out and surf smaller waves to reconsolidate the fear memories. I tried different music tracks to get me into ideal HRV (Eminem's "Not Afraid" and the Black Eyed Peas' "Imma Be" seemed to genuinely work).

By the time winter comes around, I am in the best shape of my life by far. There doesn't seem to be a wave at Ocean Beach that can rattle me, no matter how large. And when the first Mavericks-size swell finally rolls around, lighting up the horizon with nuclear force, I am . . . positive this was all a terrible mistake.

CHAPTER 7

HELLO DARKNESS, MY OLD FRIEND

"You can be free from fear, if you realize that fear is not the ogre."

—CHOGYAM TRUNGPA

Surfline's *California Surf Guide* reads:

MAVERICKS

Best Size: Triple-overhead to 80-foot faces.

Ability Level: Nothing short of Flea, Laird, or Neptune (Flea and Laird being two of the best big-wave surfers in the world; Neptune being a god).

Hazards: Death by drowning, sharks, run over by a whale, run over by a PWC, a trip through the rocks, hypothermia, broken boards, ego deflation.

Why did I open that book? I knew all this. The waves at Ocean Beach outside my window look like they could take down a cruise-liner. But seeing the dangers in print changes things. I trip and fumble as I walk around the house, wiping counters that don't need wiping. I don't eat. I find myself feverishly tossing an apple and a loaf of bread into a paper bag and loading it into the truck with the rest of my gear: the 9-foot-8-inch Mavs gun, the 15-foot big-wave leash, the 5-millimeter wetsuit, booties, wax, sunscreen, water, towel. I check and double-check that I have everything but still feel vulnerable, exposed. Something must be missing.

Music, music will help, I'm thinking—something to calm me down. Here we go, the Felice Brothers, a favorite. But the normally soothing sounds are grating. Darwin comes to mind: "When fear reaches an extreme pitch . . . the mental powers fail." I shut off the stereo, try to breathe. Fresh air. Salt air. That's what I need.

It's exciting on the road, views of these diabolical swells exploding against the craggy coast. There are even moments when I laugh out loud, feeling like Don Quixote chasing windmills. *Oh life!* But the pendulum sways back so rapidly: faith, fear. Lightness, dark.

You can't follow the expansion and contraction, I tell myself. You've made a decision, a commitment, and you're going forward: forward over Skyline Boulevard, forward through Pacifica with its perpetual gray 1950s funk, forward through the grove of eucalyptus, forward around the misty cliffs, hundreds of feet above the dark blue sea. The waves don't look so abnormally large from up here and this is better, this view from above. "Everything looks perfect from far away," I hum. But then comes the view of Gray Whale Cove, the massive warbled wall of water stretching across the bay. I see it as a stampede of elephants and envision myself trampled underneath by those leathery feet. *Splat, splat, splat!*

Forward.

Forward past the Half Moon Bay airstrip, onto Princeton Drive, past the fishing boats, and into the dirt parking lot brimming with tourists and surfers' trucks. I park next to a bearded man in a Subaru wagon with a green kayak strapped to the top. He rolls down his window. "About 10 guys out at Mavs," he says with a mischievous grin.

"You go out?" I ask.

"Nah," the man says. "I don't go out there. I know what can happen." He speeds off in a cloud of dust.

A silver Tacoma rumbles into the slot next to me with two surfers, one with a mop of bleached blond hair. I recognize the blond—baggy sweatpants, a fluorescent mesh hat—as Ryan Augenstein, a pro surfer who competes in the annual Mavericks contest. "Hellman," he is often called in the surf media. Augenstein looks casual, like he is going out to breakfast. I envy him.

"How's it look?" he asks me.

"I haven't seen it," I say, "but I hear it's supposed to bump up this afternoon." I say this with false confidence, as if I think it is a good thing that waves are supposed to get bigger. In truth, I want them small, as small as possible for Mavericks to break at all.

"That'd be good," Augenstein says. "That'd be reeeeal nice."

An SUV full of men who look like they could be the Rolling Stones' bodyguards—tatted up, black sunglasses, arms like lumber—pulls into the parking lot. Behind the wheel is Jeff Clark—the Jeff Clark who discovered these waves, whom I've only seen before in big, high-production surf movies. Clark knows Augenstein, of course. These are the gatekeepers, the Michael Jordans and Joe Montanas. They crack jokes and sip coffee, and Clark says, "The Half Moon Bay buoy's going crazy. It just hit 18 feet at 16 seconds." This means the wave faces may be around 40 feet.

What. In the hell. Am I doing here?

I push forward, walking past the lagoon, the reddened cliff, past the couple holding hands and asking—"This is where *the Maverick* happens?"—past sailboats in the harbor. I'm on the sand now and looking west, and I can see the rock garden, "the boneyard," as it's called, the black teeth I've watched men pinned to by walls of white water in surf movies, battered like rag dolls. The foam explodes against these stones. The sea is angry.

• • • •

When I was 12, among a whole bedroom full of surf photos from around the globe, I tacked up a *Surfer* magazine spread of Clark hurtling down a 50-foot green Mavericks beast. Even then, my relationship with the place was split.

On the one hand, I yearned to *be* Clark, to know what it's like to dance gracefully with one of nature's most raw and ancient powers, not to mention be part of that elite club of athletes. But when I actually thought in terms of cause and effect, and I considered the black depths Clark could be pushed into if he fell, I felt an equal and opposite chill.

In so many life events—a job interview, a speech, a white-shark dive—the physical sensation of fear, the emotion, comes first. Rational thought—a product of the modern brain—must then attempt to convince the body to approach despite those nerves. This is, in part, what's going on with me now as I pull on my wetsuit and shakily screw the fins into my board. But my relationship with Mavericks is also more complex. Like a child drawn to bright color, the emotion that hit me as a 12-year-old was an indescribable urge to approach that magnificent power, to be on that wave. Then, I didn't know where the attraction to Mavericks was coming from, but as I learned from Hanson, if there is a drive we social primates have that is as primal as fear, it's the drive to belong to the pack, and I was likely being guided by that unconscious urge to be part of the coolest pack I knew, the Mavericks crew. Fear—in this case triggered by rational thinking, rather than sense stimulation—was the one emotion that could quell this other ancient urge.

Almost 2 decades later, I feel myself split between the same complex array of thoughts and emotions. But there's also another feeling gurgling underneath them all. Maybe it's that childhood yearning finally come, after years of training, to fruition. Maybe it's a belief that this is destiny. Maybe it's a glimmer of faith. But there's a sensation in my chest—one I have also felt in the stillness of meditation—

that is utterly confident. It's as if my intellectual debate about Mavericks' danger, and even the emotional swaying I've done for years, is just the chop and pitch of waves on the surface of my mind. But underneath, deep below, there is more stability, more ease with darkness. And it's this sensation, I think, that is overriding the others, leading me into the lagoon and out to sea.

• • • •

Unlike Ocean Beach, the paddle out won't be hard. The simultaneous beauty and deception of Mavericks is that there is a deep-water channel running south of the reef, allowing surfers to literally paddle out on peaceful flat ocean, then approach the takeoff zone between set waves from the side, often still with dry hair. I recently learned the safest paddle-out route from my friend Danny Hess, a longtime Mavericks surfer who also designed my board: south through the lagoon toward mushroom rock—"the one that looks like a mushroom"—then a right turn between the mushroom and the most southerly rock outcropping, and finally a half-mile beeline west until you run into the patch of other surfers waiting for waves. (Mavericks has become a pilgrimage site for any serious big-wave surfer, so there is almost always a competitive crew.) Following these directions, though simple, gives me a sense of being prepared, not to mention occupying my modern brain so it doesn't run ahead with its usual disaster scenarios.

A blue October sky above, with each stroke toward Mavericks, I feel lighter. Dr. Lardon's technique of a "positive anchoring thought" comes to mind too, and I start chanting in my head as I paddle: "I do this every day. I do this every day" to keep the confidence flowing. Much as a little caffeine before a running race can increase performance—but too much can be detrimental—Lardon told me that a light fear response can give energy and increase focus and reaction time, but the longer fear endures and the larger fear grows, the more it stifles athletic flow.

• • • •

The anchoring thoughts, the smooth ocean, the movement: They all seem to be working to put me in a reasonable balance of faith and fear. But when I finally make it out far enough to see the pack, my stomach knots. There are maybe 15 of them, floating near a patch of kelp, practically shoulder to shoulder. People had told me that the takeoff zone was small at Mavericks, but I had no idea I'd be practically holding hands with them.

This may not sound like a big deal, but it is. Surfers are not always the laid-back dudes they're often cast as in the movies, and the more coveted a wave is, the more difficult it is to make inroads with the local protectors. I've witnessed far too many fights in the surfing world to think newcomers are welcome anywhere. I suppose you could compare the feeling of approaching a new elite break to being a fresh walk-on in a heated pickup basketball game. But missing your shots on even the toughest court is just embarrassing. Lose control of your sharp 20-pound board in the wrong place at Mavericks and you could seriously injure someone, or worse.

I know a handful of Mavericks surfers from my neighborhood, but as I get closer, I realize none of the guys out today have any clue who I am. For all they know, I'm one of the annual neophytes who turn up after a few years of surfing with something to prove and ends up leaving via jet-ski rescue or a medevac. And the way my gut is tying itself in knots, I feel like I might be.

Forward.

I paddle to the south of the pack, safely in the channel, deciding to watch for a while and avoiding eye contact so as to hide my nausea. It's deceptively flat out here between sets, almost calm. The sun is shining. Harbor seals poke their mischievous whiskers up. But when a wave finally comes, the tone changes.

When the first green wall—tall as a four-story building—marches off the horizon and pushes onto the reef, the base of the wave—*the cauldron*, as it's called—drops below sea level, sucking in its gut. It would be one thing if Mavericks were just an exceedingly tall wave that rolled in and crumbled onto sand. It doesn't. The deep-ocean surge collides so suddenly with the jutting stone reef that the wave becomes as thick as it is tall, driving forward like some angered aqueous rhino.

There is the hook as the swell boosts to full height, and then that weightless, eerie quiet as the lip falls toward the sea. When the lip connects, forming a vapid core as big as the Holland Tunnel, the explosion of white blows higher than the wave itself, 40 feet up, and the sound, Jesus—an explosion.

Nobody catches this wave, and I feel glad about this. Nobody should be getting near that whole situation. And I should definitely go back before anyone sees my ghostly frightened face. But behind this monster there's another monster, and a surfer is going. I recognize his paddle and his wetsuit. It's Alex Martins, one of the Mavericks competitors who occasionally fixes my boards at his San Francisco shop. I feel simultaneous relief that I know someone in the lineup (maybe I'm not a total outsider) and worry. I feel like calling out to Alex—*don't do it!* The wave looks like it will simply consume him or slingshot him to the moon. But Alex pops to his feet quickly, up early, before the wave goes vertical, composed even as he rides down, down, down, an ant against the green swell.

Oh dear God that looks awful. But something also just shifted in my brain, something deep in that social structure part. I know Alex. Alex is human. I am human. I have dreamed of doing this from the age of 12. People do this. I can do this.

I paddle closer to the pack, nodding and trying to look manly and confident. Nobody acknowledges me. The other faces are familiar only through surf media: Flea, Grant Washburn, Tyler Smith, Skindog. I wish Doc was here. These are all my comic book superheroes! Flipping hell, how did I end up in a surfing movie?

My strategy, if I'm really going to do this (and I'm still not sure I am), is to move slowly. Sit here on the shoulder of the pack and watch. Learn exactly what to do. More importantly—what not to do. I'm not going to try to be a hero. I tell this to my ego firmly. Know your place.

And so the minutes pass, the minutes turning to strange, trancelike hours of watching, hours of gradually moving deeper into the path of the beast, hours of hedging, second-guessing. I try to cheat inside and paddle for the smaller sets—small, meaning, oh, just a few giraffes high—but at the top, I'm looking over the edge of a cliff as it crumbles. Everything in me wants out and back and away. All I can think is that this is where fear makes sense. Mark Foo died on a day just like this, his body floating in a lagoon after catching an edge on an 18 footer. Mark Foo, who never came back—never.

But I've trained for this. The statistics are on my side, I tell myself: thousands of waves ridden by humans just like me, without incident. You must push past instinct. This is the greatest of human feats. This is philosophy, science. This is—

Oh, mother f—

A rampart of green almost twice as big as anything that has yet come, far outside, has eclipsed the sky. It's a freak set, a rogue. And so the mayhem begins, the herd mentality. Everyone scraping for the horizon. The wall is coming closer, a dreadful malice in its wedge. It grows and grows, high, high above us, and I feel it so clearly, more clearly than ever: that will to live that isn't even part of consciousness. It's something in your bones. I've never paddled so hard. The men ahead of me look like minnows leaping up the falls, just barely scooting over the crest. Most make it over, but it's too late for me. I'm in the dragon's shadow now.

Automatically, I fling my board forward and dive down into the pocket, trying to get under. Diving deep, deep, into the murk, hoping, praying, and—what's this? I'm somehow suddenly through. I breathe air, but just when I think I'm safe, I feel the tug, the slurping at my toes. My board is caught in the vortex and the leash, Velcroed to my ankle, is yanking me down. One last gulp of air, and—

Darkness.

I'm under, pulled deep, deeper than I've ever been before. The green murk turns to black, and for the first time I can understand why Mavericks surfers have always said that you don't know which way is up when you get pushed this far to the bottom. I take a guess and swim: one stroke, two, three, four. The light must be around here somewhere. Please, please, lighter, lighter, and—*inhale*. Yes.

No!

On the horizon, the next wave, equally ugly, impossibly high, is plunging down. An avalanche of foam mows me down and I'm back into blackness: punched, kicked, splayed, held under again. I completely forget to relax and there is simply no way I would. I'm gagging for air, again with no sense of direction. Where the hell is the surface?

I'm not sure how long I'm down, but eventually the water seems to push me up. I seem to have no say in the matter. The ocean just decided. I start flailing for the safety of the channel, thanking God and wondering, once again, what I'm doing out here. A couple of men lost their boards on that wave and they're swimming in. It's as if the enemy just tossed a grenade into our fortress. Now the recovery, the cleanup.

Catching my breath in the channel, I contemplate going in. That was not cool. Not cool at all. But once I see that everyone miraculously survived (including myself), another shift occurs. I have genuine information now. The horrible unknown—*What will it be like to get smashed by a four-story wave?*—is now demystified.

• • • •

My friend Karen Rogers is a world-record-holding open-water swimmer who often trains with Jamie Patrick. In the spring of 2011, Karen took a boat 12 miles off the coast of San Francisco and, at about 4 a.m., started swimming alongside a kayaker toward land. It was pitch-dark, and drizzling. The air temperature was in the low 50s, the water even colder. But the ocean was glassy and calm, and Karen felt good for the first few minutes. Having an incredible tolerance for cold, even without a wetsuit, Karen had hoped for exactly these conditions.

About 10 minutes in, Karen felt the water swirl around her in the exact way shark experts had told her it would feel if a great white was coming from below. "I thought I was done," Karen told me. "I really did. So I just said, 'Well, this might be it. Let go.'" Seconds later, something huge rammed into her thigh with a force so hard it left a bruise the size of a grapefruit. The animal rammed her two more times, but in the blur of darkness, Karen felt whiskers. "I realized it was a seal," she laughed. "Probably pissed off I'd woken him up with my headlamp."

This may not sound like such a big deal, but if you've ever observed 5,000-pound male elephant seals, one of the most testosterone-stocked animals on Earth, you can understand the gravity. Ironically, the kayaker who was supposed to be spotting Karen was up ahead seeking favorable currents when this happened and had no clue what was going on. And Karen didn't scream to notify him. She didn't even ask politely for help. In the meditative state she has to enter to do these superhuman swims, she simply swam forward, telling herself again and again: *I belong here too. I belong here too.*

The seal then left Karen alone, but 30 minutes later, she had another visitor: a great white the size of a VW bus swimming 10 feet below.

"So, you must've gotten out at that point," I said. "Obviously, this was not your morning to be out there."

"No," Karen said. "I just kept telling myself, *I belong here too. I belong here too.*'

• • • •

I'm tired and hungry. I've been out at Mavericks for 4 or 5 hours since those dramatic rogue sets rolled through, and I haven't caught a wave. Though nobody has said anything, and Alex is nice enough to chat with me, I'm quite sure most of the world-class lineup thinks I'm in the way. Part of me would like to just go in and head home. I survived being crushed by a massive wave at Mavericks. Isn't that enough for one day? But the truth is, I have physical energy left. My real fatigue goes deeper. What I'm really tired of is hedging, doubting, feeling like I don't belong, lacking the sort of faith Karen had that morning.

It's not that I want to be flippant, but Karen's story is poignant because she is actually a very cautious person in other areas of her life. Swimming, however, is what Karen feels she was put on this Earth to do, and succeeding at the types of swims she does seems to require an almost religious faith that she's meant to swim in the sea, and that no matter what happens, things are as they should be. "I'm clumsy on land," she told me recently. "I'm literally more at home in the ocean." I've always felt similarly about surfing, and I know that the same faith Karen found that morning has to be available to me now. It's increasingly clear, given how things have gone thus far today, that I have to find it.

It's obvious watching professional athletes point to the sky or cross themselves that many of them look to a higher power for strength under pressure. Studies like the one Jeong-Keun Park of Seoul University did in 2000 on Korean athletes have found that prayer both helps players cope with anxiety and often aids them in achieving peak performances. Dr. Lardon spends a whole chapter in his book *Finding Your Zone* explaining the benefits of faith—religious, spiritual, or simply faith in the near divine power of the mind and body. The benefits of prayer are mysterious, but as Anne Harrington, professor of medical history at Harvard, has said, it's likely similar to the placebo effect: "There is an innate capacity for our bodies to bring into being, to the best of their ability, the optimistic scenarios in which we fervently believe." In other words, believe God is on your side, and your body may be more likely to produce its most godly results.

I've never been a particularly religious person, but in my early twenties, I used to do intensive meditation retreats at a Chinese Buddhist monastery. We followed the ancient schedule of waking at 2:30 a.m., repeating hour-long meditation sessions with 20-minute breaks until midnight, and maintaining this schedule for a week or two at a stretch. Sitting still in lotus posture for that many hours per day can be unbelievably excruciating, and during the first few days of retreat, the majority of my meditation sits were spent trying to sneak my legs into different positions while the abbot wasn't looking. But each night, various teachers would remind us that if we ran away from the pain—squirming about each time it appeared—it would follow us through the entire retreat. But if we could sit with it, even embrace it, the pain could actually transform. Suffering, after all, is a mental interpretation of sensation, and sensation and suffering can be decoupled if the mind is still. After I became more experienced with meditation, there were times during these retreats when the pain could even flip to its opposite and I'd find myself in a euphoric, painless state for days, an experience I can only compare to finding runner's high after miles of aches and drudgery. In Zen, this is called passing through a pain gate, and it can only happen if the mind relaxes around the pain. It was having this experience that gave me faith—if not in a higher power—then in a method: Turning toward suffering is a much better way of dealing with it than running. It's a principle that I always struggle to integrate, however, and it suddenly hits me that I should be doing the same thing out here with fear.

This whole time, I've been waiting for that perfect fearless state to come first, a point where it miraculously feels right to paddle down a skyscraper of saltwater. Like avoiding pain, I've been shifting this way and that way around fear, never turning toward it, never embracing it. I've been seeing fear as a harbinger of all things bad: a reason I'm not worthy of being here (look how calm the other guys are), a reason I won't perform well, a reason I shouldn't trust my training. But the fact is the fear is not going to leave, not before I know in every fiber of my being that I can do this. And despite the fact that these other Mavericks surfers seem like superheroes, 99 percent of them felt just like I do now the first time they were out here.

I'm not in any peaceful, meditative state. In fact, after hours of botching opportunities, I'm incredibly agitated. But bobbing in the light onshore breeze, I take a few deep breaths and feel a renewed vigor in this realization. *Just let the fear be there,* I tell myself. *Don't run from it. Don't identify with it. Don't fight it.*

I'm a little hesitant to call what happens next a surrender or letting go like Karen described. It's not the usual *relax and just be* kind of surrender that I've felt on retreat either. It's a more primal surrender to whatever outcome—even, yes, death—and a simultaneous sharpening of the senses, a readiness to fight. Instead of feeling weaker by embracing fear, I'm flooded with a surge of power.

I let a few sets go by, breathing fully and deeply, collecting my energy, focusing. All day, I've felt like I couldn't get into position. I always seemed to be just a little too far to the left or right or outside. But as soon as this mental shift comes, I'm finally, almost magically, in position. The wave is coming right to me, too fast it seems, but I don't care. Let it take me down if it must.

I turn my board toward land and paddle. Suddenly I'm on my feet looking over the mountain's precipice, and when it boosts to full height, the whole ocean hiccups. The streams of foam pass underfoot while I scream down this wall so high above me it's perfectly surreal. I look over my left shoulder at the houses of whitewater, and they are just there, just houses of whitewater. Everything is big and beautiful and fast. I ride a football field of water, thinking nothing at all, the avalanche on my heels. The wave flattens, then reforms into a second frothy bowl. I drop down this ledge, half the size of the original and still far above me. It slingshots me forward with another burst of speed, and then, seeing the wave is going to close, I pull off the back, skimming and skimming and skimming across the flat sea.

Lying down on my board, there's a moment before I snap out of my trance and realize what has just happened. There are a handful of peak moments of success I've had in my life—winning an award or a big game—memories I fall back on in times of insecurity. But pulling off the back of that first Mavericks wave, still standing, trumps them all. It's as if that unhinged adolescent yearning to be part of the most elite pack, to explore the edges of my potential, has been building for 18 years, so often repressed because my critical, rational side saw it as shallow or juvenile. But the primal part of me couldn't let go of it, and now all that pent-up desire is releasing in a single burst of euphoria. I don't know it yet, but for weeks, months, even years to come, the memory of this one wave, the raw joy, will permeate my life and alter it.

I paddle back to the lineup, an uncontrollable smile plastered to my face, everything around me seeming to pulse with ripeness and life. The sky, the clouds, the sea, they all have a heartbeat. The fear has dissolved. It will be back, of course, but for now, there is this moment when only faith remains. And I belong here. I belong here too.

CHAPTER 8

FEEL-GOOD FEAR

"We must be learning if we are to feel fully alive, and when life, or love, becomes too predictable and it seems like there is little left to learn, we become restless—a protest, perhaps, of the plastic brain when it can no longer perform its essential task."

—*DR. NORMAN DOIDGE,*
THE BRAIN THAT CHANGES ITSELF

Half Moon Bay was dark and ominous on the morning of December 4, 2007. None of the fishing boats even attempted to leave the harbor. The offshore weather buoys at one point clocked 36-foot swells with a wave period—time elapsed between set waves—of over 16 seconds, a formula that could result in breaking waves cresting 80-feet high and beyond. To top it off, the entire coast was socked in with fog. You couldn't even see a few hundred yards ahead, let alone the half-mile out to Mavericks.

It looked like the swell of the decade, but Darryl Virostko, a big-wave surfer more commonly known as Flea—just the guy you'd expect to be waiting for such an event—didn't feel like going out. It wasn't the near suicidal conditions that bothered him. It wasn't the fog. It wasn't the cold. The problem was Flea had been partying a wee bit too hard. He hadn't slept in 48 hours. Or was it 72 now? He could hardly remember. His body ached. He didn't really want to do anything, much less attempt the impossible. Then again, attempting the impossible was what Flea did for a living. Fans, friends, and media would expect him to be out at Mavericks on the swell of the decade. Reluctantly, he suited up and prepared for another Tuesday at the office.

Since they were too big for paddle surfing, Flea and a smattering of the core Mavericks crew were going to attempt to tow into these monsters with jet-ski assistance. Tow surfing is a bit like waterskiing in the approach: The jet ski drags the surfer behind by a rope. The difference on this particular day was that once the surfer let go, he'd be trying to outrun a mountain of water moving at 40 miles per hour that could roll the *Titanic*. Big waves had been surfed at Mavericks, but nothing like this.

As the crew navigated the boneyard on the jet skis and broke through layer after layer of fog, Flea got his first glimpse, not just of how big the waves were, but how nasty:

straight out of the west, the most direct kind of hit. It was a war zone, the sets rising up like dark cathedrals before detonating into avalanches of white.

In video footage from that day, Flea looked almost casual on his first wave, but halfway down, he suddenly caught a rail, slammed into the face, and got sucked up to the top. You can hear the photographers in the channel shouting, “Oh no! Oh no!” with genuine panic in their voices. And it’s easy to see why. As the wave inverted and pitched, Flea’s tiny figure can be seen suspended *inside* a hook of white water that makes him literally resemble his nickname. He fell six stories and absorbed the full power of the crashing lip.

“We all thought he was dead,” surf photographer Frank Quirarte, one of the witnesses, later told the *San Francisco Chronicle*. But when the mist and foam cleared, Flea, using another of his nine lives, popped up relatively quickly with the help of his life vest. After a brief recovery, he asked to be towed into another.

When Flea dropped in on his next wave, he purposefully went right for the vortex, trying to pull *inside* the gaping mouth of what looked like a horizontal tornado. The result was just as bad as his first wave, but again he popped up and, in classic Flea fashion, wanted to be dragged into a third.

Somehow Flea had enough coherence to make the descent on this wave beautifully, but the lip exploded behind him with such nuclear force, the white water alone reached 50 feet. Flea disappeared into the chaos and seemed to be sucked under yet again. Could anyone survive three? But at the last second, he emerged from the explosion of foam, still riding.

• • • •

"My body was just *done* after that," Flea tells me, taking a sip of coffee. "I remember making it to the beach and thinking, 'Thank God I'm alive.'" I'm meeting with Flea at his local haunt, the West Side Café in Santa Cruz. With his slicked-back hair and light mustache, Flea looks more like a '50s greaser than a surfer. And at only 5-foot-9, he doesn't resemble the NFL–size big-wave celebrities he often competes with (hence, the moniker). But there's no disputing that Flea is one of the greatest big-wave surfers to have ever lived. Nobody else has come close to winning the Mavericks annual big-wave contest more than once. Flea won it 3 years in a row. The magazines might debate if Flea is *the best* ever, but you'd be hard pressed to find a surfer who would dispute that Flea is certainly the craziest. Flea is *that* guy: the one you both admired and rolled your eyes at in high school, the one you could depend on to pull off some ridiculous athletic feat in the clutch and be the last one standing at the party the same night, but also the one who was sure to get in your face if you did something that pissed him off.

"Being seen as the crazy person in the water, that's what I was all about," Flea tells me, as just about every passerby interrupts us for a standard man nod or fist bump with the legend. "I wasn't scared to die. And that's how I've been on land. If I feel something, or I think something, or if someone's fucking with me, I'll just say it. You know, a lot of people won't say it, and they'll be like, 'Thank God he said it, 'cause I was thinking the exact same thing.'"

Flea said part of that sentence in the past tense—"wasn't afraid to die"—because he has begun to regulate this no-holds-barred part of himself. Flea still surfs Mavericks with his characteristic brazenness, but a couple of years ago, he gave up a far more risky pastime: smoking crystal meth. The habit had taken over his life and was the reason he hadn't slept for 48 hours when that December Fourth swell came through. (Likely the reason he botched those first two waves too.)

"In the beginning it was just drinking on the weekends," Flea says, "just going out with friends and getting crazy." But Santa Cruz is a party town and, unlike today's environment where surfers train like Olympic athletes, Flea, now 40, grew up in an era when professional surfers were expected to party like Keith Richards. Alcohol mixed with cocaine; cocaine turned to a taste of meth here and there, until: "We were doing it every single day." At his worst, Flea would wake up in the morning, empty out a half bottle of Gatorade, and fill it with vodka, which he nursed on his morning surf checks that moved closer and closer to afternoon. He'd mix a steady flow of booze with smoking meth five or six times a day, staying up all night, yet still casually managing to ride waves that would've been thought impossible a decade ago.

For years, Flea saw no reason to question his partying. He reeled in six figures a year for his gladiator-style surfing, and his days-long, post-event hotel parties seemed to only improve his reputation as surfing's bad boy in the media. But a couple of events gave him pause. On that very same day in 2007 when Flea was out at Mavericks, a big-wave surfer named Peter Davi died at a break called Ghost Trees in Monterey. An autopsy found 0.75 milligram of methamphetamine per liter in his system, about triple the abusive level. Davi had been trying to paddle into 70-foot waves when everyone else was using jet skis. "Peter was a good friend of mine," Flea says. "So that scared me a little bit."

Not quite enough, though. A couple of years later, Flea was partying with friends on a cliff near Santa Cruz when he mysteriously lost consciousness right on the edge. Friends reported watching Flea free-fall 60 feet, completing a full backflip before bouncing off rock and dirt. His body ended up on a hunk of metal left over from an abandoned pier. Flea came to in a puddle of blood, and though he had a severely broken arm, friends had to convince him not to scale back up the cliff while they called in a medevac.

After who knows how many other close calls and an attempted intervention by some fellow Mavericks surfers, Flea checked himself into rehab in 2009. He drove to the clinic so drunk he blew a 0.28 blood alcohol content, a level that is often fatal (not to mention dangerous to others on the road). But no matter how belligerent he was when he checked himself in, Flea is just grateful he got there. Looking back, he wishes he had done it sooner. His 4-year binge took almost everything his heroics had earned. He lost the house he was making double payments on. He lost all the big sponsorships. He no longer gets paid to do what he loves and says he often has trouble making rent on his Santa Cruz studio. "If I was thinking then more like I'm thinking now," he says, "back when I was in my prime. . . ." Flea shakes his head. "Well, I don't know. But I would have had more success than I did."

• • • •

Risk taking is a double-edged sword. Coming in from that first day at Mavericks, I felt like Jamie Patrick did after his

44-mile Tahoe swim. I could do anything. My anxiety about work had largely vanished. My anxiety about my relationship with Amy vanished. I suddenly had supreme confidence. Put me in a marathon with no training, I'd be fine. Give me a job at Goldman Sachs, I'd outperform the market with ease. The waves at Ocean Beach that used to scare me felt playful.

I started surfing Mavericks every chance I got, and just like the studies suggested (and much to my own surprise), I started to feel almost comfortable out there. The death nightmares went away. My main concern was actually that my newfound hobby worried Amy and my family too much. They constantly urged me to stay away from "that horrible place." I tried to sneak out to Mavericks with nobody knowing, but Amy caught me and made me swear that I would never do it again—like it was a sin akin to cheating. I argued Doc's points to them that Mavericks wasn't nearly as dangerous as it was made out to be: I listed the car accident statistics and the fact that more cheerleaders got paralyzed and died every year than big-wave surfers (this is true, by the way).

But recent news wasn't helping me out. In January, a Southern California surfer named Jacob Trette got caught by a wave on a relatively small day—small for Mavericks, anyway. He was found minutes later, facedown in the lagoon, hundreds of yards from the break, unconscious. Luckily, a kayaker happened upon his body and photographer Russell Ord whizzed him to shore by jet ski—otherwise, he would've ended up far worse than in a medically induced coma.

Trette fully recovered after 2 days, but the following month, a famous Hawaiian big-wave rider named Sion

Milosky went down on a 60-footer just before dark. I'd talked to him at Mavericks 2 days before. Just like Trette, his body was found in the lagoon, only this time it was too late. Sion—a beloved husband and father of two young girls—was dead.

My sister tried all different angles to dissuade me from going out again. "Where is this going to *stop*?" she asked one night at dinner. "Look at these big-wave surfers. They're egomaniacs and they're never happy with what they've done. They always have to go bigger, faster, meaner. The search for the baddest, stupidest, most gut-wrenching wave. You've never been that way, and I think this is going to ruin your whole love of surfing. A lot of these guys don't even appreciate the little fun days anymore. They're addicts."

I rolled my eyes. I saw my sister's point, but I didn't want to judge all extreme athletes as adrenaline junkies. That was just a stereotype; I knew too many guys like Doc who didn't fit it. I didn't want to fall victim to negativity bias either. Just after Sion died, a surf instructor died at Ocean Beach in 3-foot waves and nobody knew why. Accidents happened and the statistics at Mavericks were still pretty safe. Plus, I didn't *feel* addicted. I surfed because I liked to. It was a healthy lifestyle, and Mavericks was just a new challenge.

But if I hadn't been so defensive, I would have admitted to my sister that I felt pulled back to Mavericks in a strange way. I also worried that my newfound confidence could easily spill into an unchecked ego. After hearing Flea's story of addiction and plain overconfidence, I started to wonder if my sister might be right.

• • • •

Coincidentally, just after meeting with Flea, I'm invited to give a presentation at a neuroscience and ocean conference called Bluemind at the California Academy of Sciences. Organized by marine biologist and neuroscience buff Wallace J. Nichols, Bluemind features a mix of ocean experts and neuroscientists for a "this is your brain; this is your brain on ocean" day. I look at the schedule and can't believe my luck. Jeff Clark, the *original* Mavericks surfer, is going to present with Dr. Howard Fields, director of the Wheeler Center for the Neurobiology of Addiction at the University of California, San Francisco.

When conference day arrives, I feel like a kid on Christmas Day. The morning consists of presentations on topics like the biology of whale songs and the psychology of ocean views: a heaven for ocean geeks. Around noon, Clark, a 54-year-old with a boyish grin, gets up and tells his harrowing tale of the very first adventure out to Mavericks, a story I've heard hundreds of times but never *in person*.

Just as the legend has it, Clark explains how at just 17 years old, he paddled out to Mavericks alone, leaving behind one of his high school buddies who stood on shore, saying: "I'll call the Coast Guard and tell them where I last saw you." There was no need, though. For 15 years, Jeff Clark surfed Mavericks alone because none of his friends would even dare approach. Later, of course, the magazines and media frenzy turned Mavericks into a Mount Everest–like destination. But even now, with all the crowds and hype, "I still can't tear myself away," Clark tells the audience. "I still love it."

Everyone is wowed by Clark's stories. Journalists surround him after his talk to ask just what in the hell was going through his mind. Then Dr. Fields gets up and says in a very calm, understated way: "Jeff thinks he can't tear himself away because he loves it, but I'm sorry to tell you, he's actually just addicted to dopamine." Fields, a silver-haired bespectacled man, announces this with a laugh, but he's serious. He then gives a PowerPoint presentation showing that the brain's dopaminergic pathways—our reward/motivation system, as it's often called—are at the core of what drives us, what makes life pleasurable, and what also forms so many of our addictions.

Dopamine, Fields explains, originates in very ancient parts of the brain like the substantia nigra and the ventral tegmental area, which are buried down there deep in the midbrain, close to the brain stem. Like the amygdala, these are gizmos we also share with our reptilian ancestors, meaning they've been with us for well over 200 million years. Dopamine is a neurotransmitter that you can picture like a three-pronged puzzle piece. When these neurons in the ancient midbrain start cranking out the little knobbed-triangle dopamine slices, they float over to the brain's dopamine receptors, fit their knobbed ends snugly in, and project signals out to the cortex and limbic system. What this process means to us is simple: *pleasure*. When dopamine fires and connects, we feel a rush of happiness that we try to seek out again and again, which is why dopamine is often referred to as a motivator.

Eating, sex, exercise, music, falling in love, even meditation and prayer—they all raise the amount of dopamine in our brains. But dopamine levels are particularly correlated with doing something novel, and the *unexpected reward* that often comes with that new thing, say: finding a new delicious bakery, listening to a brilliant new piece of music, skiing a new mountain, watching an exciting thriller, having a new fling. The list goes on. Doing something new usually requires risk, but it's also the key for learning, for rewiring the brain in novel ways. Scientists think the dopaminergic system originated to motivate us to learn new skills—*and* to be adventurous.

A dopamine rush feels so good that we've invented shortcuts that bypass our sense organs altogether so we don't have to work for it—morphine, cocaine, crystal meth, heroin, alcohol, nicotine, caffeine—these drugs all toy directly with the dopaminergic system, letting more dopamine flood the brain than usual. Humans aren't the only ones susceptible. Fields showed us photos of experiments in which a rat is hooked up to a catheter that will pump cocaine into its system if it presses a lever. The rat will learn increasingly complex patterns to get the cocaine, and gradually the cocaine will become more important to the rat than even food.

Synthetic forms of dopamine seem to attract all of us mammals, but crystal meth turns out to be the kingpin of dopamine dealers. In experiments on rats, Richard A. Rawson, a psychiatry professor at UCLA, found that sex at the moment of orgasm causes dopamine levels to jump from 100 to 200 units, cocaine to 350 units. But crystal meth catalyzes a leap up to *1,250 units,* a level that far outweighs any natural dopamine hit. Meth addicts describe a euphoria that often comes with a sense of fearlessness. But, as Rawson points out, "the brain wasn't meant to experience this level of dopamine," and once the high wears off, the user feels depressed and often paranoid or violent. Gradually, the meth actually destroys the brain's natural dopamine receptors so it's hard to feel *any* sort of pleasure, synthetic or otherwise. As Dr. Nora Volkow, director of the National Institute on Drug Abuse, has shown, if you look at the midbrains of meth addicts, they glow with less dopaminergic intensity than the brains of normal folks. The receptors can heal over time, but it's not evident that the brain ever fully heals from meth abuse.

The point of Fields's presentation at Bluemind is that our brains make quick associations with the things that brought it increased dopamine—synthetic *or* natural—and we learn how to get that hit again, just like rats learning how to press a lever for cocaine. If you learn that aerobic exercise increases dopamine—which it does—then exercise can become that natural source of pleasure. If you learn to play music, you can strive for dopamine with a challenging new piece. If you love food, you could pursue new cuisines. But if you learn, say, that getting to a new level in a video game increases dopamine—and you latch on to *only* that—then you may end up an obese kid with fast thumbs. If you win a big pot on the slot machines, your brain might urge you to spend all your free time in casinos. And if you're a Wall Street executive, after one big win, you might find yourself consulting your risk advisor less and less. "So the key," Fields says in closing, "is finding healthy ways of increasing dopamine rather than unhealthy ones."

Jeff Clark learned at a young age that his preferred form of dopamine came from big-wave surfing. There is perhaps no greater unexpected reward than still being alive after tossing yourself over the edge of a 50-foot wave: *surprise!* But along with that novel reward, you get the dopamine from aerobic exercise *and* a strong adrenaline hit from the amygdala kicking the fight-or-flight system into gear, a double upper. On top of all this, you're outside somewhere beautiful (even if the water isn't always balmy), and you're satisfying that primal desire to belong to an elite tribe. Perhaps all of this is why Clark still can't "tear himself away" and why, after just a handful of times surfing there, Mavericks has already become something I think about every day.

But why do some people like Jeff Clark and Flea seem to be especially willing to put their lives on the line for fun, while others seem content to have everything around them stay as safe, monotone, and repetitive as possible? Why do some people want to diffuse bombs or fight terrorists for a living while others don't want to leave their houses? Why do some people seek stability in relationships while others get bored after a couple of months?

• • • •

This last question has been on my mind lately as Amy and I grow closer, even broaching the dreaded "where are we headed?" talk. I've never really been firmly on one side or the other of the relationship spectrum. I've been at times the hopeless romantic, yearning to find *the one*, while at other times easily bored and seeking nothing but freedom. From what I can tell of Amy's past, she's in the same boat. She has had a handful of short relationships, and several long ones, even marriage proposals, but none of them seemed quite right. The freedom to invest in her career, or simply take off and travel spontaneously, has been more important than settling down before it feels natural. Since she definitely wants kids, it has been risky to turn down eager suitors—a couple of whom were quite wealthy—in the first half of her thirties.

In some ways, the fact that we met when she was 36 is putting pressure on our relationship to move more quickly than usual. But the pressure is currently freaking me out much less than I'd expect, and one part of this has been, oddly enough, because of Mavericks. The moment I came in successful from that first Mavericks session, I had this profound feeling of knowing I could make this relationship work, and wanting that more than anything. Of course, I'd had this thought tons of times or I wouldn't have been living with Amy, but this was the first time I'd felt it deep in my core. I'd had so many huge doubts and fears about Mavericks, but the fact that wanting it badly enough made it possible seems to have proven to my emotional brain that I can also overcome any and all of my doubts and fears about relationships and marriage, provided I want to badly enough. It's in part Amy's bravery—the fact that she has put her freedom above settling for so long, and that it's clear she puts genuine friendship and love above money and stability—that makes me want her that badly. Unlike many of my previous relationships, Amy and I seem to have a very similar novelty-seeking profile, and to find out more about the science behind this, after the Bluemind conference, I called Vanderbilt neuroscientist David Zald.

Dr. Zald specializes in neuroimaging of the dopaminergic system. He and his colleagues have discovered fascinating correlations with dopamine and personality difference, particularly that we are not all created equal when it comes to our appetite for feel-good dope. It turns out that all of our midbrains have these things called autoreceptors that *regulate* the amount of dopamine our neurons release when there has been a sufficient amount. Think of autoreceptors like chaperones. "Okay, half the party is staggering or passed out," the autoreceptors tell your neurons after a big brain party. "Let's hold off on the 2 a.m. beer run."

Zald and colleagues found that some people have fewer autoreceptors. As many of us remember from high school, the fewer chaperones you have at a party, the more willing you are to take risks. Psychologists call these people high novelty seekers, or high sensation seekers, and they tend to like new stuff more than others because their brains get flooded with more dopamine when they get that unexpected reward. (Zald points out that autoreceptors are not the only factor, but a strong one.) They tend to be more adventurous in all areas of life, which can be positive when applied to the right setting. But, as Flea found out the hard way, novelty seekers are more susceptible to unhealthy risky addictions too.

Zald tells me that the running theory is that novelty seekers evolved because the tribe needed people willing to do the hunting, battling, and exploring. Inventing new tools, philosophies, and art forms also took some social risk taking, and it was advantageous to have some sexually adventurous members of the group so we didn't all end up having children with our siblings. Some experts who study novelty seeking say it may even be the secret to the human race's survival. After all, if we didn't have the risk takers, we would have just stayed in East Africa instead of spreading out over the entire globe in a period of only about 100,000 years.

There have been great social incentives for those who are willing to take risks, provided the risks don't go too far. But not everyone got this novelty-seeking trait, Zald says, for exactly the reason that it often does go too far. "There were lots of situations," Zald says, "where those guys all got killed off in battle, and the guy who was more nervous and anxious and managed to find an excuse *not* to fight, lived for another day. So both tendencies exist in the population: very anxious and harm avoidant and those who are going to put everything on the line." Most of us are somewhere in the middle, and that's a good thing. Moderately cautious people are often the voices of reason, the ones who take the high novelty seeker's keys at the Christmas party and tell her she can have them back when she's no longer slurring.

The famous psychology professor Marvin Zuckerman first elucidated this sensation-seeking paradigm and created the Zuckerman/Kuhlman questionnaire, which tries to categorize you as either a high or low novelty seeker as well as to measure how harm avoidant or boredom susceptible you are. Although I question the accuracy of any test that asks me to choose between options like—*(a) I dislike "swingers"* or *(b) I enjoy the company of real "swingers"*—these tests have been proven to have some actual biologic validity. I should note that I also despise categorizing tests because, as we've seen, they tend to set up stereotypes that often affect our beliefs about ourselves and our performance more than is helpful. Still, it's helpful to use these tools to study ourselves. The Zuckerman test seemed to be fairly accurate. It revealed that I scored high on "adventure and thrill seeking" (10 out of 10), which explains why I took to sports like surfing and skating in the first place. But I scored low on boredom susceptibility (2 out of 10), which might explain why I tend to like geeky academic pursuits too.

According to studies on the results of tests like the

Zuckerman scale, novelty seeking is estimated to be about 60 percent genetic (from studies of twins). And interestingly, the combination of traits in people like Jeff Clark, Flea, or your average firefighter or quarterback—high novelty, low anxiety—is the same combination found in our greatest problems, psychopaths. In addition to dopamine, Zald studies psychopathic tendencies. "These guys," Zald says, "if channeled into a culturally sanctioned direction, could be heroes. They could do things that normal people can't. . . . The ones who are willing to do the work to get skillful at something, they can accomplish impressive things."

Zald's work has led him to believe that there needs to be a greater understanding of how to channel novelty-seeking behavior, particularly for high-risk novelty seeking, into more positive outcomes for society. "As a teenager, there are several ways to pursue risk," he says. "For instance, learning how to rock climb but to do it properly; to ski or bike, but wear a helmet to properly protect yourself. But the other way to pursue risk is doing things that you know are illegal, or doing things that you know you could get caught at or beat up. High novelty-seeking kids need opportunities to pursue risk in a way that is controlled so they don't go the illegal route."

• • • •

A few weeks after learning about dopamine rushes, I find myself riding up the KT-22 ski lift at Squaw Valley with JT Holmes, one of the best extreme skiers in the world. The snow is coming down in sheets, and KT-22 is a double black diamond with the occasional 20-foot cliff. When we begin our descent, I'm hot on JT's trail for about, oh, 5 seconds.

Then I realize JT isn't going to make any turns. His friend, an Australian snowboarder, informs me that JT is "taking it easy today," so, okay, change of plans. Snowboarding down at my own pace, I meet JT at the Squaw Valley wine bar.

JT strolls in wearing a black hoodie and Irish tweed cap, brushing snowflakes off his shoulders. "You scare me," one man shouts at JT through a thick beard. "You scare *me,*" JT laughs, clearly used to this treatment. JT has been skiing from the age of 2 and has developed an international reputation not just for being able to get down some of the most technical and sheer mountains in the world with speed, style, and huge air, but for—in his off-time—flying.

In 2009, *60 Minutes* featured Holmes and friends BASE jumping in "wing suits," flying squirrel–like getups that allow them to leap off, say, a 1,000-foot cliff and cover up to 2.5 feet horizontally to every 1 foot of vertical free fall. It's the closest thing to a human flying without a motor. When we sit down, JT has just finished a stunt for *Transformers 3* in which he and three others did their flying squirrel act off the 1,730-foot-high Willis Tower in Chicago. They used the suit's steering capability to make a sharp, mandatory right turn around a neighboring skyscraper called 311 South Wacker, then maneuvered their way through downtown Chicago, opening their chutes just 400 feet from the ground and landing safely on the street that had been blocked to traffic.

"We needed a beer after that," JT laughs.

He may sound blasé, but when he and fellow BASE jumper Mike Swanson got the job for *Transformers 3*, they were far from relaxed. "We were scared and we trained like hell," JT says. "Mike and I probably did 180 jumps together to prepare: skydives, BASE jumps. By the end, we could communicate without speaking. We could anticipate each other's moves. We took our fear and transferred it to focus."

Often people look at JT's videos and think he's a brazen kid with little regard for his life, but meeting him in person, I sense just the opposite. There are even times when he sounds more like a cautious investor than an extreme athlete. "If there's a way I can get from being 90 percent sure about skiing a line to 93 percent sure," JT says, "if I'm scared enough about it, I'm going to make damn sure I get that extra 3 percent. I'm going to hike the mountain and look at it from every angle. So you turn that fear not only into emotion and energy when it's go time, but you also turn it into motivation for research."

Transforming fear to motivation got JT through a lot more than skiing. As a young boy, JT was diagnosed with attention deficit hyperactivity disorder, or ADHD, and given a prescription for Ritalin, an amphetamine that increases dopamine levels in the brain. ADHD has become something of an epidemic in the United States. According to the Centers for Disease Control and Prevention's most recent statistics, one in every 10 US children has been diagnosed with ADHD, and 66 percent of them, *2.7 million children*, were receiving medication for the condition as of 2007, usually amphetamines like Ritalin or Adderall.

The neurobiology of ADHD is still being figured out, but there are some very interesting studies showing that ADHD may be affiliated with low numbers of those autoreceptors (the party chaperones) or, in other cases, low numbers of dopamine receptors. In either case, those kids would be motivated to seek adventure and novelty more than others, and indeed, ADHD kids tend to show both high novelty seeking and high boredom susceptibility. In the old world, these kids probably would have been put to work as hunters or explorers and praised. But in today's society, where they're supposed to sit still and study, they're considered problems, and labeling them as kids with a "disorder" likely doesn't help.

JT had problems concentrating and the Ritalin worked, even if it gave him headaches. Later in high school, however, the Ritalin headaches became too much, so JT stopped taking the drug and started getting more and more into skiing, and skiing hard. JT wanted to ski full-time so badly, he went to summer school and doubled his course load his junior year. The skiing, which gave him a natural supply of dopamine, sharpened his concentration enough so that he was able to graduate from high school in 3 years and move to Squaw. As he built a reputation as one of the most radical skiers in the world, he was able to also get a college degree.

It wasn't until later, when he studied more about the brain himself, that JT realized he had replaced Ritalin with skiing. "If I'm on top of the mountain and I'm scared," he says, "that fear really drives me to analyze every step of the skiing line I'm about to take. I think it through: *How am I going to do this safely? Are the conditions right?* With that fear, and that brain stimulation, I'm completely focused. I can dissect and be meticulous, and that transfers to my life off the mountain."

When I ask JT if he needs that fear in his life, if he's addicted, he laughs because it's such a common question. "Addiction is a big word," he says. "Addiction is a physical need. I'm not shaking if I don't go BASE jumping or skiing.

If I get injured and I'm down for 6 months, I don't have any major physical breakdown. A meth addict or a heroin addict is going to have physical withdrawals." What JT is addicted to, he says, is the outdoor life and a good challenge. When he can't ski or BASE jump, he likes going hiking or running or climbing in the mountains, all forms of exercise that provide their own dopamine bumps. "You get that same good feeling," he says, "but it's more fun to have an extra carrot involved like a line to ski."

• • • •

Addiction *is* a big word, and though biology certainly plays into it, our environment may play an equally big role. What JT said reminds me of a fascinating (if controversial) experiment by Canadian biologist Bruce K. Alexander. In the late '70s, Alexander built a 95-square-foot park for rats to play and live in, replete with lots of fun wheels and balls. The idea was to test his hypothesis that drugs aren't so much the cause of addiction as the environmental stressors that drug addicts tend to live with. This was an unorthodox hypothesis, but the results were surprising.

Alexander took a group of rats and force-fed them morphine for 57 days, making them addicted. Then he set them free in the luxurious rat park with options to feed their habit anytime they liked with morphine-laced water. Alternatively, they could just drink plain tap water. For the most part, the so-called addicted rats, and the nonaddicted controls, chose the *tap water*. Meanwhile, a control group of rats that were also force-fed morphine for 57 days, and then placed in isolated cages, drank far more of the morphine-laced water. The results were published in *Journal of*

Psychopharmacology. It seems what other scientists hadn't considered in earlier studies on rats and addiction is how *stressed* their test subjects were from isolation and caging. And "severely distressed animals," Alexander said, "like severely distressed people, will relieve their distress pharmacologically if they can."

Fortunately, using new forms of gradual training that take advantage of the brain's plasticity, psychologists are now finding that there are methods to improve the attention of ADHD kids in the classroom without drugs. But it's also worth noting that we may not be taking into consideration that for a child who is genetically wired for exploring, a typical classroom setting may feel like a cage, and they're going to seek to relieve their stress any way they can.

Jamie Patrick—like Michael Phelps and many other top athletes—also suffered from ADHD as a kid. Back then diagnoses weren't as common, so he wasn't prescribed the usual Ritalin or Adderall. Instead, during college, Jamie found his own version: cocaine. Cocaine completely derailed Jamie's swimming career for a time and kept him from being as successful as he could have been. But eventually he found triathlons and later ultra swimming, which helped him kick the cocaine habit cold turkey. "I'm definitely addicted to training now," Jamie told me, "and I'm probably addicted to scaring myself a little—to that challenge. But it's an addiction that allows me to focus on my job and be a good father and husband. I'm okay with that."

The day we met at the West Side Café, Flea told me he was going to surf the Mavericks contest for a few more years, but he didn't feel the need to be the crazy guy in the water anymore. He just enjoyed the exercise now. But he also said what he learned at Mavericks, that ability to act against your natural biology, managed to come back and help him when he needed it most. Very few meth addicts get clean. Some estimates are as low as 1 to 5 percent. Once he actually got to rehab, Flea was surprised how easy it was. "I'd learned from surfing that you can do anything you put your mind to," Flea told me, "so when I wanted to get clean, I just did it."

It was nice being sober. Having clean hands was cool for a change. Waking up in the morning for once. Now Flea felt bad for his friends who were still using, for those millions of meth addicts around the country who were trying to quit and couldn't. Maybe he could use his high profile to actually keep other people from walking down that road. A lot of athletes abuse drugs and never go public with it to protect their image, but just 4 months out of rehab, Flea spilled his guts in gruesome detail to *Surfer* magazine. He was on a roll, feeling grateful for getting his life back. He thought there were a couple of things he might be able to do for rehab.

"It sucks being around a bunch of people who want to get sober," Flea said. "They just sit around and smoke cigarettes. *Hey, it's time to go for a walk. Oh, cool, let's go for a walk.* It doesn't make getting sober seem fun, you know." By the time Flea checked out of rehab, he had his skateboard, his bike, his longboards, his tennis racket, his golf clubs, whatever he could use to keep him focused. It helped, radically, and that gave him an idea, a rehab center for people who actually want to do fun stuff. Why not call it FleaHab?

Recent studies have found that altruism can increase dopamine levels in the brain too, implying perhaps that novelty seekers like Flea could become as obsessed with giving as they could with taking risks. Melissa Brown, associate director of research at the Center on Philanthropy at Indiana University, has coined this our "immediate altruistic response," and while it may be unlikely that Flea was becoming addicted to rehabbing drug addicts, he seemed to be having fun.

FleaHab entails basically whatever sport the recovering addict wants to do with a surf star: surfing, hiking, biking, tennis—just getting out and staying healthy. At the time of our interview, Flea was still getting the paperwork and financing together, but he was already taking individual clients and sounded more excited about the program than he did about anything else (except the baby his longtime girlfriend was pregnant with). A guy came to FleaHab who said he hadn't played tennis since his addiction started. "He chain-smoked through the entire game," Flea laughed. "But I got him back into doing something he loved, and that's what's rewarding, just seeing that."

When I tell Amy about all this novelty-seeking research, she admits she is probably addicted to new challenges at work, and definitely travel. (Since we've met, Amy has had a new travel idea just about every week, and I've never seen someone navigate frequent-flier programs with such savvy.) She sees these addictions as mostly good since they keep her learning, but she also tries to reel herself in when she feels herself wanting to jump to the next lily pad before a project is done.

Surfing, I suppose, is one of my addictions, I admit to Amy, but like JT, I'm more addicted to the healthy outdoor life. I could give up Mavericks no problem. In fact, I tell Amy, I'm already realizing I have a lot more fun on smaller days. I don't like the heavy crowd out there, and it's not really worth the risk.

"So stop," Amy says.

"Fine," I say.

"Good," she says.

"At least until next season," I add.

Amy rolls her eyes.

CHAPTER 9

INVESTIGATING THE ELEPHANT'S FOOTPRINT

"I'm not afraid of death. I just don't want to be there when it happens."

—WOODY ALLEN

The Sacramento River, still as glass, winds between great oaks and tall grasses. Mist rises up off the water, catching moonlight. It's 3:30 a.m. and so quiet—all we can hear is the occasional sound of a paddle or hand breaking the water's skin. Between two kayaks, Jamie Patrick swims steadily. He's in about mile 55 of an attempt to swim 111 miles without stopping.

It's amazing to think that it was just a year ago that Jamie was the first to swim twice across Tahoe, 44 miles. That swim took 26 hours, and the ER doc said if Jamie had swum one more hour, he could've died. Jamie has now been swimming for 14 hours. He looks steady, but at this pace, he has about another 17 hours to go, and that's being optimistic. Only a handful of people in history have swum longer than 30 hours at a stretch. This is new territory, and it's hard to say if he'll make it.

Mark Lukach and I are kayaking alongside Jamie, feeding him water, potatoes, pasta, and the occasional piece of chicken. Though we're mostly quiet—the morning stillness seems to call for it—we chat briefly about how strange it is that just 20 months ago the three of us and Greg Larson were swimming to Alcatraz, and that Mark and I were terrified.

Mark, inspired by Jamie's Tahoe Double, has since gotten into endurance sports in a more serious way. He has been training to try his first Ironman Triathlon next month, which shouldn't be too difficult considering his rigorous training schedule—and that Jamie is coaching him. Mark says he doesn't care about getting any particular time in his Ironman. He's doing it for himself. "I need it," he says, "after the last few years."

It's true, and while we paddle through the darkness, I can't help thinking how impressive it is that Mark is even here. Earlier in the week, I was over at Mark's for dinner, and he and his wife Giulia told me the full story of their last few years, including bits and pieces Mark often left out in our casual conversations.

• • • •

Both Mark and Giulia grew up with fairy-tale lives. They were raised by well-to-do families, attended the best schools and colleges, and got great jobs after school. They married in their early twenties—Mark's family holding up a "will you marry me" sign on the beach while the two were out surfing.

"We had everything," Mark said. "Everything came to us easily, and I just expected life would continue that way. We'd have children and get to travel and do meaningful work." Both devout Catholics, Mark and Giulia always had profound faith in the benevolence of God. They often used their spare time to do things like develop a boarding school for underprivileged girls in rural Kenya called the Daraja Academy.

But in 2009, 5 years into their marriage, cracks started to appear. Giulia, a rising star in marketing, took on a new and stressful job. A perfectionist with a feisty Italian streak, Giulia couldn't turn down a stitch of the work, but she felt increasingly unable to deal. Mark began feeling more like a counselor than a husband, and it was scary how quickly things turned ugly. Giulia wasn't just stressed; something fundamental was changing within her. She had always been good with math and numbers, but she would go to work now and not be able to make sense of simple spreadsheets. She felt like her thoughts were floating inside her head. She couldn't organize them. She stopped sleeping.

Numerous studies have linked higher levels of the stress

hormone cortisol to both insomnia and lack of REM sleep. In turn, insomnia also causes higher cortisol levels, a vicious cycle. Good-quality sleep is key to a healthy stress response, so much so that one George Institute for Global Health survey of nearly 20,000 people found that those who got less than 5 hours of sleep per night were three times as likely to suffer from mental illness. It's hard to know what exactly was going on with Giulia, but within a month, she wasn't even recognizable. She was threatening to kill herself weekly. She hallucinated about demons and people trying to kill her. After her second trip to the emergency room because of threatening or attempting suicide, the doctors had no choice but to place Giulia in a mental health facility.

Mark could see his wife once per day during the ward's 7 to 8:30 p.m. visiting hours. He tried to stay optimistic that Giulia was having what the doctors called a brief psychotic episode. But Giulia was only getting worse. She refused to take her medicine because she thought the doctors were trying to kill her. The nurses had to strap her down to the bed and administer drugs intravenously. The doctors said she might have schizophrenia, which meant Giulia was likely sick for life.

Mark was trying to keep it together, but he was starting to feel crazy himself. He'd always felt in control. Why couldn't he fix this? He also felt, for the first time in his life, angry at God. No, not just angry. He was losing his faith, losing his usual calm and confidence—losing everything. He found himself panicking at times, crying, or lording over the doctors and nurses, yelling at them. If he couldn't reach his wife, he would make damn sure that the doctors were doing their jobs.

But nothing was changing. Day by day, Giulia was becoming one of the most psychotic patients in the facility (which was saying something in a place where one man thought he actually *was* God). Giulia still didn't sleep a wink. Fearing the other patients would rape her, she tried to concoct little ways to kill herself with her blanket, and might have succeeded if she wasn't checked on by nurses on 10-minute suicide watch rounds.

One day, about 2 weeks into Giulia's hospitalization, Mark's friend Austin tried to get Mark to go surfing to get his mind off things. Mark reluctantly agreed, and they paddled out into the cold, murky San Francisco ocean. Uninterested in waves, Mark paddled right past the breakers, far out to sea. Austin paddled up behind him, and the two just sat there in silence.

"You know what," Mark eventually told Austin, "if I'm a caregiver the rest of my life, it was worth it. Nine years of health with Giulia was completely worth it. I've been given everything so far, and this is what's happening now." When Mark heard himself saying this, he started sobbing uncontrollably. "It's hard to explain," Mark told me, "but I let go of the fear of death—Giulia's and my own; I let go of the guilt that I couldn't fix her. I let go of the fact that I might not even be able to stop her from killing herself. It just all washed away, right there. And maybe I was able to let go because I had to. I had no choice."

Afterward, he still felt angry about Giulia's condition, but he could see a little more of the big picture. He was going to die. Giulia was going to die. This was just the way it was. He couldn't choose when, or stop it from happening. And the more he let go, the more he felt like, somehow, things were as they should be. He felt his faith in a supportive God and even an afterlife come back to him. But in a different way from before. Of course, he was still going to do everything he could to help Giulia. But he also had to accept that he wasn't in control anymore, not completely anyway.

That very night, when Mark went to visit his wife, the doctor gave him a strange report: Giulia, for the first time, was showing signs of recovery, and after 22 days in the mental health facility, Giulia was allowed to go home.

• • • •

When I first met her, a few months after her hospitalization, Giulia was a walking zombie. She followed Mark around the house, nodding and smiling blankly. Mark had to watch her almost every second of the day, and Giulia still sometimes asked Mark to let her kill herself. It took her more than a year of therapy and heavy medication to fully recover and come off antipsychotics. Psychotic breaks can sometimes be traced to genetic abnormalities, substance abuse, or brain damage, but as none of these relate to Giulia's situation, her psychotic break seems to have been stress induced. Returning soldiers, new parents, and those who lose a loved one, for example, have also been known to suffer psychotic breaks—the word "break" in these cases often meaning a break away from reality when it becomes too painful. Giulia's case is still mysterious, but whatever the reason, you would never have the slightest clue that Giulia ever went through any of this. She's now back to work full-time as a director of online marketing. She and Mark travel often and still work on the rural school in Kenya. Giulia has her Italian feistiness back, as well as her warmth and wit. The only reason you would know about her past is the fact that she loves to tell her story. Mark has even written a memoir, *Where the Road Meets the Sun,* hoping to help others who might go through the same experience and to help remove the stigma of mental illness.

The most interesting part about reading their book is that, in retrospect, they're both *glad* that it happened. Before getting sick, Giulia and Mark both describe her as scared of the smallest things: getting a B on a test, getting criticized at work, gaining the slightest bit of weight. She was judgmental of others. She obsessed about her appearance and thought she would only be happy with the right body, the right clothes, the right friends.

"It's actually the fear that changed me," Giulia told me. "The scary experience is what turned me, what evolved me." Though she used to put on a good face, she said she wasn't ever completely happy because she was so hypercritical. Now she can feel for the people she used to judge, and for herself. "I was given a second chance," she said. "After feeling what it's like to want to throw your life away, I wouldn't give up or change being terrified in that psych ward. I wouldn't change getting held down while they put medicine in my veins. Before, I didn't understand the value of life. I took it for granted. I didn't realize the beauty of life or why I'm here. My goal isn't to become the next CEO anymore. My goal is to give hope. I really believe I can help people see the negative in a positive way. I never did that before. I was the pessimist. I was never the optimist."

On their most recent trip to Kenya, Giulia was doing just that. In a country where mental illness isn't discussed openly and is generally poorly understood, Giulia started a women's forum to both educate women and let them talk about any challenges with mental illness they were having themselves or in their families. "All of the women were in tears by the end," Giulia said. "They'd never had the chance to talk about their fears openly like that."

• • • •

Seventeen hours later, it's hard to believe Jamie is still going, but it seems he really did learn from that near tragedy in Tahoe. After consulting doctors, on this swim, he let himself digest his food longer after each feeding so that he could keep down the protein. The adjustment—along with a whole lot of training and mental preparation with Paige Dunne—worked, and after 31 hours of suffering, Jamie is again flopping and sputtering to an applauding crowd. (With the river's current, Jamie technically swam about 60 miles, which is why this swim only took him 5 more hours than the Tahoe Double.) The most shocking part is that this time Jamie looks like he could go another few hours, and he doesn't even need to go to the hospital for an IV, the doctors say.

Mark kayaked and swam with Jamie almost the entire 31 hours, and one thing I couldn't help noticing during the swim was that Mark was by far Jamie's strongest emotional support. When Jamie was in his truly dark moments, he didn't want to see anybody but his wife or Mark. It was almost like Mark was the one person who had been deeper into darkness, and he was the guy who could coach Jamie through.

The natural cycles of suffering and death give us enough fear to work with in one lifetime. There's no good reason we should all go out and swim 111 miles or climb mountains. But in a world where we try to micromanage everything, there is value, I think, in occasionally going to that edge as our exploring ancestors had to do, coming face-to-face with our mortality.

I'm thinking about this when, not long after Jamie's swim, Doc Renneker takes me on a trip to one of his secret big-wave spots far, far north. Doc was out the day Sion Milosky died at Mavericks, and we end up talking about Sion's death on the way up. Doc, ever the contrarian, thinks it wasn't a Mavericks specific fatality. He was watching the usual crew of daredevils that day and said they were sitting in a far too dangerous spot, too deep in the dragon's belly. They knew what could happen and it did—plain and simple.

Doc leaves it at that, but ends up telling me, in a clearly connected way, about his favorite polar explorers, men he has spent decades reading about. Fridtjof Nansen, the famed Norwegian explorer and Nobel Peace Prize winner, the first to cross the Greenland interior, is Doc's favorite. Doc says that unlike the other early polar explorers, Nansen was more studious, more creative, more open-minded. Instead of trying to survive on his own rations as the other polar explorer's did when they were stranded in ice, Nansen befriended the locals and learned their fishing techniques, surviving for years when the public thought he had disappeared forever. "He wasn't out to prove how tough he was," Doc says. "He was too smart for that. All the other guys died."

Doc probably talks about death so casually because it's such a common occurrence in his life. These days in his medical practice, he almost exclusively takes cases that are terminal or seem unsolvable to other doctors. He calls it the "big wave equivalent in medicine," and says that his surfing at the outer limits helps him probe the depths of his own fears. So when medicine reaches its limit—as it so often does—he can be supportive to his patients making that transition into the unknown.

Maybe Sion was being overly brazen that day at Mavericks, but the line between brazen and courageous is often gray. I'm thinking of an article I read recently about Sion in the Hawaii press—one of many articles that have sung his praises as a devoted father since his passing. Just before sundown, the powerful surf had apparently swept a woman out to sea in front of Sion's home on Oahu's North Shore. This was just months before his death at Mavericks, so Sion was at the peak of his big-wave training. While the fire crew was still unpacking, Sion didn't think anything of paddling into the darkness alone, searching for 45 minutes among the black waves until he finally found the woman alive. He paddled her to shore, never saying much about the rescue.

Out the window along Highway One, gray seas are exploding off black and green bluffs. I ask Doc if he has faith—you know, like the capital "G" kind. Doc says he doesn't adhere to any one religion, but he has studied them all. He takes what is useful to him, leaving behind what he thinks is dogmatic or blind. Doc has no specific beliefs about life after death or what God is, but he says that he knows, "in the way one does, that everyone has a spirit." He feels it. And Doc has seen how, in all his patients facing death, it's faith that allows them to go peacefully or not.

We happen to be on a section of the highway where the truck is skirting the edge of immense cliffs. The car could just fly off—over. Death will come. If it does not come now while we're driving north past these bluffs, then it will come next year, or 80 years from now—it's the one inevitable.

• • • •

In many ways, all this science research has made me realize how far we've come as humans, but it has also made me realize how much we still don't know. I find myself thinking more about the characters from my old religious studies and philosophy classes, and how they approached the problems science still can't solve.

"Of all footprints," the Buddha said, "that of the elephant is supreme. Of all mindfulness meditations, that on death is supreme."

I think of the Prince Siddhartha, before his enlightenment, wandering for 6 years as an ascetic, pushing himself to the very brink of death. Was it because he went to that edge that he was able to speak so confidently about the way out of suffering? I think of Michel de Montaigne: "Let us deprive death of its strangeness, let us frequent it. . . . We do not know where death awaits us so let us wait for it everywhere."

I'm wondering if this is, in part, our motivation to be out there in the wild seas, to look at death straight on, to get a glimpse beyond logic, or to feel our smallness, the fleetingness of it all, how we are specks of sand whirling around suns, and to come back to land like children, looking up and saying, thank you.

• • • •

Hours later, far from civilization, Doc and I arrive at the cliff's edge in front of his secret spot. You can't even really see anything—the wave breaks so far out to sea, over a mile. "How big do you think it is out there?" Doc asks with a wry grin. It's impossible to tell from here. It could be 100 feet. It could be 10. "Twenty or twenty-five feet," I guess, a shot in the dark. "Pretty good," Doc says.

We watch for 30 minutes, and then Doc spends another 45 minutes telling me about all the risks of the place, exactly how to make it through a small window in the rocks that one needs to pass through before making the mile-long paddle out to sea, what areas to avoid, and what objects to line up with on land to gauge position while out to sea.

We plunge into the cold water and paddle and paddle and paddle. It feels more like we are going out to sea, to Tortuga Island or the Fountain of Youth, than a surf spot. The wind howls and sprays salt in our eyes. Seals pop up everywhere, looking at us differently from how they would in well-traveled areas. We pass fields of spooky aqueous boils where the dark water is being swirled and gargled by the mysterious reef below. I am already exhausted, and the paddle just continues on and on. We're so far out, a whale breaches just 30 yards from our boards. How the hell is this guy almost 60? We have been paddling for an hour when we finally arrive somewhere in the middle of the ocean where Doc somehow knows the waves will line up. He is right. They come. The sets are huge and beautiful and blue and pristine. It's as big as Mavericks, but it has a completely different feeling. There is no crew to compete with, nobody to prove anything to. These waves would have probably sent me into a panic a year ago, but now I feel almost relaxed. I get a jolt of fear peering down the immense walls when I'm at the precipice, but this is fear as I expect it, right in the moment. Between the spikes of alertness, I feel pretty relaxed, happy.

There are long 20-minute lulls between sets, and Doc and I are mostly quiet. Like him, I realize that I don't have any specific religious faith in a heaven, the next life. But I do have a certain faith in nature, in what I feel and observe. Look at these huge waves, each one with such a distinctive personality and presence, but never separate from the ocean. Just like us, each wave has a distinct nature, a hardened beauty, hard enough to pound rock to sand. But at the same time each creation is never separate from its source, and when its life ends, it returns. I have no word for this source, but I do feel it, especially in moments like this, on the edge of the sea—quiet. How it holds things together, supports them.

I have no idea how I will feel when death comes. And I have no idea if freedom from the fear of death is completely possible, even for the monk or nun who sits in meditation as the last bit of life leaves the body, or the soldier who wants to die with honor, or the mother who throws herself into harm's way to protect her child. But if I've learned anything in this research on fear, I guess it's not really specifically about death, or even about fear. If I've learned anything, it's that nature has selected a whole variety of traits for us—some good, some bad, and some a combination of the two. But the brain and the mind and the body have more plasticity than we ever imagined. We are constantly evolving. We learn from events, from one another, from our own emphases and awarenesses. A single thought changes the very structure of our brains. Think about that for a moment. A single thought moves matter. And that's a good thing if we use that malleability wisely. We can take this biological mess of wild impulses, hormones, ferocious emotions, and sharp intellect that we're saddled with and do something worthwhile—maybe something beautiful.

We can't know what happens when we die, but we do

know that we'll die, and death—even the fear of death—can serve as a reminder not to fritter our time away, to appreciate the ones we love. And it's love that allows us to move, to act, even in the midst of fear. We're all different. But maybe the point is, if you start to understand what is driving you, the script that has been written into your genes and your collection of memories, you can begin to mold your life a bit more. It will be scary, but every stressor, every fear, is really just a sign that those boundaries are stretching.

I think we have to keep confronting our fears and keep telling one another the stories that come from doing that. Stories mold our brains, our selves, our future. So we have to choose our stories wisely: the ones we write, the ones we consume.

• • • •

I shouldn't be preaching. But I need this pep talk myself now that it's spring and Amy and I are up here on Vancouver Island. I'm doing a travel story, and I've brought my great aunt Jeanie's engagement ring with me. I have always been scared of this moment. But when I met Amy, something changed. For the first time in my life, I understood why people say, *When you know, you just know*. My earlier fears of commitment and having a family were shaken loose. I could picture living with this woman for our whole lives, and I started planning this engagement just months after we met. But "just knowing" hasn't taken the nerves away, and now that I'm here, I already feel part of myself wanting to back out.

I've found myself reading about marriage and commitment, which I don't recommend highly. As in sports, I have a feeling too much analysis in love might just make you choke. It's made me stay up late at night anyway, thinking far too much about the prairie vole and its cousin the montane vole. The montane is very promiscuous, writes Dr. Louann Brizendine in *The Male Brain*, but the prairie is strictly monogamous because "when the prairie vole finds his partner, he mates with her over and over in a twenty-four-hour sexual marathon. This sexual activity changes his brain forever. An area of his brain called the AH—the anterior hypothalamus—memorizes his partner's smell and touch, leading him to aggressively reject all other females." Both voles get all sorts of dopamine and vasopressin (a chemical associated with masculinity) during sex, Brizendine continues, but only the prairie vole has the vasopressin receptors to make him monogamous. When scientists block the receptor, the prairies become dirty playboys just like their cousins the montanes, and "although the brain biology in men may turn out to be more complicated than it is in voles, humans have this vasopressin receptor gene too. Some men have the long version, while others have the short one." A study in Sweden found that men with the long version were twice as likely to leave bachelorhood behind and commit to one woman for life. Great, now I have to wonder how long my vasopressin receptor is? Either way, I'm pretty sure I can't pull off a 24-hour sexual marathon.

At least I have my aunt Jeanie's ring. My parents' marriage didn't work (as hard as they tried, and wonderful people that they both are), but my great aunt Jeanie and my great uncle Bob gave us the model of a happy, lifelong relationship—with love from marriage until death. Knowing what I now know, emphasizing the love story over the fear story will sometimes be like rowing against the stream of 200 million years of evolution, but I also know that it's possible: I know that the story I emphasize and tell myself again and again will rewire the fear. It will determine how I act when our relationship hits hard times, and how much we are enjoying ourselves right now.

After kayaking around the Clayoquot Sound, Amy and I go tide-pooling at an inlet near Ucluelet. The squally waves explode against the black stones. A lighthouse shines through the drizzling fog. Amy looks beautiful in her fur-lined hoodie, the same one she wore that first night we met. I feel both stories—the story of doom and fear, the story of love and hope—inside. I think of those rats that got the shot of oxytocin, the love hormone, into their brains and were able to overcome their fearful paralysis. And though I've never been a Bible reader except in religious studies classes in college, John 4:18 comes to mind: "There is no fear in love, but perfect love casteth out fear."

I reach into my pocket and turn the diamond in between my fingers nervously. While Amy isn't looking, I hide the ring under an oyster shell and pretend to have just found it there. "What's that?" I say, obviously a little shaky and up to something.

Amy looks at me, and I get the feeling she might know. Oh well, nothing's perfect. But as she lifts the shell, her face lights up. I get down on one knee and finally ask: Amy Elizabeth DuRoss, would you spend your life with me?

"Yes," Amy says, and we both cry. The fear dissolves—for now anyway.

A month later, Amy is pregnant. We're thrilled, of course, and this is actually part of the plan. Amy is 5 years older than me, and we talked about getting down to business in an expedited fashion for biology's sake. But I didn't think it would happen quite *this* soon. We've only been trying for a few *days*. When the doctor gives us the news, Amy, sensing my nerves, jokes: "Well honey, maybe you'll need to write a sequel." We're going to be parents. How is this even possible?

I feel barely capable of getting my taxes in every year, even after the maximum extension. Now, suddenly, we're wading through the pros and cons of epidurals, which investment fund will be better for college in 2030, and what sleep/nursing schedules are ideal for newborns. As new boxes arrive on our doorstep every single day containing items like a mechanical swing, an oak crib, and a baby dresser—all of which require a few hours of assemblage—the potential for complexity once this baby arrives is starting to feel more numbing than scary. Perhaps this is the effect of too many psychological fears descending on the mind at once. I don't know. But the surprises come daily. Nobody tells you that morning sickness can be, and often is, all-day-and-night sickness. My future wife has become a gentle hue of green, cracker crumbs trailing in her wake as she orders more and more "how to raise a child" books. God, if you're out there, What is happening?

I cling to the moments of hope. Our wedding, for example. With Amy's penchant for making lifelong friends on airplanes and in grocery shopping lines, we figured we'd have to either rent out the biggest barn in northern California or have the wedding at Ocean Beach with just our families, saving our friends' party for that hazy time in the future when we come up for air. After much debate, the gods seem to smile on us for choosing the latter. Amy has recovered from her nausea by wedding day, and there are games of beach volleyball and bikini-clad Frisbee (as opposed to the usual foggy beach scene of shivering children crying in wet jeans) occurring as we say our vows across the street from our house, toes in the sand, tears in abundance. This may be the best day of weather San Francisco has produced in a century; and instead of taking out a small business loan to feed our friends (as if Amy doesn't feed them enough already), a local chef cooks up a spread of braised short ribs, garlic mashed potatoes, and a warm mushroom salad, serving all 16 of us in our living room for about the same price as a fancy dinner for four downtown.

Looking around at our dads smoking cigars, our moms discussing future family reunions, and Amy's young nieces throwing flower petals around the living room with my 6-year-old cousin, I have an epiphany: Maybe even events that most people seem to turn into ulcer-inducing extravaganzas—say, 18 years of child rearing—can be made simple, even enjoyable, with a little foresight, a little dialing down, a little letting go of societal expectations. As the sunset turns purple through our window and we sip Amy's father's stellar selection of Kermit Lynch reds, I have that deep-in-my-heart sensation of truly having done right with this whole *life thing*. We're a damn good team, Amy and me.

We have also found out it's a boy, a fact we are both unbelievably overjoyed about—Amy, partly, I think, because she can sense it will reduce my stress. Much as I'm a little embarrassed to admit it—and much as I would also be overjoyed for a girl—imagining surfing and camping with my son has had an oddly calming effect. (And yes, I'm aware I can also do those things with a girl, and I will when that day comes. But I can't deny that this father and son fantasy has been rooting spontaneously into my dreams.)

The afterglow of this discovery, the wedding, and our gorgeous honeymoon in Kauai do wonders to lighten the mood. But as the doctor's appointments mount, and my announcement to Amy and all of our friends and family that "we are having a war on stuff" does nothing to quell the flow of boxes full of objects that need assembly, the uncertainty about my ability to be a good father *and* a good husband *and* have a successful career *and* maintain marginal psychological stability *and* perhaps still have time to, I don't know, have sex with my wife, is, shall we say, on a strong and constant simmer. Amy, despite the fact that her ribs are now nearly snapping with each breath, is ever encouraging—"Of course you will be, and of course we will." But fortunately, divinely, I also get a visit from Mark and Giulia Lukach just before our due date. They're pregnant too, also with a boy. Mark is bouncing off the walls just like he was when we first swam to Alcatraz—like he usually is for that matter. "I think I was born to be a dad!" he exclaims. I try to let Mark's confidence rub off on me, and we joke that we can take turns watching the boys while the other surfs (at least until they're old enough to have their own boards). "It's going to be awesome!" Mark says.

"I know," I tell him, "but we've got to help each other. We are in this together—you hear me."

CHAPTER 10

THE PARADOX OF HAVING A BIG HEAD

"Bran thought about it. 'Can a man still be brave if he's afraid?' 'That is the only time a man can be brave,' his father told him."

—*GEORGE R.R. MARTIN,* A GAME OF THRONES

"Imagine you're having a bowel movement," says our birthing coach, Rachel, "except there's a bowling ball coming out of your butt. Everybody get that? A bowling ball."

There are 12 of us pregnant couples sitting in a semicircle around Rachel, some holding hands, others diligently taking notes. A few of the men adjust our seated positions upon the mention of the bowling ball. For the most part, however, nobody bats an eye. This is our fourth birthing class with the ever-blunt Rachel, and she has been dropping shockers like this from day one. At an earlier class, she showed us a video of a home birth in which the mother delivered twins without a drop of painkillers, and this after demonstrating how the baby descends down the birth canal with a life-size skeleton and a stuffed-animal moose.

It has been . . . enlightening. As many a man before me, I have realized that of all the athletic feats humans engage in, there is none greater than that of bringing a new life into this world. Whatever my anxieties about very soon not having enough time or money to do anything I once enjoyed, all I have to do is conjure that bowling ball to remember my sacrifice pales in comparison to Amy's—as it does, for that matter, to the sacrifices of all moms throughout mammalian time. I have the urge to go see Doc Renneker—the man who told me, "I somehow didn't get the fear gene"—and say, "Well, just to be sure, do you mind pushing this bowling ball out of your butt?"

It's going to hurt. But, after numerous birthing books and classes, we have learned that the key to getting that bowling ball out without too much excessive torture is to (a) take a lot of drugs, (b) let go of all tension and fear, or (c) some combination of the two. The "fear-pain-tension cycle" was coined by British obstetrician Dr. Grantley Dick-Read in the 1930s. By simple observation, Dick-Read concluded that the more a mother fears during labor, the more she tenses, and the more resistance there is to the baby sliding down. What many experts think is happening here is that our fear response, in its blunt way, doesn't suddenly notice that mom is in labor, and divert its extra energy to her uterus. Instead, as if mom were under threat from a tiger, it signals the reproductive and digestive organs to all but shut down, its soldiers of adrenaline and cortisol diverting to the limbs for fighting or fleeing. In other words, a scared mom's uterus, the key birth muscle, is getting starved of its usual power at a time when it needs every ounce, the equivalent of running a marathon with blood flow to your legs stymied. There are other theories about why fear hinders birth, but it's clear that, nearly a century after Dick-Read's observation, he was onto something. A 2012 Norwegian study that surveyed 2,206 women found that those who ranked high in fear of labor—determined by an elaborate questionnaire—endured longer labors by an average of nearly an hour, and that was after adjusting for factors of first-time moms and drugs during labor.

In short, the very moment we come into this world, fear is lying. It's telling mom's body to contract when it should be opening. And if there is one thing I recommend remembering from all this research, it's that *fear lies*. When you see that gorgeous girl or guy across the street and your body tenses at the thought of saying hello; as you step up to the podium to deliver a speech; while you're warming up to kick the winning field goal; while you're walking in for that job interview—in all of these instances, like laboring mothers, we should be relaxing rather than contracting. But, because of our evolutionary baggage, our brains—still worried about the tribe leaving us alone in the Serengeti—are arguing that the risk of approaching that hottie, podium, field goal kick, or interview is akin to serious injury, even death. And that is emphatically not the truth. The risk of approaching a love interest is that you will experience a simple rejection. The risk of making the speech is that you make a bad speech, which might be at least passable if you're relaxed. The risk of taking that field goal kick is missing. No more, no less.

"Do one thing every day that scares you," said Eleanor Roosevelt, which is the best advice we could ever get, I believe, if a caveat is included. First we might ask: Is fear lying? Is the risk actually lower than our ancient fear response is selling it as? If the challenge is sticking your tongue to a frozen metal pole to placate your dumb friends, then: no. Fear isn't lying. Don't do it. But if the opportunity is, say, talking to the intimidating and supercool filmmaker at a cocktail party, the key person who could catalyze your lifelong dream of an acting career, fear is selling you up the river. Go! Schmooze! Talk! Dance!

If we learn to detect fear's bald-faced lies, and make a practice of debunking them, and if we do this, as Roosevelt recommended, every single day, we will live better. I can say that with confidence now. And it doesn't have to be epic. If you're shy and tend toward social anxiety like so many of us do, have a random conversation in an elevator. Wear that outlandish pink shirt to the party. Do a cartwheel on the street. Ask the boss for a raise. Buy that expensive pair of shoes. (Actually, don't buy that expensive pair of shoes.) Experiment depending on your nature. Little by little, the murk of the mind begins to clarify; and look—so many of the boundaries we've created are just that: created.

But there is another caveat. To use the current metaphor of birth, how can fear be lying when labor is so dangerous? The World Health Organization (WHO) estimates that about 800 women die *every single day* from childbirth or pregnancy complications, most of them in the developing world but a handful in medically advanced countries too.

If we hadn't heeded our fears of losing more women and babies in labor, we wouldn't have spent centuries developing deft methods of Caesarean section, incubators, ultrasound technology. We would still be having our babies in caves and shouting at the gods when that most wonderful day of our lives turns to tragedy.

It's hard to know whether to praise our smart worrying brains or to scold them. After all, one of the reasons birth is so especially dangerous for human moms is that our skulls have grown so large to accommodate our ever-burgeoning neurons. And while baby's big brain is jamming mom's pelvis, risking her life, mom's big brain, unlike any other mammal to our knowledge, is imagining multiple horrible outcomes that are making her body tense unnecessarily, further endangering her life. The brain is clearly poor engineering from this view. But then again, it's baby's big brain that will go on to invent some new technology that will allow more big-headed human babies to survive this perilous birth stuff, and it's mom's big brain that allowed her to choose a safe hospital or midwife in order for her young genius to survive.

When it comes down to it, there are really no facile statements when it comes to fear. This is the paradox of being a big-headed, bipedal, human being. It's the paradox of trying to live longer and longer, healthy lives in an inherently risky world. But, because the scared brain needs simplicity, let's go ahead and make some facile statements anyway. As a general rule, it's often in social situations that fear tricks us. When it comes to these truly dangerous physical acts—surfing a monster wave, fighting a forest fire, giving birth—a middle path is necessary. Tensing won't help us perform better, at least not in high doses. But it *can* help us *prepare* better, which will help us relax and have faith when it's go time. If we freeze, and let fear simply spin our internal wheels, we'll stagnate. But if we harness fear as motivation to prepare, invent, train—one of its true purposes—then the fear transforms from villain to hero.

• • • •

At our 6-month ultrasound, Amy and I discover that our son—whom we've already given the Lithuanian name Kaifas, or Kai, for short—is particularly well-endowed in the cranial region. Looking on screen at that bowling ball perched atop Kai's scrawny body, Amy asks: "Is it just me, or does he have a large head?"

The perinatologist, likely knowing all about the fear-tension-pain cycle, clearly doesn't want to add an extra psychological burden. "It's not, well, small," she says, shuffling out of the room.

But our doctor, president of one of the most prestigious medical associations on Earth, seems always in the middle of saving someone's life or delivering a baby and doesn't have time for niceties. "That is not an insignificant noggin!" she says when she receives the ultrasound photos. "This makes things interesting."

Interesting?

"How big is it?" Amy asks, smiling through a tightened jaw. "Give it to me straight."

"*Definitely* in the 99th percentile."

It's in this moment that a mantra comes to me. Yes, a

facile statement, but still, a mantra that may best summarize everything I have learned about fear. It goes like this:

Prepare, prepare, prepare, flow. Prepare, prepare, prepare, let go.

"Prepare, prepare, prepare" will remind us to *act* during the worry and anticipation stages of this pregnancy and life—that is, the majority of it. "Flow and let go" will remind us that, at go time—time to push!—it's all about trusting our instincts, trusting our training, and remembering that, ultimately, we are never completely in control.

So, with Kai's huge head expanding each moment, we do it all: prenatal yoga, prenatal massage, a hypno-birthing class (where, oddly enough, the bowling ball line gets dropped). We even hire a young doula to accompany us to the hospital and help encourage as natural a birth as possible. To cover our bases, though, we attend, on our hospital's recommendation, a class that describes all our drug options in detail—from morphine to an epidural—generally encouraging these pain killers by telling us how much it's going to flipping hurt, not to mention spackling the weekend course with stories of everything that can go horribly wrong. I can imagine this class being interesting to a med student, but to give you an idea of how little the instructor heeds the psychological tenderness of this process, one pregnant mother walks out of the class in tears, her husband awkwardly trailing behind her, and another couple simply leaves and doesn't return.

In many ways, these two sides of the birthing prep spectrum—I call them the hippies and the hawks—seem to cancel each other out. The hippie classes, generally taught by nonmedical professionals, encourage us to think positively, envision a pleasant, even orgasmic, birth, and say affirmations like, "My body is the perfect size for my baby" before bed. Meanwhile, our hawkish medical team—who, I should add, are the ones who have to save moms' and babies' lives on a regular basis—keep emphasizing the plethora of risks. For us, they say that labor could take literally days with a head like Kai's, and, yes, a C-section is a good possibility, and, yes, you'll probably want the drugs.

To make matters worse, the hippies tend to despise our hawkish hospital choice, and it annoys them that our hawkish birthing instructors would plant such seeds of fear. These will clearly make our fears manifest, they say. Meanwhile, the hawks don't even like to allow these hippie doulas into the room and tend to think all these natural birthing people are living in the dark ages by encouraging women not to take advantage of advancements in science (read: drugs).

For the victims—us—these lines in the sand are frustrating. Both groups are clearly right. You have to be cautious (*prepare, prepare, prepare*). But at the same time, mom should have candlelight, Gregorian chanting, a hot tub, and as few interventions as possible (*flow and let go*) if that's what will help her avoid the fear-tension-pain cycle from spinning out of control. The hippies and hawks should be working together. Instead, they seem to hate one another's guts.

Amy and I are trying our best to learn from both groups. We're checking all those boxes in our stacks of birthing books (bags packed, baby room set up with far too many items for any baby to ever use, doctor's and doula's phone numbers written on fridge, family members on alert with roles assigned) while at the same time trying to chill with nightly comedies, shoulder rubs, and positive-guided reveries before bed.

• • • •

When Amy's water breaks, we don't actually realize it until, on our due date, we get an ultrasound, and—look at that—no amniotic fluid. The reason Amy didn't get the usual gush, we learn, is that Kai's big head is already jammed against her pelvis, allowing the fluid to escape only in tiny dribs and drabs. With her amniotic sack having been ruptured for 24 hours, and true contractions (or "surges," as the hippies call them) still having not begun, we're told we have no choice but to rush to the hospital and induce labor with Pitocin, a synthetic form of oxytocin. This is already a strike against a natural birth, our first choice, because Pitocin is known to increase pain. Perfect.

But we are not going to forget our hippie training. After a series of tests and needle pricks that raise Amy's blood pressure through the roof (one of the main reasons the hippies encouraged home birth), we enter our birthing room, ignoring any sideways glances from the staff as we roll out the yoga mats and bring out the enormous pink yoga ball, shifting Amy into various poses (cat stretch, doggie wags its tail, polar bear) all to a background of tribal African beats, MIA, and Ravi Shankar. To summarize the rather dry details of the next 24 hours, a combination of our hippie training along with, eventually, some extremely strong drugs gets Amy to 8 centimeters dilated and nearly ready to push.

He's coming, he's coming, the nurses say, any hour now. Except, 5 hours later . . . wow, he is really not coming.

The head, of course, is still jammed. Our doctor thinks that it's actually too big for Amy's pelvis. Our doula thinks that the painkillers we used are preventing a natural flow.

Who is right? Hippies or hawks? Mary Mother of God! We Don't Know! We use our hippie training to request another couple of hours to try to relax and pray, but after 2 hours with no downward progress of the great head, a whole group of hawks descend to tell us that this is a textbook C-section. We have no choice. For Kai's and mom's health, Amy must go under the knife.

We prepared. Amy flowed and let go as much as she possibly could. She has been heroic. But geometry appears to have won the day, and this is not a time to test if fear is lying. This is one of those times when hawk preparation pays off big. Amy diligently researched the best surgeons in the country, and earlier in her pregnancy we switched hospitals to be with this one, a huge relief as we enter a white and silver room that reminds me of an alien spacecraft, all of us in scrubs and surgical masks. The anesthesiologist, whom Amy says she wants to marry when this is all done (the drugs are *that* good), plays Norah Jones and talks to Amy about his recent trip to Paris, an intentional distraction, while our doctor and a team of stealth operators silently go to work.

It's scary. At one point, when Amy starts to understandably freak out because she can *feel* the incision being made, the anesthesiologist shoves some tubes up her nose, making her pass out for a few seconds. But when the frenzy dies down, just 20 minutes later, like magic, our deft doctor pulls from Amy's stretched belly skin a beautiful, beautiful, beautiful boy.

"Would you look at that head!" are, not surprisingly, the first words Kaifas William DuRoss Yogis (8 pounds, 11 ounces) will hear in this world. He should be proud. It is a beautiful head, a head for the ages, a head we would not have any other way. None of the disappointment about a C-section or the debate between hippies and hawks matters now. Here he is. Healthy. Glorious. Strapping. A boy.

I can't lay him on his mom's chest yet, her belly being sewn up, but the doctors let me place him next to Amy's face, and the two of them instantly recognize each other's voices, crooning at each other, crying oh so happily.

• • • •

"It's like falling in love and getting married all in the same day," I tell Amy when we have the wee Kaifas back in our hospital room, his little bow lips rounding out for bewildered coos and hoots. "We're committed for life to this being we've just met and completely head-over-heels happy about that."

That this parenting thing is something I have been afraid of most of my twenties and all of my thirties because—What was the reason again? Time? Money?—seems the epitome of ridiculous. Are you kidding? I would hike through a jungle of poison oak and venomous snakes for this baby. I would bodysurf Mavericks naked. I would analyze tax law under fluorescent lights 12 hours per day. And I know Amy feels the same way, especially after what she just went through. Whatever it takes, bring it on. We will do it. We will not fail. Like Jamie Patrick after his 44-mile swim, exhausted in our hospital gowns, we somehow feel like we can do anything. It's the best day of our lives. And the second day is equally best, and so is the third.

It's on the fourth day when, for the first time, through the clouds, a ray of sunlight pours through our hospital room window directly onto my cot. Amy is sleeping. I'm holding Kai, who is nodding off on my shoulder, when I realize, wait, *he has never felt sunlight.* This blood of our blood has never tasted the sweetness of the source of life on Earth. It's time to change this. We wiggle precariously into the golden beam and situate ourselves chest to chest in its warmth, quickly falling asleep in each other's arms.

In my dream, I'm in a small farmhouse, in the Old West, and, just like in the hospital, Amy and newborn Kai are sleeping. I look at them, proud and happy, but then peer out the window to see an enormous dust storm barreling toward our rickety house of old fence posts and rusty nails. It's clearly going to obliterate us. I start scrambling around the room desperately, trying to find a way to reinforce the house, trying to find an escape route. But then I remember . . . oooohhh yea, I have a hidden superpower now. As the avalanche of swirling dust engulfs the home, I simply open up my chest and, with this new love of creation surging through me, project a beam of light—just like the sunlight pouring down on Kai and me through the hospital window—shining it in all directions. The tempest is no match. It dissolves into thin air.

I wake to Kai making little chipmunk noises in the crook of my neck and can't help feeling that a huge loose end has been tied up inside me, and that this boy on my chest was the unconscious reason I began this whole fear project in the first place. He wanted to join our family. Dad just had to work out a few issues first.

This reminds me of another potent dream I had back in 2003. I was in my last semester of college, studying in South Asia. In the dream, I was a nomad of sorts—alone, as I often felt at that point in my life—and I could see this dark and horrible dust cloud destroying everything in its path. Whole villages of people were fleeing, loading up their belongings in wagons and onto donkeys. They were in a frenzy, screaming and colliding in a panic as people do. I was frozen with terror, and people were shouting to me to flee too, snap out of it. I started sprinting away. But as I fled, I kept looking over my shoulder with a simultaneous dread and fascination. Some part of me was drawn to the blackness and chaos, and also worried about the people left behind. Did I dare go back?

Then, on the safe horizon I was fleeing toward, another low billow of dust appeared. At first I thought it was another storm, but as it got closer, I saw that it was a stampede of horses. They were strong, fast, and gorgeous—white, black, and brown; pintos and stallions. They ran by so gracefully. And in the way you can be both the omniscient author and an innocent character in your dream, I knew that like rescue workers on September 11, these horses were going into the storm to save those who were injured or left behind. But they were also going simply because this is what they did—what everyone else ran from, they went toward. These were the saints, healers, heroes, teachers. I dropped to my knees and wept when they galloped past me. I knew I wasn't one of them. I was still only concerned with myself, with comfort and safety. As I realized this, the storm hardly mattered anymore. I just knelt there and cried in reverence. They were so beautiful.

I'm perfectly aware that being Kai's dad doesn't suddenly make me a saint. But holding his fragile body up in these, his first rays of golden light, I see that in a small way, all parents are bestowed with this gift from nature, which has concluded so rightly that love is essential for continuing life on Earth. There is this immediate biological imperative to stop obsessing so much about ourselves, a small taste of what true selflessness might be like. It's up to us, I suppose, what we then do with that taste.

• • • •

It's not long after Kai is born that I get to actually observe what this love is doing to my heart. Needing to make more money—immediately—I take a job for *ESPN the Magazine*, a feature about why athletes choke under pressure. My first stop is in Boulder Creek's HeartMath Institute, a research center that studies stress and how it affects heart-rate variability, or HRV, and performance. To refresh your memory, HRV is the measurement of how our seemingly constant hearts beat rather erratically. And this is good. The greater the variability, the more resilient our bodies and minds are at balancing our sympathetic and parasympathetic nervous systems—which basically means we are shifting between stress and relaxation, fear and love.

In a computer lab tucked under the shade of redwoods, HeartMath sports trainer John White, who works with a number of PGA tour and NFL athletes, hooks my earlobe up to an iPod-size device called an emWave and rigs that device to a computer screen. Suddenly, there it is, my HRV pattern on-screen, the rhythm resembling a stormy sea or jagged mountain range: high, low, then midrange, then a big spike. This is normal, White says in a Texan accent.

A 32-year-old like me should jump around from, say, 50 beats per minute to 80 beats per minute almost every other beat.

Still, the irregularity in my HRV pattern isn't ideal, probably because I'm a little nervous with a bunch of scientists observing my emotional state, not to mention extremely sleep deprived. I'm not scared, but there's that light buzz of anxiety and coffee that usually accompanies my interviews, leaving me making those typically journalistic strings of ums and uhs mid-question. Interestingly, HeartMath and other HRV specialists have found that these states—fear, frustration, anger, and anxiety—create increasingly haphazard HRV patterns that look something like mine does now.

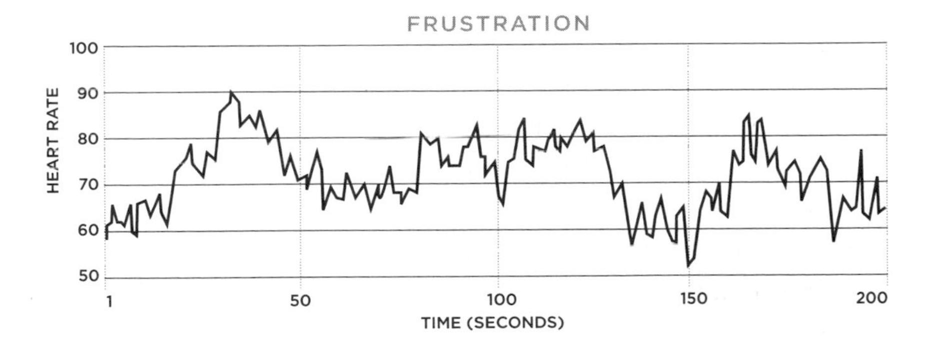

In studies, these patterns generally correlate with decreased performance, be it academic or athletic. However, when we move into more positive states—appreciation, contentment, tranquillity, love—our HRV patterns change rather dramatically. They suddenly appear more like gentle, sloping waves, a certain regular irregularity to them.

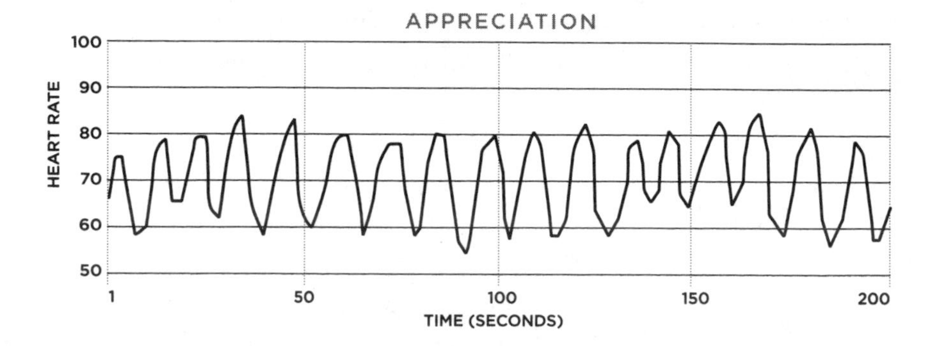

In this state, which HeartMath calls coherence, studies have shown that pro golfers can hit farther and students get higher scores on exams.

White asks me to breathe more regularly—5 seconds in and 5 seconds out, visualizing each breath entering and exiting my heart. I don't feel any different as I do, but lo and behold, instantly the pattern on screen starts looking more like those even, sloping peaks. Not perfect, but better. "Now think of your newborn baby and wife and how you feel about them," White says. It's not hard to conjure up a picture of that beautiful little nugget in Amy's arms, and when I do, the pattern immediately enters a different phase, a recurring wave, much closer to that state of high performance—not to mention, pleasant—coherence. In just 2 minutes, by mixing calm, regular breathing and positive emotion, I've taken the stormy sea inside and converted it to pristine, glassy waves.

As parents who both work full-time, Amy and I have found that the number of times in a day when we have to stop and breathe evenly and think of all the things we're grateful for seem fewer and fewer, but White tells me that it's just a matter of practicing appreciation in those brief natural breaks: before bed, as you wake up in the morning, and then, gradually expanding this feeling of coherence that comes with appreciation into times when you're under pressure. White has been monitoring his HRV pattern for more than a decade now, and when he gives speeches, he'll sometimes display his pattern on a screen above his head, letting everyone read his emotional state while giving the talk. It's not that White is able to stay perfectly calm during the speech. Like the rest of us, his heart rate increases with the stress of being on stage, but since he knows the *feeling* of coherence so well, how to incorporate stress into a more positive frame, he's able to keep those HRV lines in nice little waves of coherence, the dips and troughs slightly more dramatic than when at rest, but still even. White adds that professional athletes as well as military special forces who train with HRV monitoring have been able to do the same thing, be it during heated competition or battle simulation.

It might be a little creepy to live in a world where we all constantly monitor our emotional patterns, trying to keep them in a certain positive zone. It seems ripe for a sci-fi novel where the government makes us wear our HRV patterns on color-coded T-shirts to help predict social unrest and crime. But we don't all need some new expensive gizmo to grasp the good news that these HeartMath scientists—and so many others—are pointing to: With practice, even in the busiest of worlds, stress and relaxation, fear and love, the ancient and modern brain, and maybe someday even hippies and hawks can learn to coexist in coherence, high performance, even harmony. The facts and wisdom, both ancient and modern, seem to be laid out for us: If we can understand fear rather than demonize it, reframe fear as a natural part of our biology rather than avoiding and repressing it, stretch our comfort zones just a little every day, and walk peacefully and courageously into those scary memories of embarrassment and trauma, we will gradually learn to transform fear into focus and compassionate action, and our sons' and daughters' world can be better than the one we live in. Will we collectively freeze, fight, and stagnate? Or will we learn and act?

• • • •

As I write this, Kai is 5 months old, smiling, giggling, rolling over. Amy is fully healed and back to work, jogging, and throwing dinner parties with gusto. Just when we think Kai can't get any cuter, he learns some new quirky giggle and pulls off yet another level of adorable. I know, all parents think this about their children, but I can say with the objectivity of a balanced journalist: This kid is cute, and the big head is just part of the act.

But we've also noticed something now that we're back to work and Amy's mom has flown back to DC, ending her generous run of laundry and dishes. *This is hard.*

I remember rolling my eyes at a birth book by one of the hawk nurses that said in typical dire fashion: "Before your child is born, you don't know the meaning of the word busy." *Please, lady, spare us.* But she was right. We didn't. And along with this new level of all-pervasive, selfless, superhero love, has come a whole new level of all-pervasive fear. We must protect this little guy. He is so helpless. What if someone drops him? What if *we* drop him? Has anyone invented a helmet for newborns? I mean, for the love of God, have you felt how soft this huge head is? Our dinner conversations have migrated from which movie we will see tonight to will we be able to get Kai into the right schools? What will we tell him when he asks about drugs? How much, and for how long, should we protect him from the iPad invasion of American childhood?

We will have to be vigilant. But while we methodically round all sharp objects, remind ourselves to never again text while driving, and strive to always use compostable diapers so our son doesn't grow up in a landfill, I am—as I sensed earlier in this project—now utterly convinced that these fears are merely the necessary biological chatter on the surface of a much deeper ocean. And the fundamental substance of this ocean, its essence, is faith and love.

It's easy to see how parents' fears for their children are generated by love. But really break them down to their most basic parts, and even our deepest, most monstrous fears are generated by a desire to live—a love of the sweetness of breath and body and taste and touch. Like waves, all these individual fears, small and large, appear to have a unique, intrinsic personality. Some of them can grow quite large and destructive, and if you react to their towering appearance or try to fight them, they can hold you under in darkness. But if you see that they are actually made of the same substance as the rest of the sea, they lose their monstrous mystique. They become merely water in another form.

I want most of all to show Kaifas these depths of faith. His world, and his capabilities, will be as large or as small as his implicit beliefs about the universe and himself, beliefs we are helping him form every single day in a largely unspoken way. He observes our every move, taking in the faith we have in ourselves in our body language, in the way we gaze at him, our tone of voice.

Unlike negativity bias, which operates generally in

regard to memories, other studies have shown that many of us hold an optimism bias about the future: Basically, we tend to think it will be better than it usually turns out to be. This is clearly nature's way of helping us keep on keeping on when the odds are stacked against us. You could view it as a weakness, and it's true that it can be dangerous when it causes us to ignore real problems. But think of all the evidence of the power of true faith: its ability to heal, to break records, to keep us alive and fighting through the most dire winters. It's actually this feeling of certainty that we *will* survive, we *will* do better, we *will* fix these problems, that is likely the reason we're all still here, against the odds.

Sometimes when I'm walking with Kaifas in the forest or at the beach or in a beautiful corner of our city, I stop, hold him up toward the sky while circling, then hug him and whisper in his tiny ear: "Look at this magnificent world, Kaifas. Do you realize you can do anything?"

ACKNOWLEDGMENTS

The scariest thing I did in this book was write this book. I couldn't have finished it without daily support from my brilliant wife, Amy Elizabeth DuRoss, who not only tolerated me bringing the laptop into bed at 2 a.m. but read every draft at least twice and always found something to praise, even in the really bad sections. I love you, Nurse, and I'm so glad you're even more addicted to travel than I am.

I'm also endlessly grateful to those folks most responsible for keeping me on the straight and narrow all these years (lord knows it hasn't been easy), not to mention giving me life. To Gramp, who drilled into us to always think for ourselves, and Grandpa, who demonstrated how adversity could be powered through with silent grace. To Grammy, who taught us that real bravery is generosity, and Grandma, who showed us how fear can be love simply dressed in different clothes. To Mom, who gave us the gift of knowing how to talk about feelings, and Pa for teaching us how to keep working hard even when it sucks. To Ciel, for being my best friend through it all (not to mention blazing this path of prose long before me). And now to the great Kaifas William DuRoss Yogis: Thank you for making me get my act together each morning and reminding me to giggle a lot in the process. This would get a little ridiculous if I start listing all you fabulous cousins, aunties, and in-laws. But I love you all.

On a more practical note, this book may not have come into being if Karen Rinaldi had not had faith in it from the first e-mail exchange. My agents Andrea Barzvi and Kari Stuart at ICM were so clutch and swift in closing a great deal. Author Michael Ellsberg helped immensely with his usual "go hard or go home" wisdom. Shannon Welch and Ursula Cary served as both my editors and personal psychologists. (It was uncanny and weird how you both asked exactly the right questions. Thank you for being so kind yet firm with my psyche.) Aly Mostel is such a bright light to have in my corner, and Lisa Braun Dubbels has been tireless in keeping the faith, love, and tweets alive from *Saltwater Buddha* to present. And, of course, thank you to Stephen Perrine, Chris Krogermeier, Marilyn Hauptly, Mike Smith, and the rest of the team at Rodale.

I'm grateful to *Surfer* magazine, *The Huffington Post* (especially Elizabeth Kuster), *KorduroyTV, theinertia.com* (especially Zach Weisberg), and Dr. Arnie Kozak at *Beliefnet* for creating pre-publication momentum. Though all the material in this book is original, a handful of passages were also inspired by other articles I'd written first elsewhere. The swim to Alcatraz and the great white shark dive were both written about first on the beautiful new site, *thebolditalic.com,* thanks to their very savvy editor, Nicole Grant. The passage with John White from Heartmath was very close to an article I wrote in *ESPN the Magazine* on why athletes choke. Thank you to the great Bruce Kelley for calling.

Most of all, I have to thank all the brilliant folks who let me pick their brains and basically recycle their hard work into my book. To the scientists, doctors, psychiatrists, and psychologists, Michael Lardon, Mark "Doc" Renneker, Rollin McCraty, Peter Pyle, Rick Hanson, Philippe Goldin, Joseph LeDoux, Daniela Schiller, David Zald, and Sian

Beilock—thank you for allowing me to stutter through all those basic science questions before getting into the weeds. Thank you to sports/mental trainers John White and Paige Dunne for making all this heady stuff applicable, Karen Rogers for the beautiful mantra "I belong here too," JT Holmes for being a living superhero, and Jamie Patrick for being completely mad and full of love. Thank you to Urijah Faber for pushing me to my limits since the first grade, Noah Borrero for being ready to charge at a moment's notice, and Mark and Giulia Lukach for being so fearlessly open about their love story (and, of course, for Jonas). Thank you James Moskito and Captain Mick Menigoz for finding us one hell of a great white shark, and to the Mavericks crew, especially Danny Hess, Doc Renneker, Flea, Jeff Clark, Alex Martin, and Austin Balk. You guys frighten me. (Special, special thanks to Danny for letting me try out different Mav's guns, and to Doc for helping me survive the keyhole.)

There were a handful of fabulous interviews that were cut from the book to maintain story flow, which saddened me because they were all very insightful. The interview with one of my personal heroes, the Reverend Heng Sure, as well as Heartmath scientist Rollin McCraty, are unavailable due to technical problems, but my interviews with author and life coach MeiMei Fox, and natural healer Dr. Sarah Bamford Seidelmann, world record–breaking cave diver Mike Madden, professional runner and physical therapist Neil McDonough, and witty escape artist and actor Jonathan Goodwin are available at www.fearproject.net, among many others.

There were also a number of great books that made writing this one a lot easier: *Fear: A Cultural History* by Joanna

Bourke; *Finding Your Zone* by Michael Lardon; *The Synaptic Self* and *The Emotional Brain* by Joseph LeDoux; *Choke* by Sian Beilock; *The Science of Fear* by Daniel Gardner; *The Buddha's Brain* by Rick Hanson; *The Culture of Fear* by Barry Glassner; *Why Zebras Don't Get Ulcers* and *The Trouble with Testosterone* by Robert Sapolsky; *The Brain That Changes Itself* by Norman Doidge; *Deep Survival* by Laurence Gonzales; *When Things Fall Apart* by Pema Chodron; *The Origin of the Species* by Charles Darwin; *Feel the Fear and Do It Anyway* by Susan Jeffers; *Surf Survival* by Mark "Doc" Renneker, Andrew Nathanson, and Clayton Everline; *Dreams and Nightmares* by Earnest Hartmann; *On Water* and *The Face of the Deep* by Thomas Farber; *Breath* by Tim Winton; *Mavericks* by Matt Warshaw; *Inside Mavericks* by Grant Washburn, Doug Acton, and Bruce Jenkins; *Surfline's California Surfguide* by Sean Collins; *Memories, Dreams, Reflections* by Carl Jung; *The Devil's Teeth* by Susan Casey; *The Secret Life of Sharks* by A. Peter Kimley; *West of Jesus* by Steven Kotler; *Where the Road Meets the Sun* by Mark Lukach; *The Male Brain* and *The Female Brain* by Louann Brizendine; *A General Introduction to Psychoanalysis* by Sigmund Freud; and *The Seven Sins of Memory* by Daniell Schacter, to name a few.

Other indispensable tools included *Radio Lab's* interpretation of LeDoux and Sapolsky's work (which highly influenced the structure of my second chapter); the *New York Times* science coverage; Uri Nili's work on snakes and courage; Ron Stoop's research on oxytocin and fear; Karim Nader, Daniela Schiller, and Liz Phelps's work on memory; the Heartmath Institute; *Scientific American*; *Nature*; Livescience.com; *Psychology Today*; *Surfer* magazine; and *The Surfer's Journal*.

In a slightly different but no less important category, I want to thank Lil Wayne, Eminem, Outkast, the Black Eyed Peas, the Beastie Boys, Bon Iver, Old Crow Medicine Show, Nine Pound Shadow, and the Felice Brothers for getting me through some dark patches both with writing and surfing. To Alex Fang and *Surf for Life* for allowing my surf addiction and book selling to serve a greater purpose, and to James Mitchell at Las Olas and Danny Hess for providing stellar boards for these adventures.

I also have to thank those who helped me develop the faith and skills to live as a writer: Thomas Farber, Ari Goldman, LynNell Hancock, Judith Matloff, Bruce Porter, Bruce Kelley, Nan Weiner, Max Track, Michael Ellsberg, Brian Lam, Mark Lukach, Peter Yogis, Janice Klar, Ciel Yogis, and of course, the nonfiction novelists, MeiMei Fox, Kristen Philipkoski, Siveya Ethersmith, Nathaniel Eaton, Kate Seward, and Bill Wright. (NFN forever, bitches.)

Very special thanks to Lara Popyack and Mike Madden at Nohoch Productions for working that magic movie machine and putting up with my constant nit-picking. Many more adventures to come!

Lastly, I'd like to thank one of my best teachers, Steven Tainer. Your philosophy is really too subtle for me to ever attempt to put into my own work, but it has influenced all of my writing, and my life, immensely.

ENDNOTES

INTRODUCTION

1. **(p. ix) The Roman philosopher Seneca:** Though it doesn't apply to this passage in particular, it seems unfair to leave out the Greeks in this brief history. Deimos was the god of fear and terror for the ancient Greeks. Phobos, Deimos's twin brother, ruled over panic, flight, and battlefield rout, hence phobia. Maybe to show that fear, courage, and love are all bound up, Deimos and Phobos were born of an affair between the great Olympian gods Ares, who ruled over courage and war, and the beautiful Aphrodite, goddess of love. The twins represent fear of loss; they joined their father in battles, spreading fear with faces like lions.
2. **(p. ix) *God fearing:*** Many scholars say that the biblical term *god fearing* can also be translated as "in awe of god"—more reverent than terrified.
3. **(p. ix) He that feareth is not made perfect in love:** Also from the Abrahamic traditions, there is Psalm 23: "Yea, though I walk through the valley of the shadow of death, I will fear no evil. For thou art with me." Rumi, a mystical Muslim, who is ironically America's best-selling poet of all time, said of fear: "Why do you stay in prison when the door is so wide open? Move outside the tangle of fear-thinking. Live in silence." As for famous Jewish quotes on fear, I don't think the Hebrew Bible can beat the chosen people's modern prophet, Woody Allen: "I'm not afraid of death; I just don't want to be there when it happens." (I say this as one very proud of my Jewish heritage.)
4. **(p. ix) The Buddha apparently wouldn't have been surprised that public speaking often tops fear polls:** Another Buddhist quote on fear comes from the *Sutra of Forty-Two Chapters*. "Fear arises from worry," the Buddha tells his students, "and worry arises from craving and desire. If you abandon desire, what fear or worry could you have?"
5. **(p. ix) Utter prostration soon follows, and the mental powers fail:** I found this quote first in Joanna Bourke's *Fear: A Cultural History*. But it's originally from Darwin's *The Expression of Emotion in Man and Animals*. Darwin did say that an animal that "feared rightly" increased its chances of survival, but he added, in the same vein as Freud, that "man has retained through inheritance a relic of them [fear responses], now become useless."
6. **(p. xi) A close associate of Sigmund Freud's:** In *A General Introduction to Psychoanalysis*, Freud himself went so far as to write that, "The condition of fear is in all cases purposeless and its lack of purpose is obvious when it reaches a higher level. It then disturbs the action, be it flight or defense, which alone is purposeful, and which serves the end of self-preservation." Freud seemed to think that fight-or-flight and the

emotion of fear were separate, continuing in the same paragraph: "You don't really believe that we flee *because* we experience fear? On the contrary, we are first afraid *and then* take flight from the same motive that is awakened by the realization of danger."

Like Abraham, Freud related fear and sexuality in often bizarre ways. Also in *A General Introduction*, Freud describes a teenage girl who can't sleep unless all ticking clocks are stopped or removed. Instead of concluding that the girl might just not like the sound of clocks, he wrote that, "Our patient gradually comes to understand that she has banished clocks and watches from her room during the night because the clock is the symbol of the female genital. The clock, which we have learned to interpret as a symbol for other things also, receives this role of the genital organ through its relation to periodic occurrences at equal intervals. A woman may for instance be found to boast that her menstruation is as regular as clockwork. The special fear for our patient, however, was that the ticking of the clock would disturb her in her sleep. The ticking of the clock may be compared to the throbbing of the clitoris during sexual excitement. Frequently she had actually been awakened by this painful sensation and now this fear of an erection of the clitoris caused her to remove all ticking clocks during the night."

7. (p. xi) At a time when functional magnetic resonance imagery (fMRI): If you've never had an fMRI, you lie down in a cylindrical tube that looks something like Michael Jackson's hyperbaric oxygen chamber, except without the windows. The machine uses a strong magnetic field and radio waves to track changes in blood flow in the brain. These changes correspond with cellular activity, so even though the blood in your brain moves more slowly than your lightning-fast thoughts do, the images of blood flow give scientists a surprisingly accurate picture of which areas of the brain are working the hardest, albeit a tad delayed.

Because the tube is about the size of a coffin, fMRI scans make many people feel claustrophobic, which can complicate fear studies because some test subjects are already scared before they are asked to, say, look at a scary image. But as testament to the power of exposure therapy and so many of the studies in this book, my mother-in-law found it almost physically impossible to get into an MRI scanner the first time around. But after going back and—at the radiologist's suggestion—listening to music while inside the tube, she soon found the experience almost pleasant.

CHAPTER 1

1. (p. 2) About to become fish food: This recurring nightmare haunted me for years. But around the age of 12, I read *Lucid Dreaming* by Stanford psychophysiologist Stephen LaBerge. Lucid dreaming is the practice of becoming aware you're dreaming while still in dream, often giving yourself more control of your dream circumstances. (Many people fly or go have wild sex the first time they go lucid.) Some scientists used to think that lucid dreaming was impossible, but LaBerge has demonstrated numerous times in his lab that skilled lucid dreamers can consciously relay signals to researchers with agreed-upon eye and hand movements while brain imagery machines show they are deeply in a dream state.

There are many techniques to learn lucid dreaming. For me, reminding myself repeatedly during the day that "when I'm dreaming tonight, I will know that I'm dreaming" worked within about a week. When this Alcatraz nightmare rolled around post lucid dream training, I recognized it was that pesky old nightmare and dove happily into the bay to ride the sharks and slap some high fives with the killer whales. The nightmare never returned.

Tibetan Buddhists and Taoists have been using lucid dreaming—dream yoga—for millennia as a tool to practice different sorts of meditation within the dream state. Now studies at McGill University in Montreal and Utrecht University in the Netherlands have shown that lucid dreaming techniques can significantly reduce repetitive nightmares. When I was reporting on the subject in 2005, Patricia Garfield, a clinical psychiatrist who has written nine books on dreaming, told me lucid dreaming works in helping reduce anxiety and fear because the dream is behavioral rehearsal for confronting fears while awake. Garfield said she herself used lucid dreaming to break a recurrent nightmare that had haunted her for 15 years. "I didn't believe it was possible," recalled Garfield. "But my nightmare never came back."

To learn to lucid dream, you have to first remember your dreams regularly, and the best way to do so is to keep a dream journal and to tell yourself before going to bed, "I will remember my dreams." Other techniques for lucid dreaming can be found in LaBerge's books or in works like *The Tibetan Yogas of Dream and Sleep* by Tenzin Wangyal Rinpoche. My previous writing on lucid dreaming can be found at http://www.naplesnews.com/news/2005/mar/22/ndn_lucid_dreaming/?print=1 and http://www.yogajournal.com/health/2026.

2. **(p. 2) Best ultra swimmers:** I say *ultra swimmer* rather than an open-water swimmer or marathon swimmer because Jamie generally wears a thin wetsuit in his 20-plus hour swims. And as openwaterswimming.com put it recently, for traditionalists, wearing a wetsuit is "similar to riding a moped in the Tour de France." It's beyond sinful. Never mind that none of these marathon/open-water diehards who critique Jamie could survive a 44-mile swim in Lake Tahoe without a wetsuit—and I dare them to try. But Jamie respects the traditionalists and doesn't claim any titles. Ironically, the public doesn't seem to care who's wearing a wetsuit or not as long as you're trying really flipping hard. In 2011, Jamie was crowned World Open Water Swimming Man of the Year by popular vote.

3. **(p. 3) About Tahoe's environmental problems:** Jamie has most recently partnered with the Sierra Club to raise money for their clean water campaigns, but he has also raised thousands of dollars for Buena Vista, a Bay Area literacy program that his wife, Terry Patrick, volunteers for. See more about Jamie's Sierra Club campaign at www.jamiepatrick.com.

4. **(P. 8) Oddly enough, it works:** I didn't know this at the time, but music—playing and listening—has been found to significantly reduce stress and fear. One study by Dr. Michael Miller at the University of Maryland found that when people listen to their favorite tunes, the linings of their blood vessels actually relax, open, and produce chemicals beneficial to the heart. Another study out of the Osaka Medical Center for Cancer and Cardiovascular Diseases found that people had less cortisol, a stress hormone, in their systems when they could listen to music while undergoing a colonoscopy. I don't know if chanting "Eye of the Tiger" in your head qualifies, but researchers have discovered innumerable benefits from music for athletic performance. As far as the fear of pain goes, studies by doctors like Costas Karageorghis, who specializes in music and sports research, have shown that there is an approximately 10 percent reduction in perceived exertion for runners listening to music, at least when they're going at about 85 percent capacity. "Music makes hard training seem more like fun, by shaping how the mind interprets symptoms of fatigue," doctors Karageorghis and David-Lee Priest wrote recently in the *Sport Journal.*
5. **(p. 9) Sara had broken up with me:** I'm making light of this, but anyone who has been through a bad one knows that a breakup can be as stressful as the death of a loved one. Divorces frequently create health problems for life, even after a happy remarriage. Linda Waite, a sociologist at the University of Chicago, coauthored a study of 8,652 people between the ages of 51 and 61 and found that the divorced or widowed suffered 20 percent more chronic health conditions such as diabetes, cancer, and cardiovascular disease than those who remain married. The problem, as we'll see in the next chapter, is that prolonged stress degrades the immune system, allowing more inflammation, one of the key causes of cancer and heart problems down the line.

CHAPTER 2

1. **(p. 20) Published in the journal *Nature*:** The study, *Preventing the Return of Fear in Humans Using Reconsolidation Update Mechanisms*, can be found at http://www.nature.com/nature/journal/v463/n7277/abs/nature08637.html.
2. **(p. 23) With LeDoux's own lectures on fear:** The Amygdaloids' music video for "Fearing" can be seen at http://www.youtube.com/watch?v=AMI3hbgRj60.
3. **(p. 23) 500 *trillion* synapses:** From *The Synaptic Self*, here is LeDoux's definition: "Synapses are small gaps between neurons. When a neuron is active, an electrical impulse travels down its nerve fiber and causes the release of a chemical neurotransmitter from its terminal. The transmitter drifts across the synaptic space and binds to a dendrite, thus closing the gap. Essentially everything the brain does is accomplished by the process of a synaptic transmission."

4. (p. 25) To fit them through the chute: According to perinatal psychologist Gina Hassan, "The human infant is born less developed than any other infant in the mammalian kingdom." Some doctors call the first 3 months of an infant's life the fourth trimester, which I'm sure grammar geeks are frowning at. Shouldn't it be the fourth quadmester?

5. (p. 25) Field of epigenetics: Read *Epigenetics: The Ultimate Mystery of Inheritance* by Richard C. Francis to get a good overview on the topic. John Cloud's *Time* magazine article, "Why Your DNA Isn't Your Destiny," is also a nice summary. "At its most basic," Cloud writes, "epigenetics is the study of changes in gene activity that do not involve alterations to the genetic code but still get passed down to at least one successive generation. These patterns of gene expression are governed by the cellular material—the epigenome—that sits on top of the genome, just outside it (hence the prefix *epi-,* which means above). It is these epigenetic "marks" that tell your genes to switch on or off, to speak loudly or whisper. It is through epigenetic marks that environmental factors like diet, stress, and prenatal nutrition can make an imprint on genes that is passed from one generation to the next." http://www.time.com/time/magazine/article/0,9171,1952313,00.html#ixzz26r0XU4Hf

6. (p. 27) Cognitive tests of various sorts under stress: This is complicated. Beilock's studies at the University of Chicago, for example, show that the vast majority of students perform worse on exams when an extra stressor is introduced: video cameras being brought in, for example. And students who usually score well on such tests take the biggest percentage drop, partly, Beilock says, because these students tend to use the significant cognitive horsepower that they would normally use on the exam to worry about the extra stressors. But remove *psychological* stress, that is, worry, and the stimulating effects of the stress response may improve cognitive performance in some cases. For example, it's well known that many animals can sense fear through smell, humans included, and that smelling fear can actually induce a stress response in the smeller. Recently Dr. Denise Chen and colleagues took sweat samples from the underarms of men and women who had just watched a scary movie (*The Exorcist*) or a benign documentary. They then asked a different sample of undergraduates to smell the sweaty swabs. Though the test subjects couldn't distinguish consciously between the fear sweat or the benign sweat, when they were asked to perform a cognitive test—determining whether two words that flashed on a screen were related—those who had smelled the fear sweat performed better. Similarly, Beilock's lab has found that students with higher stress hormone levels in their saliva sometimes perform better on math tests, but only if they are students who typically love math. In other words, their stress doesn't create worry so much as excitement.

7. (p. 32) Near-death scenarios: What leapt out at me about this study is the fact that SM could survive at all. It shows that heart-thumping amygdala fear, which is so uncomfortable, is not as essential for survival as we often think. After all, SM wasn't walking off cliffs or into cars. She could still use a degree of reasonable caution, enough to raise a family.

8. **(p. 34) From PTSD to social anxiety disorder to phobias:** According to the National Institute of Mental Health: In a given year, approximately 7.7 million American adults have PTSD, 15 million suffer from a social phobia, 19.2 million from a specific phobia (spiders, snakes, blood, etc.), 6 million from panic disorder, 6.8 million from General Anxiety Disorder, and 2.2 million from Obsessive Compulsive Disorder. Many times, a person with one anxiety disorder gets diagnosed with a second. http://www.nimh.nih.gov/health/publications/the-numbers-count-mental-disorders-in-america/index.shtml

9. **(p. 34) It doesn't matter whether you call it fear, stress, or anxiety because the same bodily process is involved in all three:** This is a bit of an oversimplified statement. We can be fairly certain, LeDoux told me, that if you're feeling all the telltale signs of that amygdala-type fear-faster heart rate, tense muscles—the ancient system is involved. And it's true that fear, stress, and anxiety all speed up heart rate and increase cortisol in the body. But the representation of how each of these distinct feelings functions in the brain is still being decoded, and the amygdala itself is actually comprised of 13 separate parts, complicating matters even more. Some scientists believe that more complex fears and anxieties (like fear of a future math test) have more to do with an area of the forebrain called the bed nucleus, which is sometimes called the extended amygdala. And studies have also suggested fear and anxiety have different reactions to various drugs, including alcohol. As I wrote recently in the *Huffington Post*, psychologists Christine Moberg and John Curtin at the University of Wisconsin recently showed that getting drunk reduces our anxiety, but not our fear. They did this by getting university students drunk on 100-proof vodka mixed with juice, then gave the boozed-up students (all of age) a series of predictable and unpredictable shocks. The unpredictable shocks produced what the psychologists call anxiety because the students didn't know when the shock would come, so they were left with that annoying feeling of uncertainty. The predictable shocks created flat-out fear because the students knew for sure that something painful was coming—more like hearing a bear rustling in the bushes and knowing it's coming for you. The result was that the mixed drinks didn't change the students' fear (predictable shocks), but the drinks did reduce their anxiety (unpredictable ones).

    Each anxiety disorder is represented differently in the brain. Take Obsessive Compulsive Disorder (OCD). As I again wrote recently in the *Huffington Post*, OCD has proven to be extremely difficult to treat, but Jeffrey M. Schwartz, a psychiatry professor at UCLA, has made definitive progress in having OCD patients switch from the content of their worry and focus simply on something else—something good. As Dr. Norman Doidge explains in *The Brain That Changes Itself* (where I learned about Schwartz), what is happening in OCD is this: That feeling that you've made a mistake is usually detected by a part of the brain called the *orbital frontal cortex*, behind the eyes, which sends a message to the *cingulate gyrus*, an older part of the brain deep in the cortex, which tells our heart and gut to feel dread and worry. Usually, we're able to get through this by either correcting a mistake (locking the door and leaving, for example), if that's possible, or refocusing on something else. The part of the brain that allows us to flow to the next thought is called the *caudate nucleus* and functions a bit like a mental gearshift.

Brain scans of OCD sufferers show that all three of these brain regions are hyperactive. The gearshift is jammed, keeping them stuck in an endless loop of worry. So what Schwartz has done is create a therapy that, like meditation, gives the sufferers distance from their own thoughts. During an OCD attack, patients are encouraged to acknowledge that there is a problem but distinguish that the problem is not the situation they're worried about (germs, the door, whatever); the problem is an OCD attack. Once it's acknowledged that the problem is OCD, Schwartz encourages patients to refocus on a positive and pleasurable action or thought that is completely different from the worry: going for a walk, playing tennis, playing music, gardening. This is different from the old-school positive therapy technique where the patient might say, in the case of germs, "I'm clean and healthy" over and over again. That sort of thing tends to keep OCD sufferers stuck in the content. Changing the subject matter allows the brain to get unstuck, and amazingly, as OCD patients undergo this therapy, you can actually watch their brains return to normal, the caudate nucleus "shifting" just as it should. To see my full article on the topic, "The Science of Worrying," go to http://www.huffingtonpost.com/jaimal-yogis/the-science-of-worrying_b_1590290.html.

10. **(p. 34) Nothing is ever repaired:** From Robert Sapolsky's classic, *Why Zebras Don't Get Ulcers.*

11. **(p. 34) Learned and genetic:** The rat's "synapses are wired by nature," writes LeDoux in *The Synaptic Self*, "to respond to the cat, and by experience to respond in the same way to dangers that are learned about. It's a wonderfully efficient way to do things: rather than create a separate system to accommodate learning about new dangers, just enable the system that is already evolutionarily wired to detect danger to be modifiable by experience." It is wonderfully efficient—as evolution often is, but it's also a clue as to why forgetting to study for a math test can feel like a rattlesnake encounter.

12. **(p. 35) Feel uneasy about snakes:** A recent 2008 study by psychologists Vanessa LoBue and Judy DeLoache at the University of Virginia showed that humans even have a genetic ability to spot snakes more quickly than we spot other animals. Even preschool-age children from the UK—not exactly python territory—who had never been exposed to snakes could locate the slithery creatures faster in pictures than they could other animals, even though the snakes were equally camouflaged. Even LeDoux is scared of snakes.

13. (p. 37) sgACC: An acronym for the mouthful, *subgenual anterior cingulate cortex*. Because the brain is plastic throughout life, it follows that we can actually exercise this courage "muscle" by giving it practice, approaching what we're afraid of rather than running, and getting better at that the more we do it. Courage builds courage. Fear builds fear.

14. (p. 40) In other words, upon retrieval a new memory is formed: Having, along with 95 percent of the rest of the world, just read *The Hunger Games,* this seems like pertinent information. It means that when Peeta was brainwashed by the villain, President Snow, into thinking his true love, Katniss Everdeen, was evil and that he should kill her, that could, in theory, *actually* happen. Snow would have to trigger Peeta's memories of Katniss, then, using media, implant believable false associations of Katniss. In the book, instead of using drugs that dull the painful memory, Snow uses Tracker Jacker venom to increase the pain of Peeta's new false memories. Tracker Jacker venom is fictional, but the fact that the brain works like this is strangely true, and Peeta's recovery from the brainwashing is equally and strangely—in theory—realistic.

15. (p. 41) But the painful aspect of the memory was erased: The incredibly good *Radio Lab* episode that includes the rape story and LeDoux can be found at http://www.radiolab.org/people/joe-ledoux/. LeDoux sees experiences like the one this rape victim had as hopeful because "even if it is possible to 'erase' conditioned fear memories," he wrote recently in the *Huffington Post*, "conscious fear memories may not be altered significantly. This is very promising for therapeutic purposes since it might allow a reduction in the emotional upheaval elicited by trauma-related stimuli without interfering with the conscious memory of the trauma. With emotional arousal to the traumatic memory weakened, it might be easier to engage in successful therapy about the traumatic experience." Others feel differently. The UK's *Daily Mail* took a poll of trauma victims, asking them if they would take a memory erasure drug, and most said no. "Do I wish I could get rid of the memory?" said journalist Tim Lott, referring to a childhood trauma. "No—because then I would understand myself less . . . my instinct tells me that pain is the most profound way there is of learning. That's probably why it's there." Even Nader himself has said in the media that such drugs could do more harm than good.

CHAPTER 3

1. (p.51) He's terrified of public speaking: Shortly after Jamie's race, I interviewed an old friend of mine, Rev. Heng Sure, a Buddhist monk of more than 30 years who speaks in front of thousands of people every week. I didn't expect Heng Sure to have many fears anymore, certainly not about public speaking, but I asked him anyway if, after 30 years, he still got nervous when he was up on the podium. "Sure," he said. "But now when I get butterflies, I get excited. The butterflies are just letting me know that this talk is important, that I care about this. If you run from that feeling, it can spin out of control, but if you welcome those butterflies, they can work for you." Heng Sure noted that it's the same technique that actors are often taught to use to get over stage fright.

2. **(p. 53) We could do more than we thought possible:** When one person breaks through a boundary, it seems to influence all of us. People used to say, for example, that a human being couldn't run a mile in under 4 minutes. They thought it was physically impossible. Then on May 6, 1954, Roger Bannister finished a mile at 3 minutes and 59.4 seconds. "There was a mystique, a belief that it couldn't be done," Bannister said 50 years later. "But I think it was more of a psychological barrier than a physical barrier." Six weeks later, John Landy, who had come within 3 seconds of breaking the 4-minute barrier six times, broke Bannister's record at 3 minutes and 58 seconds. Now, high-school students run 4-minute miles.
3. **(p. 54) On an impressive experiment:** I found this study first in Gretchen Reynolds's wonderful piece in the *New York Times*, "Phys Ed: Why Exercise Makes You Less Anxious." Unlike many of the studies in this book, I wasn't able to see the actual abstract of the study, but Reynolds cites numerous supporting studies along the same lines, and I trust her reporting. "It looks more and more like the positive stress of exercise prepares cells and structures and pathways within the brain so that they're more equipped to handle stress in other forms," Michael Hopkins, who has been studying how exercise differently affects thinking and emotion at Dartmouth, told Reynolds in the piece. "It's pretty amazing, really, that you can get this translation from the realm of purely physical stresses to the realm of psychological stressors." For the full piece, see http://well.blogs.nytimes.com/2009/11/18/phys-ed-why-exercise-makes-you-less-anxious/.
4. **(p. 54) Jay Weiss did a famous series of experiments:** These experiments were found in Stanford neuroscientist Robert Sapolsky's classic, *Why Zebras Don't Get Ulcers*, a highly recommended book for anyone who wants to understand the science of stress in great detail.
5. **(p. 55) Stress gets added to the list:** The fear of fear is not only an issue for people with panic disorder and PTSD. Fear has gotten a bad rap for millennia, often getting associated with hell and Satan in religious literature. In addition, men in many cultures—certainly in the United States—have often been told that they shouldn't show fear because to do so would be unmanly, as if a very natural emotion is a disease. Just like we can be taught to fear a tone by pairing it with a shock, we've all associated the word *fear* and the feeling of fear with some negative universal force, or at least with negative experiences, making the sensation worse than it actually is. I think we need to reframe fear as simply a biological process that's natural and normal, so we don't stack more anxiety and stress onto raw fear. It's this buildup of fear that keeps the brain stuck and creates the downward spiral into anxiety disorders. Franklin Delano Roosevelt's famous line, "The only thing we have to fear

is fear itself," is a beautiful one, but psychologically, you could argue that "the only thing we have to fear is the fear of fear."

6. (p. 57) And having fun. It was weird: The full story of running away and reuniting with my dad is in my first book, *Saltwater Buddha,* which is currently being made into a film. More at www.saltwaterbuddha.org.

7. (p. 59) more meticulously cautious than most people I know: As Chris Ballard writes about in his book, *The Butterfly Hunter,* the man considered by many to be the father of sports psychology, Bruce Ogilvie, published a study of 293 "high-risk" competitors in 1973 that shifted the consensus on risky sports. Of these athletes—including skydivers, race car drivers, fencers, and aerobatic pilots—Ogilvie estimated that only 6 percent were doing it to prove something, to make up for some inferiority complex, or because they were angry. The other 94 percent, he concluded, were emotionally stable. They were also success-oriented, strongly extroverted, and compared to the general population, above average in abstract thinking ability and intelligence. Ogilvie also found that, contrary to popular belief, they were very calculating in their risks. The difference was that risk-takers had been coached by their mentors to "go for it." They were doers.

8. (p. 65) Much more frightening than big-wave surfing: dating: I have to give a shout-out to psychologist Susan Jeffers, whose best-selling book, *Feel the Fear and Do It Anyway,* motivated me to get off my butt and start dating. I especially liked her five truths about fear, which—being the proud Self-Help Queen that she is—she writes in all caps. You can critique Susan for overusing exclamation points and not citing any research whatsoever, but there is a reason she has sold millions of copies of *Feel the Fear.* Her methods are simple. And they work. Here is her Truth 5.

TRUTH 5: PUSHING THROUGH FEAR IS LESS FRIGHTENING THAN LIVING WITH THE UNDERLYING FEAR THAT COMES FROM A FEELING OF HELPLESSNESS.

9. (p. 69) Were far less likely to freeze from fear: The study, "Evoked Axonal Oxytocin Release in Central Amygdala Attenuates Fear," can be found at http://www.cell.com/neuron/abstract/S0896-6273%2812%2900034-7.

CHAPTER 4

1. (p. 74) From the deck of the *Superfish:* Readers of Susan Casey's *The Devil's Teeth* will recall that there was profound animosity between the Farallones shark researchers like Peter Pyle and the owners of the *Superfish.* One of the reasons I felt good about going out on the *Superfish* is that Captain Mick, who is longtime friends with many of the Farallones scientists, told me it's very different now. The scientists are no longer mad at *Superfish* for chumming the water (it's been illegal since 2008), and *Superfish* helps the scientists collect data and better observe the sharks.

2. **(p. 74) Swim through it:** I was also shocked that the top of the cage is completely open. It's unlikely, but a shark could easily leap into the cage nose-first if it wanted to.

3. **(p.76) Consciously experience fear:** This is from an article LeDoux wrote with NYU neuroscientist Jacek Debiec, entitled "Fear and How It Works: Science and the Social Sciences," available at http://www.thefreelibrary.com/Fear+and+the+brain.-a0129368528.

4. **(p. 77) Susan Fiske:** Read Susan Fiske's article about this study at http://greatergood.berkeley.edu/article/item/look_twice. Though racism may be hardwired, the article states that "recent research shows that our prejudices are not inevitable; they are actually quite malleable, shaped by an ever-changing mix of cultural beliefs and social circumstances."

5. **(p. 79) We can see every scar along his massive gray back:** It's not quite *National Geographic* worthy, but I actually caught a brief video of the shark before hopping in the cage. You can watch it at http://www.youtube.com/watch?v=P9KAuLp7ng8&feature=plcp. The beautiful woman in the video is Amy.

6. **(p. 80) Chomp at the bars:** In those great white videos you see on Discovery's *Shark Week,* the sharks are often chomping at the steel cage bars, looking malevolent and ready to devour the diver inside. What they don't often tell you is that the divers just dumped a bunch of blood and guts, or "chum," into the water to attract the sharks, and they're freaking out much like a dog would if you filled a room with fresh cuts of beef. In 2008, chumming the water to attract great whites was made illegal in the Farallones and other marine sanctuaries. Without baiting the sharks, it's harder to make white shark documentaries, but when the filmmakers do score a view of a white, they see its true personality. This *LA Times* story covers the new law: http://latimesblogs.latimes.com/greenspace/2008/11/no-more-chummin.html.

7. **(p. 80) They can even be shy:** James told me an amazing story along these lines about shark diving outside of the cage. As he was getting in from the side of the boat, the coast seemed clear, but when James submerged, there was an 18-foot white shark hiding right under the hull, open-mouthed. A set of jaws bigger than the top half of his body hovered 2 feet from his face. James somehow remained calm and knew that white sharks don't like to risk injury from strange creatures. (No ER in the ocean.) He nudged the shark in the snout with a metal rod, and the shark swam away. From there, James went about his dive.

8. **(p. 80) Some of the event on film:** You can watch a bit of the orca-on-white-shark action in a *National Geographic* short at http://www.youtube.com/watch?v=SS6NjdGLVZs.

9. **(p. 82) And go on their way:** Leonard Compagno, one of the foremost shark experts in the world, told *Smithsonian Magazine* that "some 'shark attacks' on humans by white sharks seem playful," with sharks

tugging humans lightly by the hand and then releasing them. See http://www.smithsonianmag.com/science-nature/great-white-sharks.html?c=y&page=3.

10. (p. 83) Peter Pyle: Pyle studied great whites at the Farallones for 23 years, often doing little but following their trails of blood after a seal attack. After all those years of observing whites in epic battles with elephant seals—which themselves reach 5,000 pounds and aren't known for cheerful dispositions—I asked Pyle if he'd grown more or less afraid of them. "Less," he said definitively. His respect for them had grown, but fear, he said, wasn't really an issue anymore. He happily surfs in shark-infested areas like Bolinas and Point Reyes. "They're not after us," he told me. "They're very efficient and don't tend to hang around unless they think there's a chance of getting some seal." That said, Pyle does know sharks can be dangerous, especially tiger sharks, he says. When he gives lectures on shark safety to groups like the Surfrider Foundation, he always notes that surfers should "trust their spook." On the rare occasions that there is an attack, the victim often reports that he or she felt spooked in the water beforehand. "It might be an ancient biologic ability to sense a predator," he told me.

11. (p. 83) Control and predictability are highly valued by mammals: My favorite anecdotal section about control and predictability was cut from the book for story flow. It went like this: Jonathan Goodwin, a British escape artist with a shiny bald head and a 007 air, has, over the course of his career: buried himself alive, bound himself in locks and chains under ice-cold water, hung himself on stage, covered his body in 200,000 bees, swum with sharks, and had a car park on top of his head. "I'm not really an office person," Jonathan says when I meet him near his home in Los Angeles.

Many escape artists are illusionists, and they always succeed at just the last second. The interesting thing about Jonathan's escapes, many of which he performed on his own Discovery Channel show, *One Way Out,* is that they are 100 percent real, and about one-third of the time, he fails, suffering the consequences. When Jonathan was covered in 200,000 bees, for example, and placed on top of a washing machine that would begin shaking if he didn't escape from handcuffs within 1 minute, he fumbled with the cuffs and was stung thousands of times. "I was sick for a week," he laughs, "really nauseated."

But even through horrible mishaps like this, Jonathan maintains the cool British wit of a skilled television host, and I'd like to know how he does it. "Basically," Jonathan says, "I never risk death in escape artistry (a) because I'm not stupid and (b) because it's a creative thing. There are lots of my predecessors, largely magicians, that would tell the audience that what they are doing is lethally dangerous and if they don't escape in such and such a time, they're going to die, and they always escape in just the last second. But it's kind of patronizing to the audience to pretend that they would actually risk that. Most of them love themselves far too much to make it plausible. So, one of the things I told myself when I started doing escapes was, I will never risk death. I will risk serious pain and humiliation. And basically, I think what is the worst thing that I would be willing to really have happen to me. And then I work backwards from there."

Then comes the intensive research. When a car was parked on Jonathan's head, he researched exactly how much weight the human skull can endure without permanent damage. When he was hung by a noose on national television, he discovered that the part of hanging that kills you is the drop that breaks the neck instantly. "If you're lifted up slowly by your neck, which I was," Jonathan says, "it hurts like hell, but you can stay up there dangling for about 20 minutes." In all of these cases, Jonathan made sure there was someone there to help him if he couldn't get out on his own and that the pain was something he was willing to tolerate. All of this kept his fear within a tolerable zone in which he could still crack jokes and look handsome. And even then, fear was still a factor. "I'm always pretty scared of what that's going to be like to be, say, covered in 200,000 bees," he tells me. "When I pitch these ideas to the producer, I think yeah, that would be great, that would be a really cool and fun thing to do, and then the moment that they go okay, let's do it, that's the moment that I go, okay, I've got to do this thing. And at that moment, it's always pretty terrifying, and where that dissipates is knowledge. That to me is the biggest single secret in how to beat fear—knowing as much about what you're up against as possible." For the full interview with Jonathan Goodwin, go to www.fearproject.net.

12. **(p. 83) Can relax between shocks:** I found this study in Sapolsky's *Why Zebras Don't Get Ulcers.*
13. **(p. 83) Another study on rhesus monkeys:** I first found this study in *The Male Brain* by Dr. Louann Brizendine. See www.ncbi.nlm.nih.gov/pubmed/16155510.
14. **(p. 84): That snakes and insects have:** www.plosmedicine.org/article/info%3Adoi%2F10.1371%2Fjournal.pmed.0050218;jsessionid=66B81B3E56F5DABADB52D86E51BE334F.
15. **(p. 85) Peter Benchley:** Benchley kept up with the evolving great white science and eventually felt terrible about giving white sharks such a false reputation. "We knew so little back then, and have learned so much since, that I couldn't possibly write the same story today," Benchley, who has become a shark advocate, told *National Geographic* in a 2002 interview. "The most common and off-base misperception is the theory that sharks target humans, that they are man-eaters. Nothing could be further from the truth. Every time you see on TV people surrounded by sharks, the chances are 99 percent that [the sharks] have been baited, and it gives a false impression because by nature sharks will stay away from people."

16. (p. 85) Terrorize the peaceful town of Amity: *Selachaphobia,* or fear of sharks, is so common, it's discussed in the oddest of places. Jessica Simpson, celebrating her 30th birthday on a yacht in Italy, wouldn't swim because, "all I could think about is that a shark would attack me." (Watch the video at http://www.popsugar.com/Video-Interview-Jessica-Simpson-About-Italy-Sharks-Price-Beauty-New-Holiday-Album-10052087.) Christina Ricci doesn't like to swim in pools alone because, according to ABC News, "I think that somehow a little magic door is going to open up and let the shark out." Justin Timberlake reportedly wouldn't go surfing with his then-girlfriend Cameron Diaz from fear of shark attack, which is especially ironic because sharks respond well to Timberlake's music. In 2007, German scientists, working from previous studies that revealed fish process music in a similar way to humans, tried to get sharks in German Sea Life centers to get into the mating mood by playing them various music genres. According to the British *Independent*, "James Last, Justin Timberlake and Salt-N-Pepa are among the artists who get the sharks in the mood for love beneath the waves but Britney Spears left them cold." See http://www.independent.ie/world-news/europe/how-do-you-make-a-shark-mate-play-it-justin-timberlake-1053552.html.

17. (p. 87) White shark protection bill in 1994: As I wrote recently in *Surfer* magazine, northern California surfers were among the most active supporters of the '94 white shark protection bill. Eric Larsen, a surfer who needed 200 stitches after being hit by a great white, wrote this letter to Congress:

"I am writing to express my support for AB 522 to protect white sharks in California. As you may know, I was mauled by a shark thought to be a Great White on July 1, 1991, while surfing near Davenport, CA. My experience with the shark convinced me that sharks are an important part of the natural order of things."

Mark Massara, then head lawyer for the Surfrider Foundation, said in the bill's commentary: "When surfers paddle out, we become part of the food chain—and we like that." More recently, surfers were on the forefront of lobbying for the Shark Conservation Act, which forbids shark-finning in US waters. In the summer of 2009, *Surfer* magazine contributing photographer and shark attack survivor Mike Coots walked into the halls of Congress with eight other shark attack survivors—some missing arms, others legs—to advocate for the bill. It passed in Congress shortly after Coots visited and was signed into law by President Obama in 2011.

18. (p. 88) With more nuance: "When I first started doing this," Sean Van Sommeran, founder of the Pelagic Shark Research Foundation, told me, "saying 'Save the Sharks' was like saying 'save poison oak,' like saying 'spread gonorrhea.'" Now, it's better, he went on. But there is still a lot of work to be done.

CHAPTER 5

1. (p. 93) His exhaustive research: Joel Best's Halloween sadism research can be found at http://www.udel.edu/soc/faculty/best/site/halloween.html.

2. (p. 94) Not Halloween sadism: Joel Best reports the following additional incidents on http://www.udel.edu/soc/faculty/best/site/halloween.html:

"*Patrick Wiederhold* (Flint, MI, 1978). Two-year-old Patrick died after eating Halloween treats. However, tests of tissue samples failed to find traces of drugs or poison, and police concluded that Patrick's death was from natural causes.

"*Ariel Katz* (Santa Monica, CA, 1990). Seven-year-old Ariel collapsed while trick-or-treating and died. Although her parents told the authorities that she had heart problems, the initial press reports blamed Halloween sadism. The coroner attributed her death to an enlarged heart.

"*Name Withheld* (Vancouver, British Columbia, 2001). A 4-year-old girl died after eating some Halloween candy, leading police to advise parents to throw out all Halloween treats. However, pathology tests showed no evidence of poisoning, and the autopsy showed she died of a streptococcus infection."

3. (p. 95) The arousal of their penises: The abstract can be found at http://www.ncbi.nlm.nih.gov/pubmed/8772014. The researchers concluded: "Homophobia is apparently associated with homosexual arousal that the homophobic individual is either unaware of or denies."

4. (p. 95) *Who Speaks for Islam: What a Billion Muslims Really Think:* For more information about the book, see http://www.gallup.com/press/104209/who-speaks-islam-what-billion-muslims-really-think.aspx.

5. (p. 96) I've done a fair amount of reporting in the Muslim world: I've reported in Israel, Palestine, Indonesia, and Bangladesh and made many Muslim friends. I know that only a small minority of Muslims are extremists, but I do think the Muslim world's views on women need to evolve. For my recent reporting in Bangladesh on this subject, see http://www.huffingtonpost.com/jaimal-yogis/fearless-girls_b_1862486.html.

6. (p. 96) I recently reported a magazine story: The story, "Meat Is Murder, Arson Is Fun," was published in *San Francisco Magazine,* http://www.modernluxury.com/san-francisco/story/meat-murder-arson-fun. To be fair, the ALF and the ELF have yet to harm a human being with their actions, and it's part of their stated philosophy not to harm any human or animal physically. But when you're burning down buildings and blowing up diesel trucks to make a statement, it's usually only a matter of time before there's an accident.

7. (p. 99) A best-selling author: Hanson wrote the bestseller *The Buddha's Brain: The Practical Neuroscience of Happiness, Love and Wisdom* with Richard Mendius, MD. It has been translated into 22 languages and was incredibly helpful for this book. All of his books and writings can be found at http://www.rickhanson.net.

8. (p. 101) *Bad Is Stronger Than Good:* The full essay can be purchased for $11.95 at http://psycnet.apa.org/index.cfm?fa=buy.optionToBuy&id=2001-11965-001.

9. (p. 104) Brain real estate: In *The Brain That Changes Itself,* Dr. Doidge calls this *competitive plasticity.* "When we learn a bad habit," he writes, "it takes over a brain map"—meaning, a series of neural pathways—"and each time we repeat it, it claims more control of that map and prevents the use of that space for 'good' habits. That's why unlearning is often harder than learning, and why early childhood development is so important—it's best to get it right early, before the 'bad habit' gets a competitive advantage."

10. (p. 105) In a fascinating study: The study was written about in *Vanderbilt Magazine*, http://www.vanderbilt.edu/magazines/vanderbilt-magazine/2009/03/obama-effect-shrinks-performance-gap/.

11. (p. 107) It's rock climbing: Hanson told me a story about rock climbing that he said he had never told anyone.

East of Los Angeles, in the dry, craggy San Jacinto mountains, above the little town of Idyllwild, a toothlike granite rock juts out of Earth called Taquitz. A sheer hike—about 800 feet of elevation in a half-mile—leads to the thousand-foot face that has made Taquitz one of the most sought-after climbs in California.

A tall, spry climber in his early twenties, Rick Hanson was leading climbs at Taquitz in the '70s, and though he didn't like to show it, he occasionally got spooked. Certain routes had up to seven pitches. A fall could mean careening 20, 30, 40 feet down, even more if his gear popped.

Then one day, halfway up the face, it happened. One second, Hanson had a good handhold behind a thick flake of granite. The next, that granite had chipped and Hanson was airborne—tumbling, cartwheeling—the support he'd carefully laid somehow gone. Between Hanson and a slab of rock, nothing but air. All he could do was watch his demise zooming closer, closer, closer, and. . . .

He was in his tent? A dream? Or half-dream really, right at that moment of passing through the veil of consciousness: one of those full-body quakes that leaves you breathless. Hanson didn't think much of it. A little fear of falling was normal for a passionate climber. Except that when he tried to go back to sleep, the same thing happened again. Then on subsequent climbing trips too: "I'd start falling through the air," he says, "panicking, terror stricken, certain death, and then just before I hit that slab to splatter, I'd pull out of it again."

Hanson was doing what most young men do when they're up to something scary and supposed to look tough. "I suppressed my fear," Hanson says. But that realization came only after he'd become so fed up with not being able to sleep that, within the dream, he became lucid and spontaneously decided to let himself hit. "I let go," Hanson says, "and just before I smacked the granite, there was a powerful emotional release. I realized I had suppressed the fear of falling, and it was just coming back up again and again. I needed to find more of a middle path, of not tightly squeezing fear down, nor being totally overwhelmed by it—that middle place." For my full interview with Hanson, go to www.fearproject.net.

12. **(p. 110) And doesn't make it personal:** For my full interview with Urijah, go to www.fearproject.net. Urijah has a fantastic book out, *The Laws of the Ring*, much of it having to do with living courageously. His fights, book, and more can be viewed at http://urijahfaber.com.

13. **(p. 111) Associated with positive emotions:** From John Geirland's article in *Wired,* "Buddha on the Brain."

14. **(p. 113) Doesn't take 10,000 hours...to start seeing benefits:** In her book, *Choke,* psychologist Sian Beilock has even found that 5 minutes of meditation before an exam can increase test scores. In *Psychology Today,* she recently wrote about why a little meditation can have a big effect. See http://www.psychologytoday.com/blog/choke/201110/meditation-small-dose-big-effect.

15. **(p. 113) *Military Medicine Journal:*** The two studies leading to this result had a very small sample size, making them inconclusive. But as Steve Vogel wrote in a May 2012 article in the *Washington Post,* the pilots are leading to larger studies with bigger sample sizes. "The VA is spending about $5 million on a dozen clinical trials and demonstration studies of three meditation techniques involving several hundred veterans from a range of conflicts, including Iraq and Afghanistan," Vogel wrote. "Results from the studies will not be available for 12 to 18 more months." See the story at http://www.operationwarriorwellness.org/va-testing-whether-meditation-can-help-treat-ptsd.html.

16. **(p. 113) Philippe Goldin:** Goldin's Clinically Applied Affective Neuroscience (CAAN) group at Stanford recently finished two 5-year randomized control trials (the gold standard in neuroscience and psychology) comparing the effects of cognitive behavioral therapy, aerobic exercise, and mindfulness meditation on social anxiety disorder. All three are helpful in alleviating the symptoms of SAD, but Goldin wanted to know why and how the treatments differ. More about the studies can be found at http://caan.stanford.edu/current_research.html. Here are some excerpts of what Goldin told me about the results. Being, I think, a genius (the man speaks fluent Tibetan and Sanskrit), he tends to speak in long-winded sentences. See the full interview at www.fearproject.net.

CHAPTER 6

1. **(p. 118) Most powerful waves on the planet:** For more on why Mavericks breaks the way it does, see Sean Collins's Surfline piece, "The Mechanics of Maverick's," http://www.surfline.com/surf-news/mechanics-of-mavericks_62313/.

2. (p. 119) Mark "Doc" Renneker: Doc was the subject of what is widely considered the best piece of surf writing in history, a 40,000-word, two-part feature in the *New Yorker* by William Finnegan called "Playing Doc's Games." The writing is superb, but Doc hates the piece, saying that Finnegan, an old friend, got too many facts wrong. It can be found at http://www.newyorker.com/archive/1992/08/24/1992_08_24_034_TNY_CARDS_000362217.

3. (p. 120) Mark Foo: Foo was a Chinese American, Hawaiian big-wave legend with heaps of charisma and talent—one of the best big-wave riders on the planet. After riding far bigger waves in Todos Santos and Hawaii, he died on his fourth wave ever ridden at Mavericks, belly flopping at the base of a 20-footer, cycloning back over the falls, and then—nobody knows for sure. His body was found 2 hours later in the lagoon, almost a half-mile from the spot of the tumble.

The tragedy gave Mavericks the reputation of one of the most dangerous waves on the planet. Jon Krakauer wrote *Outside*'s cover feature about Foo's death. *MTV*, the *New York Times, Dateline, NBC,* the *Sydney Morning Herald,* the *New Yorker*, and countless other publications covered it in detail too, all of them, along with every Mavericks documentary and book, speculating how it happened: wind knocked out of him? Leash caught on the reef? Board impact to the head? (He had a gash above his eye.) Simple drowning? (His lungs were filled with saltwater.) After the autopsy, the generally accepted version, as Matt Warshaw describes in detail in his fantastic book, *Maverick's: The Story of Big-Wave Surfing,* was that because "the tail section of his board was smashed and laced with thin strands of sea-grass, it seemed likely that Foo had been tethered to the bottom, just below where he'd wiped out, by either his board or his leash. At some point he floated to the surface—released from the bottom by a small underwater eddy, perhaps, or a shift in the current—and drifted off toward the harbor . . . Maverick's, plainly put, did him in." Whatever the case, those who were there that day say Foo looked peaceful, a slight upturn at the sides of his mouth. Everyone recalled him telling *Surfer* magazine, "It's not tragic to die doing something you love."

4. (p. 120) Is simple: preparation: Aside from preparation, Doc is very logical, and statistics also play a role in his fearlessness. When I asked him if he thinks the danger of Mavericks is overhyped, he said: "Absolutely. It has been from the get-go." This was a rare response. Most Mavericks surfers will say that it's more terrible than you could ever imagine. (Evan Slater, the former editor of *Surfer* magazine who used to compete in the annual Mavericks big-wave invitational, wrote in *Maverick's: Portrait of a Monster Wave* that, "I still have no clue why there's a 99.9 percent wipeout survival rate. . . . Every time you go through one, you wonder in midthrashing, 'Is this the end for me?'")

To be clear, Doc wasn't saying Mavericks isn't dangerous, and he isn't suggesting anyone go out there until they've trained rigorously for years. "You can do everything right at Mavericks, and still get completely fucked," he told me. But Doc has been treating surfing injuries for decades, and he said that big waves are deceiving. The most dangerous type of surfing, in his mind, is done in ultra-shallow, shore-break kind of waves where people are likely to snap their necks in the shallows. These aren't the scariest-looking waves. "But they're the cause of the serious paralysis injuries I see again and again," Doc told me. "At Mavericks, it's deep, and if you look at the sport of surfing on the whole, it's pretty safe. Cheerleading is more dangerous."

I was pretty sure Doc was joking when he said this, but as it turns out, 93 cheerleaders were either killed or permanently disabled through head, neck, or spinal injuries between 1982 and 2007, according to The National Center for Catastrophic Sports Injury Research, usually, no doubt, performing those high-risk flips and tosses. The center states that the numbers translate into a rate of 2.68 catastrophic injuries for every 100,000 female high school cheerleaders, which exceeds the rate for most other high school sports.

Exact statistics on surfing deaths and injuries aren't logged, but a look through the newspaper archives shows you they are few and far between. Most happen to beginners who drown in mellow conditions, or to old-timers who die of heart attack or stroke while paddling around. It would be more accurate to tally these deaths with the 3,000-plus per-year drowning fatalities in the United States since the deaths have little to do with the sport of surfing. And there are far more dangerous water sports that nobody thinks of as *extreme,* by far the most dangerous being the placid sport of fishing. As Brad Melekian recently reported in the *Surfers Journal,* according to the US Coast Guard, angling accounts for nearly 200 deaths each year. Melekian also found that most high school sports do more damage than surfing, including, yes, cheerleading, gymnastics, and pole vaulting. (There are only 50,000 pole vaulters in the United States, compared to somewhere around 5 million surfers, Melekian notes, and a pole vaulter is sadly lost just about every year.)

Doc may be on to something. When you run the numbers, you can count the number of big-wave surfers who have died actually surfing in the last 60 years on two hands: Dickie Cross (1943, Waimea), Mark Foo (1994, Mavericks), Donnie Solomon (1995, Waimea), Todd Chesser (1997, Alligator Rock), Malik Joyeux (2005, Pipeline), Peter Davi (2007, Ghost Trees), and Sion Milosky (2011, Mavericks). And these seem more like black swans when you consider that Joyeux, who braved disgustingly huge and dangerous waves, died on a run-of-the-mill 6-footer at Pipeline. Davi was high on meth and likely not thinking straight, and other notable big-wave surfers—Jay Moriarty, Eddie Aikau, Andy Irons—died when they weren't even surfing.

The statistics make you wonder if the things we often call crazy—big-wave surfing and skydiving and extreme skiing, for example—might be less dangerous than the things we do every day without much thought. There are usually more than 40,000 car accident fatalities every year in the United States. That's 13.3 deaths for every 100,000 people, far more than skiing or surfing. (See http://www-fars.nhtsa.dot.gov/Main/index.aspx.) But as Greg Long, one of the best big-wave surfers ever, pointed out in Melekian's piece, "Statistics are deceiving. Just because the number of people dying while riding big waves is relatively low doesn't mean that it's not a deadly thing to do. If you put me on a motorbike and ask me to do the things that Travis Pastrana is doing, there is no question—I'm going to die. And it's the same thing here. The people who are riding big waves have a solid foundation of how to operate in the ocean. If you took someone from down at the local beach and put them in those situations, you'd have a lot more fatalities."

5. **(p. 123) Slow it down:** The full transcript of my interview with Doc can be found at www.fearproject.net.

6. **(p. 125) Thinks it's no big deal:** I read about the study in Sapolsky's *Why Zebras Don't Get Ulcers.*

7. **(p. 126) Some get tunnel vision:** Tunnel vision, or a narrower field of vision, is common with any amount of stress, and the reason for this seems to be what psychologists call perceptual narrowing. In a study done in 1971 (which I found first in Malcom Gladwell's *New Yorker* piece, "The Art of Failure"), scientists put test subjects in a 60-foot pressure chamber. Participants were told that the pressure would be turned up while they were performing a visual acuity test. Simultaneously, the subjects were supposed to hit a button when they saw a light flash in their peripheral vision. The pressure was not actually turned up on anyone, but the high-pressure test subjects thought it was and had higher heart rates than the control group. Both groups performed about the same in the visual acuity test, but the high-stress group was much worse at noting the peripheral lights. See http://www.ingentaconnect.com/content/hfes/hf/1971/00000013/00000002/art00002.

As our level of arousal increases, our ability to spot relevant cues seems to narrow. Arousal—often but not always catalyzed by fear—helps you focus and gives you an energy boost. Relaxation, on the other hand, lets you see more options. While playing basketball, for example, relaxation may help you see more passing options, more lanes, more bank shots. You're like Magic Johnson. But because you're so relaxed, picking up on so many potentially relevant cues, you make a clumsy routine pass. A little heat from Coach could help you narrow your field just enough to block out the crowd and start hitting your shots and passes, and remain pretty creative. But as soon as that arousal level gets too high—*10 seconds to go and you need a three-pointer!*—it can become extreme perceptual narrowing. In this condition, the brain fixates on the tiniest number of relevant cues: must get ball in hoop. So you take a terrible shot with three men on instead of hitting your wide-open teammate. You panicked.

8. (p. 129) Has found in studies on soldiers: From *On Combat,* a book by Grossman and Loren W. Christensen. See http://www.killology.com/book_oncombat_summary.htm.

9. (p. 130) 175 beats per minute: It's important to note that this scale only applies for *psychologically induced* heart-rate increases. If you run sprints and get your heart rate to 175 beats per minute, you won't have nearly as difficult a time threading a needle as you would if your heart rate hit 175 due to stress.

10. (p. 131) Tiger Woods: "At least, the old Tiger," Lardon added.

11. (p. 132) Before making a putt or taking a kick: See my *ESPN the Magazine* story, "The Science of Choking," for more details on how NFL kickers Nate Kaeding and Billy Cundiff, as well as PGA golfer Charlie Wi, have been using HRV technology to train: http://espn.go.com/nfl/story/_/id/7649003/nfl-science-why-ravens-kicker-billy-cundiff-choked-afc-championship-game-espn-magazine.

12. (p. 137) Mike Madden: I was sad to have to cut Mike's section for the sake of story flow. The original went like this:

Mike specializes in cave diving, and the freshwater cavern system he was the first to explore, Nohoch Caverns in Mexico, goes on for miles in complex, labyrinthine patterns, hundreds of feet beneath the earth's surface. Some of the tubes are only big enough to wiggle a human body through, meaning divers have to take their oxygen tanks off and push them through ahead of themselves to continue deeper. It's also pitch-black down there. If a light fails, if you lose the line you've laid to follow out, you can easily get lost and run out of oxygen. Alternatively, the visibility can go from crystal clear to nothing in seconds. Or the cave can just collapse on top of you, in which case you lose a lot more than your visibility. Hundreds of cave divers have perished since 1950, and the one thing we all know about cave divers is that there aren't all that many cave divers.

So, though these caverns are remarkably beautiful, the stress level is extremely high. And because there were a limited number of experienced cave divers around in Mexico in 1986, Mike had to train rookies all the time. How did he end up not having to pull out a bunch of dead bodies? "Well," Mike tells me as we drive along the coast on the way to do a dive of our own, "one of the first things I used to tell my team is that stress is good."

"Isn't stress what usually kills divers?" I ask. Mike clarifies. "A little stress is good," he says. "It keeps you attentive. It keeps you thinking about what could go wrong, the what ifs, because, as I also told my divers all the time, the situation that is going to kill you in the cave is the one you haven't thought of." The key, Mike says, is to find the space where you can be completely attentive to dangers—avoiding cocky overconfidence—while not stressing so much that it turns into panic. Because panic, he says, will kill you faster than anything.

Panicked divers can use up their air three times as fast, which, way down in a pitch-black underwater cave, might kill them by itself. Panicked divers also just do crazy stuff: Even very experienced divers, when panicked, have been known to try to rip their partner's mouthpiece right out instead of relying on, say, an extra one that's right there with them. While scuba diving, relying on hoses and knobs and dials for survival, you never want to lose rationality or options. So, besides telling his team that stress is good, similar to the way Doc Renneker trained for Mavericks, Mike would meticulously train his divers in every possible scenario that he knew could go wrong and how to get out of it. The idea was not so much that the problem scenarios were so difficult to repair. If you lost visibility, you just had to find the line you'd laid and follow it back to the entrance. The idea was to make all of these scenarios routine, so that the divers could keep their stress in a healthy zone.

Every diver knows that panic can kill them, but fearing fear only makes more fear. Stressing about stress only turns it into severe stress. Getting angry about stress has a similar result: more arousal. The trick with diving, Mike says, which rings true with what you also hear from many therapists these days, is realizing that fear has good intentions. It's there to help. Stress is there to help too. You don't need to encourage stress or turn away from it: Just notice it, let it be, and focus on the task at hand.

Realizing that fear is not the ogre paid off for Mike's Nohoch cave diving team. When his crew started poking around the Nohoch caves in 1986, the longest underwater cave system ever explored was 30,000 feet, Blue Caverns in the Bahamas. When Mike finished exploring Nohoch in 2000, they had uncovered 275,000 new feet of never-before-seen gorgeous caverns, setting a world record for the time. Mike was inducted into the *Guinness Book of World Records* and the Explorer's Club in New York, made 17 documentaries for National Geographic and the like, and was a finalist for a Rolex Award for Enterprise. All wonderful accomplishments, but the one Mike is most proud of is that not a single fatal accident ever happened on his watch. "Some people say they want to die doing what they love," Mike says. "Not me, I want to die of old age with a clear conscience."

13. (p. 137) 2 minutes to 4 minutes: Four minutes may sound like a long time to hold your breath, but it's child's play to professional free-divers. Stephan Misfud, a free-diver and the current world-record holder in static apnea, held his breath for 11 minutes and 35 seconds in 2009. From our aqueous past, humans have retained a bit of the so-called mammalian reflex that, among other things, makes our hearts begin to slow as soon as our faces hit cold water, allowing us to hold our breath longer in cold water than on land. So, counterintuitively, the fact that Mavericks is in cold water can actually help with breath retention.

Mike Madden, my professional diver friend, taught me how important technique is in breath retention. "The reason you feel like you're going to die when you've held your breath for a minute," Mike said, "isn't because you're running out of oxygen. It's because, as your body burns off oxygen, carbon dioxide builds up in the lungs, and that gives you that gaglike urge to breathe." Through a process called breathing up, a near hyperventilation state that comes from hard and fast inhalations and exhalations before retention, you can expel excess carbon dioxide from your lungs and nullify some of the false urge to breathe. You don't want to practice this more than a couple of times in a row. Lung damage can result, or you can pass out. And if you practice in water, use a partner—even in a tub. ("He drowned in a bathtub" is such an embarrassing obituary.) Prime example: After practicing my free-diving with Mike for an afternoon in Hawaii, I fainted. Fortunately, we were already back at the house.

(Mike is also the producer and incredible water cameraman of the documentary being made about my first book, *Saltwater Buddha.* You can see a snippet of our underwater training at http://www.saltwaterbuddha.org/.)

CHAPTER 7

1. (p. 139) 80-foot faces: The fact that Surfline says 80-foot faces and not 80-foot waves is important to surfers, many of whom use "Hawaiian measurement." By this standard, a wave's height is measured from behind, making it half or a third of the size of the face. I've used faces in this book because (a) you usually can't see the back of the wave from shore; (b) some "slab" waves like Teahupoo in Tahiti have almost no back whatsoever but can have a 15-foot face that carries the power of a 50-foot Mavericks wave; (c) the macho posturing can get ridiculous (you come in from surfing 20-foot waves and some guy shrugs and says, "Ah, it's only about 6-foot"); and (d) using the Hawaiian system, the general public has no clue what you're talking about.

2. (p. 142) Jeff Clark: After I finished writing *The Fear Project,* I did a long video interview with Jeff Clark. I asked him if he felt afraid when he was first surfing Mavericks alone. Like Doc, Clark said he never felt fear. "I felt desire," he told me. "Pure desire. Fear is a negative. Desire is a positive." My bet, though, is that if you could peak into Clark's and Doc's brains while they're out at Mavericks, they're getting the same amygdala response as people who say they are afraid, but Doc and Clark have trained themselves to frame that physiological sensation as excitement rather than fear. My interview with Clark can be found at www.fearproject.net.

3. (p. 145) And the way my gut is tying itself in knots, I feel like I might be: The faces in the crowd that day seemed stern and menacing, but how menacing were they really? Dr. Louann Brizendine, in *The Male Brain,* points to studies that show vigorous exercise increases the amount of a hormone called vasopressin which, along with testosterone, enhances masculinity: It rules over territoriality and protectiveness, and seems to be the reason men will defend their families to the death. So all of us men get jacked up on this vasopressin stuff when we're competing, which doesn't always help us make friends. In 2006, psychologists at Bowdoin University found that a boost in vasopressin made men see neutral and friendly faces of strangers as more antagonistic. So a group of vasopressin-heavy men will mistakenly see more grouchy faces and, in return, make unnecessary grouchy faces back, which will then be read as even more grouchy than they are. You wonder how many wars have been started this way. Fortunately, there are women. In the same study, the same vasopressin increase in women made them rate the faces as more *friendly* even though in both males and females, the vasopressin increased anxiety. The researchers concluded that women are more likely to try to make friends to diffuse the anxiety (a habit called tend-and-befriend), whereas men are more evolutionarily trained to fight or run (fight-or-flight).

4. **(p. 152) Believe God is on your side, and your body may be more likely to produce its most godly results:** This belief in the power of the mind and spirit is not new. In Mark 11:23, Jesus says: "Truly I say to you, whoever says to this mountain, 'Be taken up and cast into the sea,' and does not doubt in his heart, but believes that what he says is going to happen, it will be *granted* him."

CHAPTER 8

1. **(p. 158) In video footage:** Watch the Powerlines Productions footage of Mavericks (including Flea's wipeouts) and Ghost Trees from December, 4, 2007, at http://www.youtube.com/watch?v=imArpSkBPDE.
2. **(p. 162) Called in a medevac:** I originally got these details on the pier and the medevac from *Surfer* magazine's profile of Flea, "A Searching and Fearless Moral Inventory." I then confirmed them with him in our interview. http://www.surfermag.com/features/surfer-profile-flea-darryl-virostko/
3. **(p. 162) When he checked himself in:** The first words out of Flea's mouth upon entering rehab, according to *Surfer* magazine, were: "Where are all the bitches? I thought there was supposed to be chicks in rehab." http://www.surfermag.com/features/surfer-profile-flea-darryl-virostko/
4. **(p. 163) This is true, by the way:** For statistics, see footnotes in previous chapter.
5. **(p. 163) Jacob Trette:** Video footage of Trette's tumble can be viewed at http://www.youtube.com/watch?v=PZX4H7fYx4c&feature=related.

   A detailed account of Trette's rescue, with photos of the fall, is documented by kayaker Matt Krizan at http://www.youtube.com/watch?v=ubAi6rCZwgw.
6. **(p. 164) Was dead:** A tribute to Sion's life can be viewed at http://vimeo.com/21173687.
7. **(p.165) Bluemind:** The Bluemind project is ongoing. To learn more about it, go to http://www.wallacejnichols.org/122/bluemind.html. I have to personally thank Wallace J. Nichols for asking me to speak at the 2011

Bluemind conference with Stanford neuroscientist Philippe Goldin. It was my first introduction to Philippe, who ended up helping immensely with this book.

8. (p. 168) Than the brains of normal folks: See Rawson's explanation of meth and dopamine and an image of a meth user's brain at http://www.pbs.org/wgbh/pages/frontline/meth/body/methbrainnoflash.html.

9. (p. 170) Amy and I seem to have a very similar novelty-seeking profile: In *The Brain That Changes Itself*, Dr. Norman Doidge talks about using dopamine as a way of keeping a relationship healthy. "When a couple go on a romantic vacation or try new activities together, or wear new kinds of clothing, or surprise each other," he writes, "they are using novelty to turn on the pleasure centers, so that everything they experience, *including each other,* excites or pleases them. Once the pleasure centers are turned on and globalization begins, the new image of the beloved again becomes associated with unexpected pleasure and it's plastically wired into the brain, which has evolved to respond to novelty."

10. (p. 170) David Zald: For Dr. Zald's study in the *Journal of Neuroscience,* see http://www.jneurosci.org/content/28/53/14372.

See the full transcript of my interview with Dr. Zald at www.fearproject.net.

11. (p. 172) Marvin Zuckerman: Zuckerman summarizes his research in this *Psychology Today* piece: http://www.psychologytoday.com/articles/200011/are-you-risk-taker.

12. (p. 172) Zuckerman/Kuhlman questionnaire: A version of the questionnaire is given by the Australian government and can be taken online for free at http://www.rta.nsw.gov.au/licensing/tests/driverqualificationtest/sensationseekingscale/index.html.

13. (p. 174) *60 Minutes* featured Holmes: The footage can be viewed at http://www.youtube.com/watch?v=bGOJbXOJrZM.

14. (p. 174) *Transformers 3:* The stunt can be viewed at http://www.youtube.com/watch?v=H-9a6SNxc_E. It's by far the most amazing and highly skilled stunt that has ever been pulled off in a wing suit, according to science writer Steven Kotler, who writes about the jump in detail in his forthcoming book.

15. (p. 176) And that transfers to my life off the mountain: In a related study to fear helping narrow focus, psychologists at Finders University in Australia gave 70 novice skydivers a list of words, some relevant to their dive, other completely irrelevant. The group was then split in half, with 35 of them completing their hair-raising first jump, and the other half staying on the ground. Following the dive, the ones who jumped could recall as many relevant words as the grounded group, but they could remember fewer irrelevant words. See the study at http://www.ncbi.nlm.nih.gov/pubmed/16343419.

16. (p. 177) If controversial: Alexander's results from Rat Park are controversial because scientists have not always been able to replicate them. A study from New Mexico Tech, for example (see http://www.ncbi.nlm.nih.gov/pubmed/9148292?dopt=Abstract), found that environment was not the most important factor in morphine addiction. However, other studies seem to confirm Rat Park's results. This study from the Uniformed Services University of the Health Sciences in Bethesda found that "nicotine's chronic effects depend on subjects' sex and living environment": http://www.ncbi.nlm.nih.gov/pubmed/11072395?dopt=Abstract. Alexander continues to speak widely in support of the idea that addiction is more environmental than physical. He addressed the Canadian senate, for example, citing many of the sources that support his view. Here is the paper: http://www.parl.gc.ca/Content/SEN/Committee/371/ille/presentation/alexender-e.htm.

CHAPTER 9

1. (p. 184) Left out in our casual conversations: For more of the details on how Mark and Giulia made it through, and stayed in love, see Mark's *New York Times* piece, "Out of the Darkness," at http://www.nytimes.com/2011/11/27/fashion/out-of-the-darkness-modern-love.html?pagewanted=all as well as Mark and Giulia's book trailer for *Where the Road Meets the Sun,* http://vimeo.com/30030016. (Also, Mark did finish his Ironman Triathlon.)

2. (p. 185) Daraja Academy: By its own description, "Daraja Academy is a boarding secondary school for Kenyan girls with top academic scores and exceptional leadership skills but no means to continue their education. The academy provides shelter, food, healthcare and counseling services which allows students to focus on their academic and personal potential, without being hindered by the everyday barriers of poverty." More at http://daraja-academy.org/.

3. (p. 190) Applauding crowd: For finishing his 111-mile Sacramento River swim, and for completing the Tahoe Double, Jamie Patrick was awarded the 2011 World Open Water Swimming Man of the Year award. In September 2012, he attempted to swim the 70-mile circumference of Lake Tahoe, but huge waves thwarted the swim after 28 miles. Jamie is planning to return in the summer of 2013 to try again. More at www.jamiepatrick.com.

4. (p. 193) Pushing himself to the very brink of death: This, of course, is a reference to the story of the Buddha, which goes, in a nutshell, like this. After the Prince Siddhartha abandoned his palace to seek an end to suffering, he lived with a band of harsh ascetics, eating seeds in the forest and nearly dying of starvation. The experience frustrated him. "By this racking practice of austerities I have not attained any superhuman distinction worthy of the noble ones," he said. "Could there be another path to enlightenment?" His frustration led him to accept an offering of milk from a village girl, which gave him his famous insight of the middle way. "If the string is too tight, it will break. If it is too loose, it will not play." With his newfound strength, he was able to meditate beneath the

Bodhi tree for 3 days and 3 nights, attaining full enlightenment on the third night. Upon seeing the truth, the Buddha is said to have seen that all beings are endowed inherently with the wisdom of a Buddha, but the ignorance of the muddled mind blinds them from seeing it.

5. (p. 196) *The Male Brain*: I was also thinking about *Uta stansburiana,* the side-blotched lizard, and wondering if I was really a "blue throat." "Conveniently," writes Dr. Brizendine, "the males come with three different colored throats that match their mating styles. Males with orange throats use the alpha-male harem strategy. They guard a group of females and mate with all of them. The males with yellow throats are called sneakers because they slip into the harem of the orange throat and mate with his families whenever they can get away with it. Males with brilliant blue throats—my personal favorites—use the one-and-only strategy. They mate with one female and guard her 24/7. From a biological perspective, the approaches of the orange-throated harem leader, the yellow-throated sneaker, and the blue-throated one-female type are successful mating strategies for lizards and for human males too."

6. (p. 199) A few hours of assemblage: As comedic writer Dave Barry puts it: "All of us are born with a set of instinctive fears—of falling, of the dark, of lobsters, of falling on lobsters in the dark, or speaking before a Rotary Club, and of the words 'Some Assembly Required.' "

CHAPTER 10

1. (p. 205) A 2012 Norwegian study: The study, "Fear of Childbirth and Duration of Labour," was published in *BJOG: An International Journal of Obstetrics and Gynecology.* It can be found at http://onlinelibrary.wiley .com/doi/10.1111/j.1471-0528.2012.03433.x/abstract.

A description of the study in the *New York Times* noted that "some factors were more common in women who feared labor—for example, never having had a baby before, using drugs to speed labor, and having had a previous vaginal delivery using instruments. But even after adjusting for these and other factors, women who ranked in the upper half on the fear-of-childbirth scale had an average labor 47 minutes longer than those in the lower half. Fear of childbirth was itself an independent predictor of longer labor." More at http://well.blogs.nytimes.com/2012 /07/02/fear-makes-labor-longer-study-finds/.

2. (p. 205) *Fear lies:* Also, see my article, "Fear Lies! And Other Reasons Not to Listen to Your Inner 'Fear Factory,' " at http://www.huffingtonpost .com/jaimal-yogis/fear-rejection_b_1609337.html.

3. (p. 205) Body tenses at the thought of saying hello: When I was just starting out as a magazine reporter, I accepted an assignment for *San Francisco Magazine* to attend a "pickup artist" workshop in San Francisco that taught hopeless guys how to meet girls. I assumed it would be awful, embarrassing, and degrading (and it did have some low moments), but to his credit, Lance Mason, the suave professor of pickup, did understand exposure therapy. He forced his students to go out into Union Square and approach women over and over again, ingraining in them that rejection just isn't that big of a deal. It was incredible to watch these men lose their fear over the course of the weekend and watch many of them get dates. See the full story at http://www.modernluxury.com/san-francisco/story/what-does-it-take-get-date-town.

4. **(p. 206) Most of them in the developing world:** According to the World Health Organization: "Every day in 2010, about 800 women died due to complications of pregnancy and childbirth, including severe bleeding after childbirth, infections, hypertensive disorders, and unsafe abortions. Out of the 800, 440 deaths occurred in sub-Saharan Africa and 230 in Southern Asia, compared to five in high-income countries. The risk of a woman in a developing country dying from a pregnancy-related cause during her lifetime is about 25 times higher compared to a woman living in a developed country. Maternal mortality is a health indicator that shows very wide gaps between rich and poor, both between countries and within them." http://www.who.int/gho/maternal_health/en/index.html

5. **(p. 206) handful in medically advanced countries too:** For its wealth, the United States has an embarrassingly high rate of maternal mortality: 11 deaths per 100,000, according to the World Health Organization, which puts us behind 40 other countries. In California, according to ABC News, "the number of women who died in the state after giving birth has nearly tripled over the past decade, from 5.6 deaths per 100,000 to 16.9 per 100,000 in 2006. See http://abcnews.go.com/WN/changing-life-preventing-maternal-mortality/story?id=9914009#.UGGokhifr8A. Experts think the high rate of obesity and scheduled C-sections in the United States may be the reason for more deaths.

   On a positive note, newborn deaths have declined over the past 20 years from 4.6 million in 1999 to 3.3 million in 2009. But the United States still has a shockingly high number, ranking again below 40 other countries, including Malaysia, Poland, and Cuba, according to a study published in the journal *PLoS Medicine,* http://www.plosmedicine.org/article/info%3Adoi%2F10.1371%2Fjournal.pmed.1001080. See the news analysis at http://abcnews.go.com/MillionMomsChallenge/us-newborn-mortality-rate-higher-40-countries/story?id=14420009#.UGGmfBifr8A.

6. **(p. 207) For her young genius to survive:** Regarding how fear and anxiety have helped us survive in other ways, Frederic Neuman, director of the Anxiety and Phobia Center at White Plains Hospital, wrote an article recently about why Obsessive Compulsive Disorder may have helped with human survival. Neuman gets at why all genetically based anxiety disorders have likely stuck around in the gene pool as long as they have. See the article here: http://www.psychologytoday.com/blog/fighting-fear/201209/the-survival-advantage-ocd-tale-edna.

7. **(p. 209) I call them the hippies and the hawks:** Medicine is different, but when it comes to politics, hippies and hawks, liberals and conservatives,

Republicans and Democrats (however you like to divide them) do seem to have fundamentally different brain structures. In a 2011 study published in *Current Biology,* researchers at University College London showed that self-described conservatives had a larger "right amygdala," an area associated with fear and other emotions, while self-described liberals had more gray matter in the anterior cingulated cortex, a region associated with memory, learning, and coping with complexity. This research corresponds with other psychological studies that show conservatives have a natural inclination to focus more on risks while liberals tend to be more open and novelty-seeking. In the September 2012 issue of *Scientific American,* Emily Laber-Warren recounts a study in which "a team led by psychologist Michael Dodd and political scientist John Hibbing of the University of Nebraska–Lincoln found that when viewing a collage of photographs, conservatives' eyes unconsciously lingered 15 percent longer on repellent images, such as car wrecks and excrement." Laber-Warren also writes that when folks feel more threatened, they become more conservative and vice versa. "People of all political persuasions became more conservative in the wake of the terrorist," she writes, and in an upcoming Yale study, "asking Republicans to imagine that they possessed superpowers and were impermeable to injury made them more liberal." There is, however, some hope that hippies and hawks can come together, and it's all about how issues are framed. Laber-Warren recounts how Irina Feygina, a social psychology doctoral student at New York University, found a way to bring conservatives and liberals together on climate change. Feygina and colleagues "reframed climate change not as a challenge to government and industry but as 'a threat to the American way of life.' After reading a passage that couched environmental action as patriotic, study participants who displayed traits typical of conservatives were much more likely to sign petitions about preventing oil spills and protecting the Arctic National Wildlife Refuge." Read Laber-Warren's full article at http://www.scientificamerican.com/article.cfm?id=calling-truce-political-wars.

8. (p. 214) It dissolves into thin air: The dream reminds me of one of my favorite Zen stories that plays out between master Hsueh-feng and a visiting monk.

Master: "Where did you come from?"

Monk: "The Monastery of Spiritual Light."

Master: "In the daytime we have sunlight, in the nighttime we have lamplight. . . . what is Spiritual Light?"

Monk: no answer

Master: "Sunlight, lamplight."

9. (p. 216) A feature about why athletes choke under pressure: My ESPN article, "I Think, Therefore I Choke," can be found at http://espn.go.com/nfl/story/_/id/7649003/nfl-science-why-ravens-kicker-billy-cundiff-choked-afc-championship-game-espn-magazine. Malcom Gladwell also wrote an interesting article on the topic in the *New Yorker* back in 2000: http://www.gladwell.com/2000/2000_08_21_a_choking.html.

10. (p. 216) HeartMath Institute: The HeartMath Institute has been diligent in recording its extensive research and making it all public. See http://www.heartmath.org/research/research-home/research-center-home.html.

11. (p. 221) His capabilities: Babies teach us a lot about emotions, especially fear, because the ancient limbic system, which includes the amygdala, develops before the cortex in mammals. Because of this, babies essentially experience and show emotion that is unregulated by the more modern, logical layers of the brain.

A brief anecdote along these lines: From 5 to 7 months, Amy and I were lucky enough to travel around Portugal with Kai, and since we were always sleeping in different houses and hotels, we let Kai sleep with us in our bed. It was wonderful snuggle time, but as soon as we got home, Kai had developed a deep detest and fear of his crib. He would not fall asleep unless he was in the bed with one of us, period. Not being fans of the "cry-it-out" method, Amy and I tried gradual exposure therapy. Taking *The Baby Whisperer*'s advice of getting into the crib with the baby if he really hates it, I actually napped with Kai in the crib a couple of times, which was terrible for my back, but it changed Kai's relationship with the crib almost immediately. Once this foundation was set, we encouraged him to occasionally play in his crib with various toys, trying to show him that the crib is a fun place and not punishment. After about a week of this, Kai was napping in his crib, but he still wouldn't fall asleep on his own. So, following Dr. Marc Weissbluth's method (*Healthy Sleep Habits, Happy Child*), we let him experience just a few minutes of crying at a time in the crib—to show him that his fear of being alone in there is not really that bad—letting him go an extra minute each time before going in to comfort him. It required some sleepless nights and some tears, but within a week, Kai learned to soothe himself and was soon after sleeping through the night in his own crib.

Most parents experience something similar, but we don't always apply the wisdom we use with our babies to ourselves. I think it's helpful to remember that our fear systems are basically still like a baby—raw emotion—and our modern brains are much more like a parent, able to reason. To overcome any fear, the baby part of the brain simply needs to be gently guided by the parent toward positive exposure to the object of fear. And to avoid too much crying, baby steps seem to be key.

12. (p. 221) Optimism bias: Neuroscientist Tali Sharot's book, *Optimism Bias: A Tour of the Irrationally Positive Brain,* is summarized well in her *Time* magazine story, "Optimism Bias," which can be found at http://www.time.com/time/health/article/0,8599,2074067,00.html.